Simón Bolívar

Simón Bolívar, painted by José Miguel Figueroa soon after the Battle of Boyacá, with allegorical Indian princess. (Courtesy of Quinta y Museo de Bolívar, Bogotá)

David Bushnell

University of Florida

Simón Bolívar

Liberation and Disappointment

The Library of World Biography

Series Editor: Peter N. Stearns

New York   San Francisco   Boston
London   Toronto   Sydney   Tokyo   Singapore   Madrid
Mexico City   Munich   Paris   Cape Town   Hong Kong   Montreal

Vice President and Publisher: Priscilla McGeehon
Acquisitions Editor: Erika Gutierrez
Executive Marketing Manager: Sue Westmoreland
Production Coordinator: Shafiena Ghani
Project Coordination, Text Design, Electronic Page Makeup, and Art
    Studio: Sunflower Publishing Services
Senior Cover Design Manager/Designer: Nancy Danahy
Cover Image: Painting of Simón Bolívar by Gil. © Bettman/CORBIS
Publishing Services Manager: Alfred Dorsey
Printer and Binder: RR Donnelley and Sons Company/Harrisonburg
Cover Printer: Coral Graphics, Inc.

Library of Congress Cataloging-in-Publication Data

Bushnell, David, 1923–
    Simón Bolívar: liberation and disappointment / David Bushnell ;
        edited by Peter N. Stearns.
        p. cm.
    Includes bibliographical references and index.
    ISBN 0-321-15667-6
    1. Bolâvar, Simân, 1783–1830.   2. Venezuela—History—War
of Independence, 1810–1823.   3. South America—History—War
of Independence, 1806–1830.   4. Heads of state—South
America—Biography.   I. Stearns, Peter N.   II. Title.

F2235.A.B955 2004
980.′02′092—dc21
[B]   2003044606

Please visit our website at http://www.ablongman.com

ISBN 0-321-15667-6

2345678910—DOH—0504

Contents

Editor's Preface

"Biography is history seen through the prism of a person."
—LOUIS FISCHER

It is often challenging to identify the roles and experiences of individuals in world history. Larger forces predominate. Yet biography provides important access to world history. It shows how individuals helped shape the society around them. Biography also offers concrete illustrations of larger patterns, in political and intellectual life, in family life, and in the economy.

The Longman Library of World Biography series seeks to capture the individuality and drama that mark human character. It deals with individuals operating in one of the main periods of world history, while also reflecting issues in the particular society around them. Here, the individual illustrates larger themes of time and place. The interplay between the personal and the general is always the key to using biography in history, and world history is no exception. Always, too, there is the question of personal agency: how much do individuals, even great ones, shape their own lives and environment, and how much are they shaped by the world around them?

PETER STEARNS

Author's Preface

Among Latin American historical figures, only Fidel Castro can match—and in some quarters exceed—the name recognition enjoyed by Simón Bolívar. Yet the fame of Bolívar, as the Liberator of half a continent, is likely to prove even more durable than that of Castro, whose own country was transformed under his auspices but whose revolution never became the model for Latin America as a whole that he had hoped to see. Not all of Bolívar's hopes were fulfilled, either: the countries he led to independence proved unable in the short run to attain either domestic stability or a place of general respect among the nations of the world. However, unlike Castro, Bolívar today inspires well-nigh universal admiration. Though sometimes dubbed South America's George Washington, he in fact greatly overshadows his North American counterpart in number of books written about him and places (even one entire republic) named for him. He likewise overshadows other leaders of Latin American independence such as Argentina's José de San Martín, a more professional military officer but an overly cautious leader quite lacking Bolívar's charisma, and Mexico's warrior-priest Miguel Hidalgo, whose career was cut short by capture and execution.

Part of Bolívar's appeal to later generations derives precisely from the contradictory aspects of his life and image. Born into the highest rank of the colonial aristocracy, he proved capable of empathy with less privileged groups and readily adapted to all the hardships of campaigning through flooded tropical plains and Andean peaks. A sincere believer in abolition of slavery and in legal equality for all races and social classes, he nevertheless feared the growing influence of nonwhites in his homeland. Essentially a freethinker in matters of religion, in the last stage of his career he forged a close tactical alliance with the Roman Catholic Church. Convinced that the new Latin American states must protect their independence by joining together in close alliance, he hoped to obtain a British protectorate over any such alliance. And though he was steeped in the eighteenth-century Enlightenment's hatred of arbitrary rule and defense of basic human rights, there was also an authoritarian streak in his makeup that suggests a remote kinship with such enlightened despots as Spain's own Carlos III and that has been noted in justification of both right- and left-wing dictatorships in modern Latin America. Nor is that all—there is a Bolívar for almost every taste and ideology. Of course, in his contradictions and in other qualities, Bolívar, too, was a product of his times, but few if any of his contemporaries ranged so far as he did in both thought and action. Nor has there been a Latin American whose work covered so broad a geographic area or had so many dimensions, from war to constitution making to literary expression.

There is a vast literature on Bolívar, of which all too much consists of hagiographic paeans, attempts to claim him as precursor of some contemporary cause, or the merest trivia. As Germán Carrera Damas, one of Venezuela's more critical historians, has observed, present-day Venezuelans see Bolívar as so all-important that no detail concerning him can possibly be considered unimportant. In the present volume, I hope there may be just enough trivia to convey some flavor of the times but not so much as to obscure the subject's lasting importance.

DAVID BUSHNELL

Acknowledgments

I want to give explicit thanks to some of the many individuals who made this work possible. I start with my wife Ginnie, who got to visit the tomb of the Liberator before I did, because back then (1970, I think) they were requiring coat and tie to go in, which I was not wearing in the Caracas warmth. There follows our son John, a Russianist who nevertheless remembers some of the Spanish he learned as a seven year old in Bogotá; our son Peter, the family librarian and born in Bogotá; our daughter Cathy, bilingual educator and on numerous occasions a traveling companion on summer research trips; and Angus, our dog, who has not yet had the benefit of Latin American travel but who gave great moral support, and never ate the manuscript. Then I must add the Venezuelan historian Germán Carrera Damas, somewhat hesitantly, lest he be blamed for any excesses I have committed; Jaime Jaramillo Uribe, dean of Colombian historians, part of whose originality consists in having written little on the independence movement but whose eminent rationality has much influenced my understanding of his country's history; General Alvaro Valencia Tovar, whose views of the Liberator as a military figure I have liberally stolen (in most cases, I hope, accurately enough); Hermes Tovar Pinzón, with whom I have often argued over the history of the period but who remains a friend (while those arguments helped me refine my ideas); and the extended Hosie and Osuna clans, who welcomed us so generously in the Colombian heartland and guided us in the exploration of both Bolivarian and non-Bolivarian pathways.

Last, I pay homage to some favorite places: Caracas, a much-maligned metropolis that nevertheless delighted me from the first visit despite that brush-off at the National Pantheon; Paipa, just over the hill from the battlefield of Pantano de Vargas and up the road from that of Boyacá, set in a beautiful part of the eastern Andean Cordillera that is today our favorite part of Colombia, and a good bit safer as a matter of fact than Washington, D.C.; Bogotá itself, like Caracas always an acquired taste but for me acquired even sooner; and Cartagena, whose colonial core is a must for any professional or amateur historian to see, including non-Latin Americanists, before going on to further research in the great archive in the sky.

DAVID BUSHNELL

Simón Bolívar

Spanish American independence: the Bolivarian theater.

Origins and Early
Adventures (1783–1808)

Simón José Antonio de la Santísima Trinidad Bolívar y Palacios—Simón Bolívar for short—was born in Caracas, capital of
the Spanish **captaincy-general** of Venezuela, on 24 July 1783.
That same year, as his nineteenth-century biographer Felipe
Larrazábal pointed out, Great Britain formally recognized the
independence of its former North American colonies. These had
broken away from their parent country with the diplomatic and
military aid not just of France but of the Spanish monarch, Carlos III, who saw an opportunity to strike a blow thereby against
a traditional European rival. Larrazábal added: "Who would
have told him that the one who was to snatch away his colonies
as well had just been born!"

The same author in his romantic exuberance did not hesitate to suggest that the coincidence in dates was the work not
of chance but of divine Providence, for the coming into the
world of the child Simón was truly a gift from God. "In those
times of obscurantism and oppression, God took from the
treasures of his goodness a soul that He endowed with intelligence, justice, strength, and gentleness. 'Go,' He said, 'carry
light to the mansion of night; go make just and happy those
who do not know justice and are unaquainted with liberty.
That soul was Bolívar's; this is the charge that Providence entrusted to him." Providence was careful, moreover, to place

Birthplace of Bolívar (the "Casa Natal") in Caracas, with schoolchildren leaving, having paid their respects. (Author's collection)

Bolívar in a corner of Spanish America that was destined to become one of the primary foci of the independence movement, as well as in a social milieu where it would be only natural for him to aspire to leadership. Much like Argentina, which would play a similar role as revolutionary focus at the other end of South America, Venezuela was a colony whose agroexport economy was seriously inconvenienced by Spanish imperial trade restrictions and that in addition was relatively open to outside influences, intellectual and cultural as well as economic. And the particular family into which Bolívar was born belonged to the very highest stratum of colonial Venezuela's landowning class.

The Bolívars formed part of the elite group that was known as the **mantuanos** because of the *manto*, or type of cape, worn by their ladies; generally speaking they were also **grandes cacaos,** or "big cacaos," in recognition of their plantations' principal crop. (The fame of Dutch chocolate ultimately rested on cacao smuggled out of Venezuela to Curaçao, in the Netherlands West Indies.) Some of the *mantuanos* descended from the first Spanish conquerors and settlers, and some held Spanish titles of nobility: Caracas boasted five marquises and three counts. Indeed the father of Simón Bolívar was marquis of San Luis, even though he never used the title, and when his widow tried to revalidate it for their oldest son, Juan Vicente, the bureaucratic red tape and associated expenses foiled her attempt. At the same time, there is reason to believe—though no conclusive evidence—that one of Bolívar's great great grandmothers was of part Indian or part African descent, and certain authors have made much of the detail. It was not really unusual for Spanish American creoles (native-born whites) to have some American Indian or even African traces in their gene pool, but the Bolívar family's denials of racial taint, if not always believed, were at least accepted, in view of their wealth and other distinctions. They in any case owned not just extensive rural properties but numerous slaves, both for domestic service and for agricultural field work. Slavery was something as much taken for granted as the sun and rain, and it did not preclude the development in Bolívar of a deep and lasting affection for his slave wet nurse Hipólita.

Young Simón spent his first years either in the comfortable city mansion where he had been born or on one of various family estates. It was certainly a comfortable life. His father died when he was only three, and his mother when he was nine, but he did not lack close relatives who were prepared to manage the interests of both Simón and his older brother, Juan Vicente, as well as their two sisters. When the family properties were divided among heirs, the older brother obtained the largest share, including theoretical succession to the title of marquis. Nevertheless, Simón possessed not only his personal share of his parents' legacy but, in his own right, an entail consisting of various properties and established specifically for him by a wealthy uncle. He was the owner of houses in Caracas, plantations and herds of cattle, and of course slaves—as of 1795, approximately 160, including infants and runaways. Simón Bolívar was easily one of the richest persons in the colony.

Bolívar was also a youth of lively and independent character who, particularly after the death of both parents, was never very amenable to the control of others and caused his relatives and various private tutors a succession of headaches. The fact that the uncle with primary responsibility for his care was an unsympathetic middle-aged bachelor did not help. More than once, Bolívar absconded from the house of a guardian with whom he was staying, in one case observing that if slaves had the right to choose a master to their own liking—as under Spanish law they did in certain circumstances—then he should not be denied the right to live where he wished. The comment revealed at that point less a sense of solidarity with slaves (even though Bolívar would eventually become a decided advocate of abolition) than a strong disposition of self-will. On still other occasions, he would wander off through the streets of Caracas, mixing freely with members of other social classes in a way that no doubt helped prepare him for his later role as a leader of ragged conscript armies but in the meantime much annoyed his oldest sister. It would further seem that the young man's dedication to his studies was just a bit superficial. Nevertheless, he learned to read and write acceptably, despite the grievous spelling errors that appear in his earliest correspondence, and he absorbed the necessary fund of basic knowledge.

In addition to his other education, Bolívar received some—even if not much—formal military training. Starting at age fourteen, he was enrolled in the militia of the valleys of Aragua, where some of his family's important properties were located. There was in this respect a certain parallel with his North American counterpart, George Washington, who served in the colonial militia of Virginia, and the parallel can be extended to the social antecedents of the two men, because Washington was likewise a colonial landowner, agroexporter, and owner of slaves. However, the Virginian by no means came from a family as wealthy and distinguished as that of Bolívar. And as a militia officer Washington received a bit of practical fighting experience, unlike Bolívar, even before the war of independence, in the frontier struggle between England and France for control of the North American interior. The teenage Bolívar successfully attained the rank of *alférez,* or sublieutenant, but his military performance was thoroughly unremarkable, with no indication of future glory.

The mere fact of growing up in the capital and chief city of colonial Venezuela was, broadly speaking, another educational experience for Simón Bolívar. As an important exporter of coffee and indigo as well as cacao—indeed, after Cuba, the most successful *plantation* colony Spain had—Venezuela had an active foreign commerce that in turn reinforced other types of relations with the outside world. Venezuela was in addition the South American colony closest geographically to the parent country or to Europe generally; and it maintained multiple relationships with the nearby non-Spanish Antilles, derived in considerable part, though not exclusively, from contraband trade. Whereas trips abroad were truly exceptional among the inhabitants of Santafé (de Bogotá), capital of the **Viceroyalty** of New Granada—of which Venezuela nominally formed part—they were not uncommon for leading families of Caracas. Santafé, in effect, was separated from the sea over primitive Andean trails and the mosquito-infested Magdalena River, but Caracas was located in the Venezuelan coastal range at a mere thirty minutes today from the Caribbean by freeway and, even two centuries ago, less than a day's journey. Unlike Santafé, Caracas did not even have a printing press of its own, but it was usually the first Spanish American capital to receive foreign news. It was in fact exposed to the rapid penetration of new fashions and ideas of every kind, including those that emanated from the Anglo-American and French Revolutions.

The ideas in question permeated Venezuelan society unevenly, and their reception varied. The revolution of the English colonies, which seemed to have resulted in a political regime whose salient characteristic was liberty practiced in due moderation, was quite widely admired, whereas for most Spanish Americans who had even heard of it, the French Revolution conjured up visions of savagery and impiety rather than political and social redemption. Yet both of the great eighteenth-century revolutions did, at a minimum, reinforce a growing feeling that the Spanish monarchy had become an anachronism. After all, it was still an absolute monarchy at least in theory, with all power vested in the king and his ministers, no representative institutions at all save at the municipal level—and far from democratic even there. The general lack of interest in establishing an independent republic for Venezuela was made obvious by the total failure in 1797 of the conspiracy hatched for that purpose by Manuel Gual and José María España, but this did not prevent increasing numbers of people from feeling entitled to a greater share of power even within the framework of the existing monarchy. To be sure, the colonial upper class enjoyed de facto some extensive and often decisive influence on the conduct of affairs, but this was due in part to the venality of top officials, most of whom were "**peninsulars**" (Spanish-born, from the Iberian Peninsula), and in part to the mere fact that it was easier and less stressful to manage the colony by getting in the good graces of the leaders of local society. Despite royal restrictions on the practice, many high-ranking peninsular judges or administrators married local women, and with them they produced children who were, by birth, creoles.

There was one other eighteenth-century revolution with repercussions in colonial Venezuela. This was the Haitian revolution, which began in 1791 as a slave uprising but developed into a movement for independence as well and in the end did away not only with French colonial rule in Haiti but with the white landed and slaveowning class that had thrived under France's protection. The Haitian revolution magnified the fear of slave rebellion that had long been the worst nightmare of the white population throughout the Caribbean Basin. In Venezuela the slave population represented only about 7 percent of the total, which was not a particularly high proportion for the colony as a whole; but the figure was more like 15 percent in the north-central region, comprising the Caribbean coast and valleys of the Andean coastal range, where not only the capital city but the most important agricultural estates were to be found. The highest percentage of all—over 20 percent—was in the city of Caracas itself, where slaves performed domestic and artisan services, as well as represented a form of conspicuous consumption to underscore the honor of aristocratic families: a well-born lady of *mantuano* rank might require a coterie of female slaves simply to accompany her to mass, carrying her missal, a piece of carpet to spread out on the floor of the temple, and other such paraphernalia. In the countryside, slaves were by no means the only laborers, because there were also free workers—

hired hands, tenants, or independent peasant farmers. Nevertheless, slave labor was an indispensable, even if not entirely sufficient, resource for the functioning of the plantation economy. This was one more reason to fear the spread of the Haitian example, and such fear seemed all the more justified in light of the 1795 rebellion of José Leonardo Chirino, a free *zambo* (of mixed African and Indian ancestry) who had been in Haiti and proceeded to stir up some slaves and free people of color in the Coro region, to the west of Caracas. The rebels were harshly punished, and after the authorities finished hanging the leader, they cut off his head and hands to set them up in different places as warnings to anyone who might think of trying the same thing again. Yet the white population's worry did not go away.

For a good many whites, a threat to the existing order as great or greater than possible slave unrest was the rise of the *pardos,* or "browns" (free persons with at least some African ancestry who made up almost half the total population of Venezuela). They worked as salaried employees in towns and in the countryside, though in general they disdained handicrafts, which typically remained in the hands of free blacks. Also some *pardos* managed to acquire small rural holdings. All of them— and free blacks even more so—were denied access by colonial legislation to higher education and thereby to the professions; they were forbidden to marry whites and were exposed to other forms of racial discrimination by law and social custom. But the discriminatory regulations were not always enforced to the letter, and some fortunate *pardos* were beginning to accumulate modest wealth and to enter professions that were theoretically closed to them. The tendency was not welcome to the colony's white population. Still less welcome was the fact that the colonial authorities appeared to encourage it, recruiting *pardos* for militia service, with a limited version of the *fuero,* or legal privileges enjoyed by the military generally, and in the case of certain individuals, formally granting a dispensation from the condition of *pardo* so that they might enjoy the same rights as Spanish or creole subjects. The most notorious example was the so-called *cédula de gracias al sacar* of 1795, a decree whereby, in exchange for payments of money to the royal treasury, a select minority of *pardos* became legally equal to whites. This measure was denounced as an "outrage" by the municipality of Caracas, representing the cream of the white upper class, both creole and peninsular; and it was seen not simply as an insult to racial honor but as a sign of dangerous weakening of the social order, whose end result could well be caste war or even slave uprising. Yet scorn for the *pardos* was not an exclusive trait of upper-class whites. The whites of middle or lower social standing, who occupied lesser government jobs, owned small properties, or lived as salaried workers, were set apart from the *pardos* less by their quality of life than by the prestige of being reputed as white (something that not all of them were in a very strict sense), and it did not suit them to lose the distinction.

There is, of course, no reason to assume that young Bolívar necessarily shared the indignation of the Caracas city fathers over the coddling of the *pardos*. While in later life he expressed frequent concern that the *pardos* were becoming too influential, he was no less insistent in his support of legal equality between the races. Indeed, concerning the political and social ideas that were taking shape in Bolívar's mind, we have for the most part only indirect indications and speculative efforts to read later attitudes back into his early years. In this regard it is customary to single out (and perhaps exaggerate) the influence of one of his early tutors, Simón Rodríguez, a pedagogue enchanted with the thinking of French philosophers, Rousseau in particular, as well as a man of highly idiosyncratic temperament himself. Rodríguez gained the sincere admiration of his pupil, even though one of the latter's various escapes was precisely from the home of Rodríguez. Presumably, the tutor helped plant some of the seeds of ideas that would flourish in a more mature Bolívar, but their relationship was rudely interrupted when Rodríguez came under suspicion of involvement in the abortive conspiracy of Gual and España and in his turn fled to Jamaica. Thence he went on to the United States and Europe, where eventually he would be reunited with his former pupil.

Bolívar's own experiences of residence and travel in Europe, of which the reunion with Rodríguez—which did not occur on his first visit—was only one aspect, clearly had much to do with the evolution of his ideas. He personally had for some time harbored an ambition to know the Old World, and his family relations did not doubt that he had the necessary talent to begin the conquest of further fame and fortune at the Spanish court. Indeed, quite apart from his intrinsic ability, whose precise extent was still a matter of conjecture, he had the necessary self-confidence, not to mention an engaging extroverted personality. He was a good-looking youth, with a high forehead, dark hair and dark eyes, regular features, and excellent teeth, though he was also slight of build and, at five feet six inches, a bit shorter than many of his future comrades-in-arms (like Napoleon, one is tempted to say). The fact that Bolívar's maternal uncle Esteban Palacios was living in Madrid was naturally a factor in the decision to let him go. So he set sail from the port of La Guaira, in January 1799, bound for Spain, though by way of the Mexican port of Vera Cruz—a traditional market for Venezuelan cacao—and Havana.

On finally reaching Spain, Bolívar proceeded to Madrid, where he lost little time in making himself known in circles of high society. In his favor he had his own reputation as a rich colonial, along with the sponsorship of his uncle and of other eminent Spanish Americans resident in the Spanish capital. One of the latter was the marquis of Ustáriz, also born in Caracas, in whose home he eventually came to live and who became both guide and mentor. Once installed in the home of Ustáriz, Bolívar applied himself more seriously than he ever had before in Caracas to deepening his knowledge through reading both ancient and modern literature. At the same time, his direct observation of the intrigues and corruption of the Spanish court could only reinforce whatever critical thoughts may have been already forming in his mind with regard to political injustice and social abuses. Spain was no longer ruled by the enlightened despot Carlos III but by his well-intentioned but weak successor, Carlos IV, and the latter's favorite, Godoy, who happened to be one of the queen's lovers. Though Godoy did not lack talent, his dual role contributed to the court's generally unsavory atmosphere.

Needless to say, Bolívar did not devote all his time in Madrid to reading and to forming unfavorable opinions of the Spanish royals. He lavishly spent part of his own wealth in acquiring everything that was necessary (and some things that were not) for life at court, from fine clothes in the latest fashion to special dancing and riding lessons. And he met young María Teresa Rodríguez del Toro, born in Madrid but the niece of still another Venezuelan marquis. Although she was two years older than Bolívar and not known for beauty, she had enough grace and intelligence for Bolívar to fall madly in love with her. Without much delay he proposed marriage, and despite some reservations of family members based on his tender age, he obtained the requisite consent. Before the wedding took place, Bolívar himself first made a quick trip to France—and it would seem that he came away with a rather favorable impression of the government of Napoleon, who had not yet crowned himself emperor. The young couple were then joined in marriage at Madrid in May of 1802. Almost at once, they took leave of friends and relatives in Spain to travel to Venezuela, reaching Caracas about the middle of the year and a little later moving on to the Bolívar family estate of San Mateo, where the romantic idyll of the young lovers was combined with the oversight of agricultural operations and commercial transactions. But it ended in tragedy, with María Teresa falling gravely ill, most likely from yellow fever or malaria. When she returned to Caracas it was only to die, just eight months after the wedding.

The loss of his wife was psychologically a traumatic event for Bolívar. As a sign of fealty to her memory, he resolved never to marry again, which meant not that he renounced all future sexual relationships but that he could never have legitimate heirs. Neither, apparently, did he ever have any of what were euphemistically referred to as "natural sons," or if he did, he never recognized any as his own, in the way that other warriors of independence did on behalf of the offspring of their occasional liaisons. And although there has been no lack of individuals in the countries liberated by Bolívar who have claimed direct descent from him, no case has ever been confirmed beyond doubt. But obviously the lack of personal descendants was no obstacle to his earning the title of "father" of a whole series of new countries. As he himself would later point out, his condition as a permanent and childless widower was actually a positive factor from the standpoint of his political and military career, freeing him from commitments and responsibilities that could at times have limited his total concentration on Spanish American liberation.

But the time had not yet come for giving birth to new countries; and neither did Bolívar feel inclined to go on living simply as a rich colonial landowner. He therefore determined to journey once more to Europe. He arrived in Cádiz at the end of 1803, from there continued to Madrid, and, while in Spain, took care of some pending commercial business. However, during this second trip to Europe he did not long remain in the parent country. Instead he spent time above all in France, and in particular Paris, a city that he had enjoyed before and where he now established himself to live in comfort. He had servants, lovers, and money to squander at the gambling table; he assiduously frequented social and cultural events; and without much difficulty he gained access to the company of leading political and intellectual figures in the French capital.

Bolívar, while living in Paris, was again a voracious reader, his eclectic tastes spanning (he would later say) "the classicists of antiquity, whether they be philosophers, historians, orators, or poets, as well as the modern classics of Spain, France, and Italy, and not a few of the English." The classical and English authors he generally read in French translation, for that was the one foreign language of which he had full command. Notable, in any case, among the talents that the future Liberator was already demonstrating, and that he had been refining at least since his tutelage under Ustáriz in Madrid, was the ability to combine a life of elegant luxury with a dedication to study. He likewise took advantage of the golden opportunity to watch in person the unfolding of European developments, in which respect he did not conceal his growing disillusionment with the figure of Napoleon, whose coronation occurred during this stay of Bolívar's in Europe. He was captivated by, and frankly admired, the cult of glory that was so important a trait of the French leader and that Bolívar would not hesitate to imitate in due course. But he bitterly criticized Napoleon for subordinating other concerns to personal ambition—having betrayed the republican ideals of the French Revolution even before the formal ceremony of his coronation.

Bolívar's pursuit of pleasure and his more serious interests found mutual reinforcement in the relationship that he developed in Paris with Fanny du Villars, the young wife of a mature military officer in Napoleon's service. As a lover, she inspired in him something more than passing infatuation, but she also helped orient him in the ways of the French capital and, through her justly famous soirées, brought him into contact with all manner of interesting persons. It is quite possible that it was in Fanny's house that Bolívar became acquainted with the noted German scientist Alexander von Humboldt, known among other things for his travels of study and observation through Spanish America, including Caracas (which he had visited during Bolívar's absence). Between the two men there was a notable difference of age and experience but a similar zeal for knowledge and a somewhat similar approach to political questions. Although the German was not by instinct a revolutionary, his ideas were liberal, and he was not blind to the shortcomings of Spanish colonial rule: with Bolívar he even appears to have spoken of the possible independence of the colonies.

Among still other things, Bolívar engaged in Paris in a tentative exploration of Freemasonry, and he joined a fully accredited Masonic lodge rather than one of the Masonic-type political clubs that a number of Spanish Americans wandering about Europe had already found to be a useful venue for exchanging revolutionary ideas and plotting agitation. It would appear, however, that Bolívar could not take the Masonic rituals very seriously and soon abandoned the flirtation. Nor is it possible to tell to just what extent Bolívar personally harbored revolutionary intentions at this point, but the evolution of his political thinking was surely hastened by his reunion in Paris with Simón Rodríguez, the ardent admirer of Rousseau and convinced republican. The high point in the association between former teacher and disciple came when they set forth together on another adventure, consisting of a sentimental journey from France to Italy in which they crossed the Alps on foot, admired both romantic scenery and Renaissance monuments, and conversed about pretty much everything along the way. The two arrived finally in Rome, the "eternal city" that at different times had been a model both of austere republicanism and of imperial glory and in both of these aspects powerfully captured Bolívar's imagination. While in Rome, Bolívar made some new friends and reencountered old ones, including Humboldt; and like any tourist, he visited the principal historic monuments. But by far the best-known episode of his Roman pilgrimage was the "oath on Monte Sacro," when in August 1805, accompanied by Rodríguez, he climbed one of the hills of Rome and, after steeping himself in the beauty of the view and in the historical memories that it evoked, made a solemn promise not to rest until he saw America liberated from the chains of Spanish imperialism. There is a long and tiresome polemic among historians of the traditional school over the exact identity of the hill where the oath was sworn, and naturally his words were not at once reduced to writing, so that there are slightly differing versions of what he said (originating with Rodríguez as well as Bolívar himself). Even so, there is no doubt of the historicity of the event, which clearly ranks as a milestone in both the intellectual formation and the political awakening of the Liberator.

Bolívar did not begin immediately, from Rome, to prepare the struggle for independence. First of all, he returned to Paris, where he renewed his various acquaintances. However, he apparently talked now more clearly than before of his political aspirations, and he informed his Parisian friends of his irrevocable intention to return to Venezuela. He even stated that he was bored with life in Paris—something that would have been hard to imagine a short time before. Without doubt, Bolívar felt a certain nostalgia for Venezuela and for the friends and family members he had left behind there. But his latest thinking about the future of Spanish America could only hasten the decision to return, particularly when he learned of the plan of Francisco de Miranda, the arch-conspirator otherwise known as the Venezuelan "Precursor," to unleash an anticolonial insurrection in Venezuela without further delay. To judge from a letter written by Bolívar to a French correspondent, his reaction to Miranda's project was ambiguous: he could hardly object to the aim of liberating Venezuela, yet he stated that he feared the planned invasion would bring "much evil to the inhabitants of the colony." Bolívar's fears presumably concerned the timing and leadership of the project, and they were not unwarranted, but as things turned out the calamities were less than expected, simply because Miranda's expedition was almost from the outset a total failure.

That outcome was hardly due to lack of revolutionary experience on the leader's part, because Miranda had accumulated a long record of anti-Spanish intrigue and agitation since deserting from the Spanish army in 1783 to take exile in the United States and later Europe; he had obtained practical military experience in the armies of Spain, under whose banner he fought in the War of Anglo-American Independence, and in the service of Revolutionary France, which awarded him the rank of general. For several years, he received a modest pension from the British government, which sought to have him on hand in case the occasion should arise to use him in some action against Spain. But Miranda grew tired of waiting. He therefore crossed over to the United States, recruited some adventurers, contracted and armed a brigantine, and even bought a printing press, an artifact still nonexistent in colonial Venezuela that he meant to use to grind out proclamations in favor of general insurrection. Miranda sailed from New York for Venezuela in February 1806, and when his expedition approached Venezuela, the Spanish coast guard was ready for it. Miranda escaped in his brigantine, but the two schooners he also had with him were seized, and ten of his followers hanged. Rather than accept defeat, Miranda reorganized his small force in the British Antilles, made a new invasion attempt, and succeeded in taking the city of Coro, in western Venezuela.

However, he did not long keep it, for the general uprising of oppressed inhabitants that Miranda was counting on still did not occur. His unfounded expectation that Venezuelans would welcome him with open arms and join his small band of adventurers largely explains the inadequacy of the preparations he made for the invasion. And the fact is that Miranda, though superficially qualified for the enterprise, had not been in Venezuela for decades and had neither sufficient personal contacts in the land of his birth nor reliable information about conditions there. He was not mistaken in thinking there were motives of discontent with the colonial regime—they had always existed, and they concerned not only political rule but taxation and trade policy—but this did not mean that a majority or even a significant minority of inhabitants were yet determined to shake off the imperial yoke. Neither was Miranda helped either by his image as a fighter in the French Revolution or by the suspicion that he was now a pawn of the British.

Bolívar's brother, Juan Vicente, was just one of the distinguished creoles who offered their services to the colonial government in repelling Miranda's invasion attempts. Simón was still in Europe. However, he did eventually settle his affairs there and depart toward the end of 1806, going by way of North America for a detour both touristic and informative. He set sail from the German port of Hamburg for Charleston, South Carolina, and remained roughly a half year in the land of Washington. He arrived apparently short of funds and in poor health, and little is concretely known about what he did in the United States—there is not even agreement as to the places he visited, though it seems clear that he finally sailed home from Philadelphia, where he left in school his nephew Anacleto Clemente, who had traveled with him from Europe. Years later, Bolívar remarked to the U.S. chargé d'affaires in Bogotá that in the United States he had for the first time observed "rational liberty," and to the diplomat he also extolled the hospitality he received from a fellow passenger who on their arrival in Charleston had helped him to solve his foreign traveler's problems. But references to this visit in Bolívar's own writings are conspicuous for their absence, so that one can only speculate to what extent the experience may have influenced the ideas and attitudes concerning the United States that he later would express, not all of them positive.

Despite the little that is known about Bolívar's visit to the United States, the mere fact of his having visited the country is illustrative of the increasingly close relations between the North American republic and the Spanish possessions of the Caribbean Basin toward the end of the colonial period. Even though the Spanish monarchy's formal policy was to prevent direct trade between its colonies and foreign ports and to limit other relations as well, there had always existed some dealings, above all in the form of contraband trade. But lately, commercial contacts had much intensified, and not only by illegal means, because the condition of more or less permanent European warfare existing since the start of the French Revolution, with Spain repeatedly involved on one side or another, greatly complicated normal trade with the parent country and led to the granting almost routinely of special permission to trade with neutral nations, of which by far the most important was the United States. As was only natural, increasing commercial traffic directly or indirectly facilitated other contacts with the northern neighbor—such as Bolívar's returning home by way of the United States or his nephew's going to school in Philadelphia.

The traveler was again in Venezuela in June 1807. He devoted himself seriously to his rural enterprises, and he became involved in a bitter legal dispute with one neighboring landowner who objected to his plan of building an access road over certain lands in dispute, all for the purpose of introducing improvements to his indigo plantation in Yare, west of Caracas. Things came to the point of an armed confrontation between slaves and hangers-on of the two landowners. Bolívar's insistence on upholding his personal interests and honor was similarly demonstrated when he was named (as various of his forebears had been) to serve as magistrate of the Yare district and he proposed to take possession of the post in question by means of a representative. The municipality of Caracas, within whose jurisdiction Yare lay, demanded that Bolívar appear before it in person, and with indignation over what he considered an intolerable slight, Bolívar lodged a complaint with the highest authority of the colony, the captain-general of Venezuela.

Even amid such concerns, Bolívar abandoned neither the gambling and other diversions of his previous life nor his passion for reading and enlightened discussion. He met often with friends and relatives of like interests—among them his brother, Juan Vicente, and another former teacher, the future grammarian, jurist, and first rector of the University of Chile, Andrés Bello—to talk of travels, literary criticism, and philosophy in the broadest sense. Without doubt their conversations also touched on news of the day and Venezuela's general circumstances, though with the necessary discretion so as not to provoke a forceful reaction from the authorities. There is no indication that Simón Bolívar himself was yet a cause of official worry as a potential subversive. But with the ideas and experiences that he had accumulated in his youth and early adulthood, he very soon would be.

From Imperial Crisis to the First Republic of Venezuela (1808–1812)

On 19 April 1810 a bloodless revolt in Caracas deposed the captain-general of Venezuela and established a governing junta essentially composed of members of the creole elite. This is the date conventionally observed as the beginning of the Venezuelan independence movement and thus also of a new, more open phase of Bolívar's revolutionary vocation. But in fact these events were only the culmination of a crisis that had been incubating for some time—or better yet, the strictly Venezuelan climax of a crisis affecting the entire Spanish empire. At the beginning of the nineteenth century, Spain's was still by far the world's largest empire, yet in the European concert of nations Spain was a distinctly second-rank power. Economically, it was increasingly outpaced by France, Great Britain, and the Low Countries, and the British, in particular, were steadily conquering the markets of Spanish America despite the restrictions of Spanish imperial policy on trade with foreign ports. Spain's political control over its American possessions was shaky, as well. British intruders had moved into a wide swath of Central America's Caribbean coast, and settlers from the United States were beginning to penetrate the periphery of New Spain, or Mexico; also, in 1797, as a by-product of one of the many European

rench Revolutionary and Napoleonic era, a British
the island of Trinidad, which had been a depen-
onial Venezuela.

term perspective, however, the empire's vulnerability
to ᴄ.. encroachment was a lesser problem than a weakening of internal control. For three centuries Spanish rule had
rested not so much on force as on the spontaneous obedience offered to a monarch whose authority as traditional father figure
was reinforced by the unqualified support of the holy church.
But now, above all in the view of an educated minority, the traditional monarchy was losing its legitimacy. As noted in the previous chapter, the Spanish style of absolute monarchy was an
obvious anachronism in the era of the French and Anglo-American Revolutions, and the unedifying conduct of the royal family
and many of the crown's high servants was naturally an aggra-
vating circumstance. The result was a deterioration of the
monarchy's image that was felt in Spain itself as well as the
American colonies.

For Venezuelan creoles, there were in addition a number of
concrete grievances, which were touched on in the first chapter.
One of these concerned the discrimination in favor of peninsulars, or European Spaniards, in the distribution of high office, a
problem that existed in all the Spanish colonies, though it was
less serious than later claimed by patriot propagandists. Complaint over the apparent coddling of *pardos* by the colonial authorities was more specific to Venezuela and to certain other areas of substantial Afro-Latin American population. Imperial
commercial policy, whose theoretical objective was to prevent
direct trade with non-Spanish ports, likewise gave rise to complaint. Again as noted before, that policy was widely evaded by
contraband, and its implementation was highly erratic because
of the frequent granting of temporary exceptions. The agents of
the Spanish monarchy themselves recognized the practical impossibility of Spain's supplying all the colonies' needs and taking
all exports in a period of almost constant European warfare,
and without the customs duties collected on trade with foreigners, there would have been a critical shortage of funds in colonial treasuries. Hence commerce was in fact freer all the time.
Nevertheless, the existing system produced irritants and frustra-

tions, easily apparent in a colony like Venezuela that specialized in the export of bulky agricultural commodities, and the only effective remedy would have been a stable regime of commercial opening.

Instability affected still other aspects of colonial administration, due to the often contradictory orders coming from authorities in Spain and frequent disagreements among officials at the American end. Such problems were perceived as additional symptoms of imperial weakness. And members of the creole elite in Venezuela in particular felt the need for more effectiveness not only in routine administration but for the defense of a social order that they considered to be menaced on the one hand by the pretensions of free *pardos* and on the other by the specter of slave rebellion. If the colonial rulers were not capable of fulfilling their duty, then their American subjects had to weigh the possibility of assuming responsibility themselves. Before 1810 only a few Venezuelans, such as Francisco de Miranda and Simón Bolívar, actually favored independence; but among a wider segment of the population the continued acceptance of imperial ties, for either sentimental or practical reasons, was not incompatible with the conviction that creoles should have more direct participation in making decisions.

Autonomist sentiment was first truly put to a test following the events of 1808 in the parent country, when the intervention of Napoleonic forces compelled the abdication of the Spanish royal family. First Carlos IV was induced to give up his throne, and then his son, having been acclaimed as Fernando VII, saw fit almost at once to follow his father's example and, like him, accept internment in France. In their place Napoleon's brother Joseph was set up as José I. *Afrancesados,* or "Frenchified" Spaniards, accepted the change happily, believing it would lead to the adoption of some liberal reforms in line with the French model but without the turmoil and excesses that had marked the French Revolution. However, there were many more Spaniards, whether partisans of absolute monarchy or liberal constitutionalists, who flatly rejected the solution imposed from beyond the Pyrenees. Armed resistance broke out, and a series of juntas were established that proposed to exercise the functions of Fernando, their "captive" king, until such time as he could assume them in person. A Central Junta, established in Seville, claimed primacy over the others and further claimed to exercise all the rights of the Spanish monarchy in governing the overseas colonies.

Agents both of the *afrancesados* and of the Spanish resistance quickly traveled to the colonies, seeking to make sure that Spain's American subjects would recognize the legitimacy of their own cause and hoping for material help as well. A few colonials were inclined to favor the intrusive government of José I, but an overwhelming majority of those who knew and had an opinion about what was happening in Spain declared their loyalty to the king who was now captive in France. However, those who professed loyalty to Fernando VII did not necessarily accept the claims of the Central Junta, because it occurred to many of them that they logically had as much right to take the reins of power in their hands during the monarch's unfortunate absence as did any bunch of Spaniards in Europe. From Mexico to the Río de la Plata, there were efforts to establish governing juntas in America. But at first the opposition or indecision of other Spanish Americans, together with the firm resolve of almost all peninsular officials in America to back the Seville junta, caused the failure of those attempts.

Even if unsuccessful, the attempt to create an American junta that took place in Caracas in 1808 was one of the most serious. Initially the captain-general, Juan de Casas, wavered between recognizing José I and accepting the authority of the Central Junta in Seville as temporary representative of the legitimate monarch; but a noisy demonstration in the streets of Caracas, whose participants shouted '*vivas*' to Fernando VII and insults against the French, helped Casas decide for Fernando. The question then was whether to establish a local junta to govern in the king's name or simply obey orders from Seville. The Caracas city council asked for a junta in Caracas—and, while at it, for greater freedom of trade. At the same time, agitation was growing both among elements of the common people, stirred up by anti-Spanish slogans, and among young members of the *mantuano* aristocracy like Juan Vicente and Simón Bolívar. In the Bolívar family mansion, meetings were held to discuss the new state of affairs and possible solutions to the crisis, which were not necessarily limited to the mere setting up of a local junta. Indeed these deliberations smelled clearly of subversion to the authorities, who indicated to the Bolívar brothers and various of their associates that it might be a good idea to withdraw for a time to their estates. Casas then for once and all rejected the possibility of a Caracas junta.

Although Bolívar and others did retire to the countryside, agitation continued, and in November 1808 there occurred the final act of what has been called "the conspiracy of the *mantuanos,*" when forty-five members of Venezuelan high society (including two marquises and a count) again petitioned for the creation of a junta in Caracas. However, the captain-general, having made up his mind, saw no reason now to change it. Instead he placed on alert the *pardo* militia, whose officers pledged him support, just in case forceful measures were necessary; and the tactic proved effective, as well as deeply offensive to the creole elite. There followed the arrest of the petitioners, some of whom were briefly imprisoned while others were temporarily confined to their estates.

The future Liberator was not among the petitioners/conspirators of November 1808; indeed he was still absent from Caracas at the time. For another year, he continued taking care of his own estates and exchanging protorevolutionary ideas with kindred spirits. On occasion he expressed himself in public in terms not entirely discreet; but essentially he was content to observe and wait. He even became a friend of the new captain-general, Vicente de Emparán, an affable military officer of rather liberal views, who arrived in May 1809. But at the beginning of April 1810, with the authorities suddenly alarmed over a new threat to public order, Bolívar was again among those invited to leave Caracas. Thus he was absent on 19 April, when the movement began that, despite all setbacks and interruptions, would ultimately lead to independence.

Just as in 1808, the events of April 1810 were triggered by external developments. The situation of Spain itself had continued to deteriorate until, at the start of the year, Napoleonic forces dominated almost all the Iberian Peninsula except the port of Cádiz in the far south. Under these circumstances, the Central Junta dissolved itself, giving way to a Council of

Regency that, like it, claimed to act in the name of Fernando VII. In addition the new body invited both Spaniards and Spanish Americans to elect deputies to a meeting of the Cortes, the Spanish parliament of medieval origin that in practice had not met for generations. The Americans were not offered anything like proportional representation. Even so, in view of the changes occurring in Spain, the colonies again faced the necessity of making a decision: whether to recognize the authority of the new Council of Regency and send a token representation to the Cortes or to try to arrange things on their own.

Like its predecessor, the Central Junta, the Council of Regency, now holed up in Cádiz, proclaimed the birth of a new era of equal treatment for Spaniards and Spanish Americans. But the latter had reason to doubt the sincerity of such words. Quite apart from the lack of representation in proportion to population—in which case American deputies would have been an outright majority in Cortes—the rhetoric of equality was not accompanied by a genuine devolution of authority from the imperial center, because the Cortes would be legislating, from Spain, for the entire empire. By 1810, moreover, there was even some question as to the survival of a Spain independent of French control. For all these reasons it is not surprising that efforts were redoubled in America to set up governments, autonomous in fact even if in theory still committed to the rights of captive Fernando. Governing juntas were now set up, in one colony after another. That of Caracas was first, for the simple reason that it was normally the first colonial capital to receive news from Europe, but juntas sprang up the following month in Cartagena and Buenos Aires and in July in Santafé, where the viceroy of New Granada, titular highest authority over the Venezuelan provinces, was deposed. In continental Spanish America the main exceptions were Peru, where pro-Spanish loyalists led by an exceptionally tough-minded viceroy retained control, and Mexico, where the first blow for autonomy was struck by the radical priest Miguel Hidalgo, whose appeal to the provincial masses so frightened well-to-do creoles that they mostly threw their support to the existing authorities.

In Caracas, the revived junta movement was led by members of the city council and other creole aristocrats, one of whom took it upon himself to act as representative of the *pardos* in the *cabildo abierto,* or open town meeting, which was called to consider the latest developments and choose the course of action. There was no resistance, given the state of discouragement existing among Spanish loyalists since the arrival of the latest news from home and the lack of serious opposition from Captain-General Emparán. So the latter was peacefully replaced by a Supreme Junta of twenty-three members, which followed the same course as other American juntas of acting ostensibly in the name of Fernando VII: it merely rejected subordination to the Council of Regency. In this way it technically retained the monarchical system and, through the figure of the monarch who was so conveniently absent, a connection with Spain and the rest of Spanish America. It thus satisfied the desire of the *mantuanos* and their collaborators within the ranks of bureaucrats, lawyers, and other groups to take charge of their own destiny; yet at the same time the new regime could take advantage of the traditional respect for the emblems and mystique of monarchy among the general population.

There were some, whose number is impossible to estimate, who would have preferred an independent republic and supported the de facto autonomy now achieved as a first step toward that goal. One who felt this way was of course Simón Bolívar, who quickly journeyed to Caracas after the 19 April coup and placed himself at the disposition of the revolutionary authorities. The Junta accepted his services and awarded him the military rank of colonel, but there did not seem as yet to be much need for military preparations. Hence the first mission entrusted to Bolívar was diplomatic, for the new government decided to take advantage of his ample personal experience of the European world. The fact that he offered to pay the costs of the mission from his own pocket no doubt also influenced the Junta's decision. His destination was London, to explain to the British government the aims and justification of the Caracas revolution and to seek diplomatic and moral support. A similar mission was entrusted to Juan Vicente Bolívar and another commissioner to go to the United States, where inevitably the events in Venezuela were seen as a wholesome imitation of the glorious example of the Anglo-American colonists—without, however, the northern republic on that account wanting to make any real commitment to help. The Spanish minister in Washington, in any case, by plying the Venezuelan agents with misleading information, managed to convince them to cut short their stay; Juan Vicente then died tragically and prematurely in a shipwreck while sailing back to Venezuela.

British attitudes were a bit more complicated than the Anglo-American. There was ideological sympathy among liberal publicists, optimism among merchants concerning the possible implications for British trade, and some tacit approval in official circles. The government in London could only look favorably on a political change that might open South American markets to foreign commerce without the limitations imposed by Spanish policy; yet since the Napoleonic invasion of Spain, the latter had automatically become an ally of Great Britain in Europe. From the British standpoint, the ideal solution was therefore de facto independence, with a proper opening to foreign trade, but without abandoning formal allegiance to the Spanish crown. The formula adopted in Caracas appeared to fulfill this requirement, but as was only natural, the cabinet in London was following events with caution.

Simón Bolívar was accompanied to London by a deputy commissioner almost twice his age and, as secretary to the delegation, Andrés Bello, who until the eve of the revolution had been serving as a civil employee of the captaincy-general. A man of even temperament and moderate ideas, Bello was one of those who with perfect sincerity hoped for autonomy within the wider framework of the Spanish monarchy, something that agreed perfectly with the instructions given to the commissioners by the Supreme Junta in Caracas—and with the interests of the British government. The ulterior intentions of Bolívar were somewhat different, as the British foreign minister, the marquis of Wellesley, came to realize in the first audience he granted Bolívar after his arrival. The Venezuelan complained at length of the outrages committed by Spain in America, emphasized the impossibility of recognizing the Council of Regency, and spoke more as the representative of an independent nation than as a loyal subject of Fernando VII. Wellesley pointed out to Bolívar the contradiction between his apparent attitude and the Junta's instructions, which as a novice to diplomacy he had carelessly handed to the minister along with his credentials. Nevertheless, the discussion ended amicably, and it was followed by additional sessions over the next few weeks. In these, Wellesley flatly rejected Bolívar's request that he allow the export of arms to Venezuela but did not hesitate to offer full British protection to Venezuela in the highly unlikely event of a French attack. He also offered the good offices of his government in working out a peaceful settlement with Spain and in that connection kept urging at least formal recognition of the Council of Regency, something Bolívar as insistently rejected. The tangible diplomatic results of the mission were thus relatively modest. But the mere fact of its having been made won the Venezuelan revolutionary regime international attention, not to mention primacy among the junta movements that were now sprouting up throughout Spanish America.

Nor were the mission's objectives strictly limited to diplomacy. In London, Bolívar and his companions could sound out the state of British and European opinion concerning Spanish American developments; and up to a point, they were in a position to influence such opinion in a favorable direction. Bolívar in particular became, as before in Paris, an assiduous frequenter of social and political gatherings. He met members of the royal family and Parliament, journalists and intellectual figures, and he could express his ideas more frankly in informal conversation than in meetings with the foreign minister. Among others, he met the educator Joseph Lancaster, proponent of the system of "mutual teaching," whereby the more advanced pupils acted as monitors for the rest in order that education might reach a greater number of children with the same number of trained teachers. Years later, Bolívar would subsidize introduction of the method in Caracas, under the direction of Lancaster himself. He also met William Wilberforce, leader of the antislavery movement, although it is not known whether this encounter played any role in the later adoption of an abolitionist position by Bolívar, who in any case did not immediately free his own slaves after he returned to Caracas.

The most important of all Bolívar's meetings was with the inveterate conspirator Miranda, now again established in London, whom he had never before seen personally. Because of the "Precursor's" record of militant support for independence, the Supreme Junta had warned the commissioners to proceed with caution in any dealings with him. Yet Bolívar, being equally committed to independence despite having at times to use ambiguous language as representative of the Junta, with characteristic impetuosity urged Miranda to return to Venezuela and there take a leading role in the revolution. Miranda, of course, needed no arm-twisting on this score: he was more than ready to go. The British government, which considered him in the present circumstances a destabilizing element, did not favor his return, and not everyone in Venezuela was disposed to bid him welcome. However, he began his preparations without delay.

Amid his rounds of formal and informal diplomacy and planning for the return of Miranda, Bolívar himself did not wholly overlook the entertainments that the English capital had to offer. He saw the sights of the city and attended the theater as well as private parties. He did not even neglect to explore the brothels, giving rise to one curious episode that he later told on himself, concerning the prostitute who conceived the totally erroneous notion that he was homosexual, took great offense at what she imagined he wanted from her, and when he tried to pacify her with a handful of banknotes, angrily threw them into the fireplace. The misunderstanding must have been due at least in part to his limited command of English and her total lack of Spanish. Fortunately, in official business he could always use French.

Bolívar was in any case no less eager than Miranda to get back to Venezuela. He accordingly embarked in mid-September, just a little ahead of the "Precursor," reaching the port of La Guaira on 5 December 1810. He immediately gave his report to the Junta and was now able to observe personally how the country had developed since the previous April. It had in fact changed in a number of ways. For one thing, the new government had introduced a series of reforms intended to extirpate abuses, win popular support, cause a good impression abroad— or all these things at once. The ports were thrown open to the vessels of friendly and neutral nations without artificial restrictions, though with the prohibition of importing slaves. Nothing was done toward the abolition of slavery itself, but abolition of the trade would please the British especially and would not seriously inconvenience the Venezuelan plantation economy, which was not rapidly expanding and thus did not have the same insatiable demand for additional manpower as the Cuban sugar industry. The new government further abolished the *alcabala,* or sales tax, on basic foodstuffs, as well as export duties on farm and livestock products, all without creating new sources of revenue to replace those abolished. With a view to giving the country also some sort of permanent organization, the Junta called elections for a Venezuelan congress that was to meet the following year. But the social orientation of the new government's leadership was made clear in the regulation of the right to vote, extended only to adult males who owned 2,000 pesos (then equivalent to dollars) of property or who exercised some profession in an independent capacity. There was no open discrimination against *pardos,* but few of them could possibly meet the requirements.

Unfortunately, the situation of public order had deteriorated. As successor to the captain-general and other Spanish authorities, the Supreme Junta in Caracas expected automatic obedience from the rest of Venezuela; and it was disappointed. The central region recognized its supremacy without major problems, but in outlying provinces the result was mixed. In eastern Venezuela there was dissension and some uncertainty until at length Barcelona and Cumaná pledged obedience, but Guayana—claiming for itself the same right of self-determination as Caracas—recognized not the Venezuelan Junta but the Council of Regency in Cádiz. In the west, Coro and Maracaibo did the same as Guayana, while the Andean cities Mérida and Trujillo gave their backing to Caracas. Coro was the most recalcitrant district of all, because its people had not forgiven Caracas for having replaced Coro as capital of Venezuela in the early colonial era. And the first bloodshed of the revolution occurred precisely in an unsuccessful attempt to reduce Coro to obedience.

Even before conflict began between Caracas and Coro, the break between Caracas and Cádiz had become seemingly irreversible. In response to the refusal to recognize its authority, the Council of Regency denounced the followers of the

Caracas Junta as rebellious vassals and decreed a blockade of their ports. This was a largely symbolic blockade: it affected almost only the much reduced legal trade between Venezuela and Spain, because Spain lacked the naval power to make it effective, and the Anglo-Saxon powers, which controlled most of the trade with Venezuela, did not accept its validity. Nevertheless, the intransigence of Cádiz inevitably hardened attitudes in Venezuela, where both the revolutionaries and their opponents began to prepare for possible civil war. Thus when the Caracas Junta in November 1810 dispatched a military expedition of 3,000 men against Coro, it was basically as a preventive measure or preemptive strike. The commander was Francisco Rodríguez del Toro, marquis of Toro and another relative of Bolívar, and the campaign ended in humiliating defeat, in part because of the commander's commendable desire to hold bloodshed to a minimum and in part because of his sheer inexperience.

For various reasons, then, the panorama facing Bolívar on his return and likewise Miranda, when he arrived a few days later, was less than satisfactory. Both men were convinced, however, that what was most needed was to deepen the revolution itself. With this in mind, they entered fully into the activities of the Sociedad Patriótica, which had been founded in Caracas as a forum for discussing questions of economic improvement, public works, and anything having to do with the good of the country. The participants were typically enlightened *mantuanos* or members of the professional middle sectors, though there were some from other social groups, not excluding *pardos;* even some women attended the sessions. And in the society's debates or the pages of its newspaper, *El Patriota de Venezuela*—Caracas had finally obtained a printing press in 1808–discussion turned ever more insistently to the need for a democratic republic, with total independence from Spain.

On 2 March 1811 the first Congress of Venezuela met, having been elected according to the socially restrictive criteria already mentioned but geographically representing all the territory controlled by the Junta Suprema. At its installation the deputies swore among other things to uphold the rights of Fernando VII, which obviously differed from the tone set in debates of the Sociedad Patriótica. Indeed, disagreements within the patriot camp were already becoming evident—and in them lay the seeds of later political disputes. But at this point the drive for independence could not be stopped. In early July the issue was discussed simultaneously in Congress and in the Patriotic Society, and in a night session of the latter on 3 July, Simón Bolívar made the first of his significant political addresses, calling eloquently for absolute separation from the former parent country. Two days later Congress showed itself in agreement by declaring Venezuela an independent republic. It was the first outright declaration of independence anywhere in Spanish America.

In view of the short time that elapsed between deposition of the captain-general and the declaration of independence—little more than a year—it might be thought that the declaration of loyalty to the captive monarch as made in April 1810 and repeated on numerous occasions had been only one more example of the use in Spanish America of "the mask of Fernando"—an insincere façade of monarchism that served both as transitional formula and as an expedient to gain time while overcoming the traditionalist preconceptions of the uneducated masses. Such an interpretation would no doubt be applicable to the cases of Bolívar and other advanced thinkers but not necessarily to all the others who acclaimed the creation of the Junta Suprema and at the same time swore fealty to Fernando VII. The fact still remains that Venezuela, sooner than any other Spanish colony, came to see the unbridgeable gap between the organizers of juntas in America and those who held on to power in whatever portion of Spain was not controlled by Napoleonic forces. Venezuela's geographic position had much to do with this: the proximity of the Spanish Antilles and the presence of a Spanish fleet in the Caribbean (even if unable to mount an effective blockade) made the intransigence of Cádiz more obvious to supporters of the new regime while giving encouragement to its enemies, who were inspired sometimes by love of Fernando, sometimes by jealousy of Caracas, or more likely both.

Naturally the logic of events did not cause any last-ditch monarchists to embrace the republic, and those who had supported monarchy out of mere habit or pragmatism while otherwise accepting the rule of the Junta did not all like this latest change, either. In particular among those Spanish-born residents who had gone along with the coup of April 1810 and initial establishment of the Junta, there was a clear tendency to reject the declaration of independence. Some Spaniards did continue to support the revolution, but more numerous were the creoles and Venezuelans of color who now turned against it. The king to whom previously they gave allegiance had been, after all, a concrete being, his effigy on coins something visible and the formal similarity between his role as head of state and that of the father in any human family easily comprehensible, whereas "republic" was an unfamiliar abstract concept. To complicate matters further, nothing had happened to lessen the rivalries between Caracas and various peripheral provinces. For that matter even the concept of "Venezuela" as a single political entity had no very deep roots in popular consciousness. The captaincy-general of Venezuela had been cobbled together from provinces formerly subject to other jurisdictions only in 1777, and though after that date they all answered to a single official in Caracas, there had not been enough time for any strong sense of Venezuelan identity to be consolidated over and above regional loyalties.

There was dissension also between Caracas and some lesser population centers of its own immediate province, as was the case in the first serious challenge to the new order following the independence declaration. It appeared in Valencia, a town harboring ambitions to become a provincial capital in its own right, and this time Miranda, whose formal military credentials no one could match, was chosen to command the punitive expedition. Bolívar went, too, and in the attack on Valencia on 23 July (the eve of his twenty-eighth birthday) he received his baptism of fire. Bolívar fought with distinction, as Miranda noted in his report on the battle, but the revolutionists suffered considerable losses and had to withdraw. On returning to the offensive, Miranda systematically prepared a siege of Valencia and this time took it in a bloody encounter that was followed by a general sack of the city.

There were some, apparently including Bolívar, who felt the patriot forces should without delay go on to strike such other royalist redoubts as the hostile provinces of Coro, Maracaibo, and Guayana. But this did not happen. Miranda, as generalissimo, was in favor of such an offensive in principle. Nevertheless, he was forced to spend time defending himself against the attacks of jealous rivals and prideful *mantuanos* who looked on him as both a dangerous radical and something of an upstart, and who in addition found his character traits less than appealing: Miranda did not easily unbend, and he clearly lacked charisma. He was furthermore a man of strictly European military training, so that much of the criticism had to do with his efforts to impose greater discipline. Indeed Miranda had genuine doubts concerning the state of preparedness of the republican forces, which needed more rigorous preparation before committing themselves to a definitive campaign.

Meanwhile, attention turned to the deliberations of Congress, which after declaring independence devoted itself to giving the country a presumably permanent organization along republican lines. The first step was to be adoption of a written constitution, and one was promulgated before the end of the year. But the discussion of its terms stirred up new controversies, and the final product has been the target of strong criticism by most Venezuelan historians, who in this matter have basically echoed objections formulated in the first place by Bolívar, among others. Bolívar had not been elected a deputy to the Congress, yet obviously he followed the debates with close interest; and in his view there was more than one grave defect in the way the First Republic of Venezuela was structured by the Constitution of 1811.

The first national constitution adopted anywhere in Spanish America (though for Latin America as a whole, Haitian constitution makers had already taken precedence), Venezuela's fundamental law had as its most salient feature the creation of a federal republic, in which the provinces were given ample faculties to deal with local affairs while the central authorities took charge of matters of general interest. The influence of the U.S. federal model was obvious in this respect, though other examples of federative organization were not lacking in either modern times or antiquity; and Bolívar, for one, firmly believed that the choice of federalism reflected an unwholesome fascination with foreign models that were inapplicable to Venezuela. Federalism appeared inapplicable above all in the midst of a struggle for existence, which he felt required a highly centralized regime with strong executive power.

In truth, there was more involved in the adoption of federalism than mere imitation. As mentioned earlier, the political entity now being organized as a sovereign republic was a recent invention, dating only from the establishment of the captaincy-general in 1777 and resting on no long tradition of loyalty and obedience. The deficiencies of internal communication and sociocultural differences from one region to another were additional factors favoring some degree of decentralization. But it was also true that the Venezuelan proponents of federation had insufficiently pondered one other facet of the North American experience—the way in which the autonomy of the former colonies, loosely confederated during the very war for independence, had been a source of countless headaches for General Washington. In this last regard, Bolívar and other critics obviously had the better case.

What is more, the framers of the Venezuelan constitution signally failed to imitate one fundamental detail of the North American constitution as finally written after the war was over: a national executive branch headed by a single person. The Venezuelan charter of 1811 instead entrusted executive power to a triumvirate, thus further undermining the new government's capacity to organize institutions and to defend the liberty so recently proclaimed. But federalism and the nature of the national executive were not the only points of disagreement. On another controversial matter, the Congress adopted an article abolishing all *fueros,* or special privileges, of the clergy and military. Adopted over some bitter criticism, this reform was enacted in the name of the civil equality of all free inhabitants, and sooner in Venezuela than in any other part of Spanish America; it was therefore an indication of the intellectual liberalism of the new Venezuelan ruling groups. Such liberalism had its limits in that the constitution left intact the institution of slavery. But the deputies did again precede other Spanish Americans in expressly eliminating all legal discrimination between racial categories. *Pardos* and even blacks (obviously meaning free *pardos* and free blacks) received exactly the same rights and obligations as whites and Indians, and the contrast with the creole population's earlier attitudes is impressive. Probably, however, so brusque a change was not due solely to the penetration of enlightened ideas. For many, it was undoubtedly seen as a tactical necessity to convince the overwhelmingly nonwhite majority that the revolution—led no less overwhelmingly by whites—was for the benefit of all. Up to a point, it was only recognition that the old caste society was already crumbling through the action of the *pardos* and blacks themselves, who after various rebellions and protests in the colonial period had burst onto the political scene since April 1810 as demonstrators and combatants (on both sides of the struggle) and in a few select cases even assumed positions of responsibility, for example, as members of Congress itself. The *pardos'* advance did not cease to generate friction, but neither was it difficult to see that it was largely irreversible.

To be sure, the constitution provided only formal legal equality of the races. It retained a suffrage marked by severe socioeconomic discrimination, which supposedly was not in conflict with enlightened ideas. Equally revealing was the adoption by the same Congress of certain "ordinances of the **llanos**" designed to facilitate the extension of private ownership over the llanos, or plains, of the Orinoco Basin—and thereby, too, over the wild cattle that roamed the plains and that the existing population of **llanero** cowboys, mostly *pardos* and mestizos, had been exploiting freely. One aim was to convert the *llaneros* into hired hacienda peons by requiring them to obtain and carry a document attesting to their stable and honorable employment. For the moment there was no practical way of implementing this regulation, but it again suggests what group enjoyed greatest political influence in the new regime.

For the rest, the revolutionary government was increasingly desperate for money. It now had important military expenditures and, to cover them, was dependent above all on the customs revenues, which in turn depended on the flow of foreign trade. The suspension of trade with Spain created no serious problems, but the interruption of trade with *New* Spain—that is, Mexico—was another matter, because Mexicans were heavy consumers of Venezuelan cacao and customarily paid with hard currency. Even more serious was a downturn in the market prices of Venezuelan produce exported to the United States and the British Antilles, which inevitably reduced Venezuelans' ability to import and to pay duties on what was imported. To try to overcome the fiscal crisis, Venezuela had recourse to issuing unbacked paper money, which rapidly devalued and made matters worse. Such mismanagement of financial affairs was just one example of the inevitable stumbles incurred by a government that was weakly constituted and faced challenges without precedent in colonial experience. In military matters, furthermore, conscription was decreed to fill the ranks—a measure as deeply unpopular as it was unavoidable. There was widespread resistance to the draft, not least because there was no money to pay the conscripts adequately; not surprisingly, they tended to desert en masse.

The rulers of provinces still under royalist control faced similar problems. Their resources were even less than those of Caracas, and they could expect no significant assistance from European Spain, whose highest priority continued to be its own struggle against Napoleon. Yet the Venezuelan loyalists had not lost contact with Spanish-held Puerto Rico, and from there the naval captain Domingo de Monteverde arrived early in 1812 to give aid. Taking charge of the situation, he used Coro as a springboard to move against neighboring towns under at least nominal control of the revolutionaries. Monteverde had about 1,500 men under his command, some of whom had come with him from Puerto Rico but most of them Venezuelans. He met little resistance, for the republican cause had as yet sunk no deep roots in popular sentiment, and the apparent incapacity of the republican government further undermined its prestige.

The fatal blow was not long in coming. In the afternoon of 26 March 1812, which was Thursday of Holy Week, a powerful earthquake shook Venezuela, causing enormous destruction in Caracas and other centers. The death toll was apparently between 15,000 and 20,000, and the number of wounded greater. Buildings collapsed and small streams changed course. The psychological impact was also profound. It being obvious that the earthquake had been sent as punishment by God, many persons resolved immediately to correct their sinful ways, whether in gratitude for having been spared or as insurance in case of aftershocks. There were not a few cases of sudden marriages of people who had been living together without the church's blessing; some Venezuelans even married their slave concubines. Nor was it hard to reach the further conclusion that the sins provoking divine wrath were not just personal but political. Was not the fact that royalist-held territories were mostly unscathed a clear sign that God did not approve of Venezuelan independence?

Even before the political affiliation of affected and unaffected regions was known, the enemies of independence had drawn the inference in question and were proclaiming it to the four winds. Among them were a good many clergymen, though by no means all of them, contrary to the frequent allegations of anticlerical authors. In any event, no sooner had geology seemingly aligned itself with the king than Simón Bolívar entered again upon the scene to combat its effects. He was in Caracas on the day of the quake and immediately set forth to offer aid to the victims and counteract anti-revolutionary preaching. He threatened one royalist friar with his sword, and with good scientific sense recommended setting fire to ruined houses even if there were still cadavers within, as a means of preventing epidemic disease. His most famous gesture was the cry (as recorded by a royalist witness) in which he boldly defied the adversity of fate: "If Nature opposes us, we shall fight against her and make her obey us." To enemies of the revolution the words were blasphemy, and without question they were the words of a skeptical religious freethinker. At the same time, they demonstrated what would be one of the lasting traits of Bolívar's personality, a refusal to bow to reverses of any kind.

Shortly afterward Bolívar returned to active military service, in an increasingly desperate situation. Monteverde had continued his advance, and in an effort to turn the tide, the republican authorities took the extreme measure of naming Miranda commander of all their forces with dictatorial power. However, the royalist leader kept up his offensive, though he had even fewer troops under his command than the patriots and similar shortages of military equipment; he was finally stopped halfway between Valencia and Caracas. But Miranda showed more interest in disciplining and organizing his forces than in shifting rapidly to a counteroffensive. Neither did Bolívar take part directly in the fighting against Monteverde. Instead Miranda put him in charge of Puerto Cabello, a coastal stronghold with an imposing fortress and Venezuela's second leading port. Bolívar accepted the assignment apparently without enthusiasm, for a stationary command was not quite in keeping with the young colonel's restless temperament. But the post was of critical importance, both for the protection of commerce and because of the strategic location of Puerto Cabello, along the coast just to the north of Valencia, which made it a threat to Monteverde's rear as he advanced toward the capital. Not only that, but its fortress contained a deposit of arms and a significant group of royalist political prisoners.

The enemy was equally aware of the importance of Puerto Cabello and, in the weeks that followed Bolívar's assumption of command, kept threatening the city from the nearby highlands under royalist control. Worse yet, the royalist prisoners in the citadel took to plotting with members of the garrison and seized the castle of San Felipe, which was the key to the city's fortifications. For a few days Bolívar and the troops that remained loyal to him kept up resistance under a deadly fire from the batteries of the castle. Amid growing demoralization, there was a rush of civilians to flee the city. Trying to avoid the inevitable, Bolívar orchestrated the noisy celebration of imaginary patriot victories, supposedly to frighten the enemy in the castle, but to no effect. On the land side, other royalist forces tightened their siege of the city. The remaining patriot garrison had little choice but to surrender on 6 July, though Bolívar and a handful of his officers escaped, with difficulty, by sea to La Guaira.

Bolívar cast blame for the disaster on the traitors in the fortress and the "cowardice" of the civilian population that had jumped to the conclusion (not without justification) that the patriot cause was lost. Others have cast blame on Bolívar, arguing that, while he was dreaming of breaking out from Puerto Cabello to take the offensive, he had neglected the defense of the castle. It is impossible to say at this point where the greater truth lies, but there is no doubt about the extent of the disaster. As Bolívar himself said in a letter to Miranda, "After having lost the state's last and best stronghold, how can I feel anything but crazed, my general? Please do not compel me to see your face! I am not to blame, but I am miserable, and that is enough." Miranda felt equally miserable and exclaimed to his officers, though in foreign tongue, "Vénézuéla est blessée au coeur"— "Venezuela is wounded to the heart."

Loss of Puerto Cabello was not the only wound. A lieutenant of Monteverde had meanwhile been organizing guerrillas in the llanos to fight against independence, and bands of slaves and free blacks rebelled in the region east of Caracas. The latter had been duly incited by royalist planters and merchants, as well as by parish priests acting on secret instructions of the archbishop in Caracas. However, they were also reacting against republican military conscription: Miranda had decreed a general muster of free men, and the Caracas provincial authorities extended it to slaves, offering them liberty in return for four years' service; but it seems this was no adequate incentive. So far, the royalists on their part had done nothing for either slaves or free *pardos,* but the balance of forces in the conflict was tilting in their favor, and as yet the colored castes had seen no convincing evidence of the benefit they would derive from independence. The army under Miranda's orders remained impressive on paper, but day after day it became more demoralized. Desertions multiplied. Because Miranda no longer saw a realistic chance of victory, he entered negotiations for an armistice, proposing a series of conditions that Monteverde mostly rejected out of hand until finally, on 25 July, a surrender agreement was reached.

Even before the definitive capitulation was signed, Miranda had taken steps to have a ship ready at La Guaira, to carry him again into exile. And on 30 July, with Monteverde at the outskirts of Caracas, he went to the port, intending to embark the following day. His papers and luggage were already on board; he also had taken with him some 22,000 pesos from the republican treasury plus a quantity of gold ounces. But in the early morning of the 31st he was awakened by a group of civil and military officers who arrested him, thus preventing his departure from Venezuela and paving the way, indirectly, for his capture by Monteverde. There are different versions—and no certainty—as to the intentions of the men who treated the "Precursor" in this way. At one extreme is the view that they were trying to put themselves in the good graces of the royalists and thereby gain leniency in defeat. At the other extreme is the traditional interpretation of Venezuelan patriotic historians, to the effect that Miranda's captors were punishing him for his apparent betrayal of the republican cause. The considerable confusion and rumors that circulated concerning the precise terms of the capitulation, which had not immediately been published, combined with the news of Miranda's treasure stowed away on shipboard, seemingly gave credence to the charge of treason. But there are still other conceivable interpretations—and the possibility that not all participants in the affair were driven by the same motives.

Much of the controversy surrounding Miranda's arrest is due to the mere fact that among his captors was Simón Bolívar. It appears that Bolívar had also been considering the possibility of escape from Venezuela, in view of the near certainty that almost all of it was about to fall into enemy hands. But when he on his part went to La Guaira, whether to organize a patriot counterattack (as he later claimed) or to take ship for temporary exile, he had the unpleasant surprise of finding that his supreme commander had gone ahead of him and had his own possessions stowed on board. Such being the case, Bolívar did not hesitate to join the plotters. He was not one of those who had previously dissuaded Miranda from spending the night in the safety of the ship waiting in the harbor, but it was he who personally communicated to Miranda the order of arrest. The Spanish historian Salvador de Madariaga, author of a well-documented if somewhat tendentious biography of Bolívar, had no qualms in associating his role in the capture of Miranda with the relative leniency subsequently shown toward him by the restored colonial regime, which gave him a passport to peacefully leave the country. According to Madariaga, Bolívar was therefore one of those who acted with a view to winning the favor of the victors—an interpretation clearly applicable to several of the others. However, it does not seem most in keeping with the otherwise intransigent personality of Bolívar or with his later conduct, once he inherited Miranda's role as preeminent leader of the struggle against Spain. The one thing about which there can be no doubt is the sincere indignation Bolívar felt concerning the surrender Miranda agreed to and the precipitous flight he was preparing to undertake. For the rest of his life Bolívar never showed the least remorse over his part in the affair: if the choice had been left to him, he would have ordered Miranda shot without further ado.

If Bolívar really thought of fighting on without interruption, hoping to spark a general reaction against Monteverde, it is obvious that he had not accurately assessed the military and political state of Venezuela. The very same day that Miranda was captured, royalist forces without serious opposition took possession of La Guaira, where they arrested a great number of people. They did not arrest Bolívar, who managed to return to Caracas undetected and temporarily took refuge in the house of the marquis of Casa León, an aristocratic intriguer always ready to collaborate with the government in power, be it republican or royalist. Miranda himself by the end of 1813 had been taken to Spain, where he died in prison in 1816. But of course this was hardly the end. The Spanish reconquest turned out to be as ephemeral as the Venezuelan First Republic had been; and in its collapse Bolívar would play an even more important role than the one he played, as unlucky commander of Puerto Cabello, in the collapse of the Republic.

III

Resurrection and New Collapse of the Republic (1812–1814)

The very rapidity of Monteverde's successful restoration of Spanish rule in Venezuela inevitably entailed some superficiality, which in itself raised the possibility that it might not last—particularly because the revolutionary movement that had taken hold in neighboring New Granada was still intact. Moreover, the counterrevolution in Venezuela coincided with the adoption in Cádiz of the Constitution of 1812, which converted the Spanish empire into a liberal constitutional monarchy. The constitution did not give true autonomy to the American territories, but it endowed them with popularly elected municipal and provincial corporations for the management of local affairs; and it gave them limited representation in the Spanish Cortes. In the view of a good many creoles as well as Spanish liberals, it had at least the potential to serve as basis for a peaceful solution to the conflict between Spain and its colonies. But because Monteverde did not like the constitution, he delayed its promulgation in Venezuela, and in fact his conduct was both unpredictable and erratic. He not only hesitated about the constitution but harshly repressed some defeated revolutionists while ignoring or minimizing the faults of others. In the concrete case of the young rebel Simón Bolívar, there had been no confiscation of his property; neither was there any guarantee that he would not be arrested the minute he left his sanctuary in the house and under the protection of the marquis of Casa León.

41

Bolívar made no precipitous attempt to leave the country, but neither did he seek full reconciliation with the triumphant royalists. Indeed he had good reason to be somewhat undecided about his course of action, given the ambiguous situation of Venezuela in the aftermath of the royalist reconquest. However, he finally arranged his departure from the marquis's house and from Venezuela thanks to the intercession of a Spanish friend, Francisco Iturbe, who held a position in the colonial bureaucracy. Iturbe asked Monteverde for a passport permitting the defeated adversary to peacefully depart, and the royalist leader granted it following a meeting with Bolívar in which—according to the traditional version—the recipient objected strenuously, with renewed profession of republican faith, to Monteverde's assertion that he was giving it in recognition of Bolívar's service to the king in the capture of Miranda. There is no formal documentation of that exchange, but Bolívar received his passport and on 27 August 1812 set sail from La Guaira to Curaçao.

Bolívar remained in Curaçao two months, only a few kilometers from the coast of Venezuela and paying close attention to what happened there. Among other things, he was interested in the status of his property and in the possibility of lifting the embargo placed on that of his brother, Juan Vicente, which unlike his had been seized by the royalists. Because of Juan Vicente's premature death on his return voyage from the United States and the lack of legitimate heirs, his possessions would now be inherited by Simón. In correspondence from Curaçao with his royalist friend Iturbe, Bolívar emphasized his political good conduct, as if that might increase the chances of favorable treatment, and before leaving Caracas he had let it be known that he planned to go to Spain to take part in the struggle against Napoleon, though enlisting for that purpose in the British army of the duke of Wellington rather than a strictly Spanish force. It is not impossible that he seriously considered doing just that. But there is no reliable evidence of his intent, and when at the end of October he left Curaçao, it was for Cartagena, in New Granada, to throw himself once more into the fight against Spain. According to his detractors, he changed his mind on receiving word that Monteverde had finally seized his property.

For others, the confiscation was at most a factor hastening his return to the struggle.

In the New Granada that Bolívar found on landing in its principal port, the revolution had not gone as far as it had in Venezuela before its collapse. Neither had the revolutionaries been faced with so strong a counterattack as that launched by Monteverde. In the one province of Cartagena, the revolutionists had declared absolute independence in November 1811, but other provinces still had not followed its example, even though the majority were enjoying de facto independence. And it was independence not just from Spain but from Santafé, the former viceregal capital. The United Provinces of New Granada, a loose confederation established toward the end of 1811, was in reality an alliance of sovereign provincial governments, for it lacked a central administration with power of its own. And the province of Santafé, whose leaders aspired to take the place of the former viceroys as rulers of all New Granada, flatly refused to enter the confederation. Officially renamed Cundinamarca (indigenous names being a fashionable way to point up the break with the colonial heritage), Santafé was headed by the New Granadan "Precursor," Antonio Nariño, who had spent the last years of the colonial regime as either a fugitive from or a prisoner of the Spanish authorities. Nariño launched a campaign in favor of strong centralized government as the only way to ensure survival of the revolution; but by keeping the central core of New Granada out of the confederation, he simply exaggerated its weakness.

There were social and racial tensions too, though less severe than in Venezuela and also less serious than the proliferation of regional conflicts, for not only did outlying provinces refuse to accept the leadership of Santafé but some of them suffered their own internal divisions, pitting provincial capitals against lesser cities. New Granada's patriots still managed to adopt a number of institutional reforms, roughly comparable to those of Venezuela's First Republic, though on a province-by-province basis in the lack of any true central government. In Cartagena, which had been one of the three American headquarters of the Spanish Inquisition, the revolutionists decreed its abolition and made a bonfire not of heretics but of Inquisitorial paraphernalia.

Cartagena had also been the principal entry point for the slave trade, which it prohibited, as well.

Happily for the New Granadan revolutionists, they attracted less attention from the Spanish Antilles or Spain itself than did their Venezuelan counterparts. Located at the edge of a high Andean plain, Santafé was the most isolated of all the viceregal capitals of Spanish America: its reconquest could wait. Most of the other population centers were also tucked away in distant Andean valleys or plateaus. Cartagena was an exception, but it had the protection of its legendary fortifications, which once completed, had never been taken by assault. There were nevertheless a few counterrevolutionary strongholds, created by local initiative and generally having little contact with each other or with royalists outside the colony. One was the province of Santa Marta, a traditional rival of Cartagena for commercial primacy on the Caribbean coast but marginalized by the latter's greater success. If in Cartagena the forces loyal to Spain had prevailed, without much doubt Santa Marta would have embraced the patriot cause; with Cartagena a focus of revolution, Santa Marta chose the other side. There were some other royalist redoubts, including Pasto in the southwest, but at the time of Bolívar's arrival Santa Marta posed the greatest danger. It was an area of scant population and resources but had received an influx of royalist refugees from other provinces and even some aid from Spanish Cuba. Thanks to these reinforcements and to negligence on the part of Cartagena, the royalists of Santa Marta seized the eastern bank of the Magdalena River and thereby managed to cut the chief artery of communication between the coast and interior. The rulers of Cartagena were accordingly delighted to accept the help offered by fugitive Venezuelan patriots—among them Bolívar.

Before his first military action in New Granada, Bolívar had time to draft two documents of historical importance. The first was a petition that he and another Venezuelan refugee submitted to the federal congress of New Granada imploring aid for the recovery of Venezuela. In it they underscored "the identity of the cause of Venezuela with that defended by all America, and principally New Granada," and the grave danger that New Granada faced as a result of Spanish reconquest of the neighboring colony. The other document, known as the "Cartagena Manifesto" and dated mid-December 1812, repeated the message of American solidarity and the call for help in recovering Venezuela. Identifying himself as "a son of unhappy Caracas," Bolívar further discussed in some detail what he considered the fundamental causes of the loss of his homeland. He decried the patriots' lack of energy in combatting such enemies of the revolution as the people of Coro, who should have been harshly repressed at the first sign of opposition. Closely related to this error, in his view, was that of seeking guidance in the framing of laws and institutions from "certain worthy visionaries who, conceiving some ethereal republic, sought to achieve political perfection on the presumption of the perfectibility of the human species"—a presumption that Bolívar, it must be emphasized, never once allowed himself to make. Worst of all was the adoption of federalism:

> The federal system, although it is the most perfect and the most suitable for guaranteeing human happiness in society, is, notwithstanding, the form most inimical to the interests of our emerging states. . . . [I]s there a country anywhere, no matter how sensible and republican it is, capable of ruling itself during times of internal unrest and external warfare by a system as complicated and weak as a federalist government?

That system obviously was copied not from any "ethereal republic" but, insofar as it was a copy of anything, from the quite solid republic of the United States. Bolívar did not explicitly make that connection in the manifesto, yet a constantly recurring theme in his political writings would be the inapplicability of the seemingly successful Anglo-American model to the conditions of Spanish America.

Before the year was out, Bolívar had gone into action on behalf of the "state" of Cartagena. Initially he was given the strictly defensive assignment of guarding the miserable small town of Barranca (today Calamar) on the west side of the Magdalena River—something hardly to the liking of a Venezuelan officer whose sight was firmly fixed on the reconquest of Caracas. And so, ignoring orders and with total confidence in his own judgment, Bolívar improvised a river flotilla of canoes and

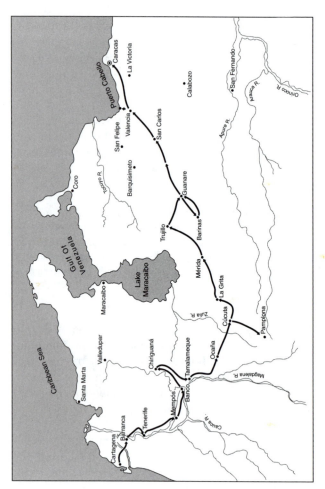

The "Campaña Admirable" of 1813, with Bolívar's prior movements. (Adapted with permission from Alvaro Valencia Tovar, *El ser guerrero del Libertador* [Bogotá: Instituto Colombiano de Cultura, 1980], p. 49)

anything that would float, set forth up the Magdalena River, and by surprise seized the town of Tenerife from a superior royalist detachment. Taking time barely to catch his breath and gather up the arms abandoned by the enemy, Bolívar continued upstream, occupying still more of the chain of Spanish positions that had cut communication with the patriots of the interior. In this series of engagements the forces were small on either side, but Bolívar's success was impressive: in just two weeks, he broke the blockade of the river. He also lifted republican morale to the extent that the government of Cartagena happily overlooked his disobedience.

By mid-January 1813 Bolívar had left the Magdalena Valley and was in Ocaña, a small city of the eastern Andes whose royalist garrison fled before the advance of this suddenly famous warrior. There Bolívar received a plea for help from Colonel Manuel del Castillo, who with a small force was guarding the route that led toward Santafé from the border between New Granada and Venezuela. This time Bolívar did seek the prior consent of the government of Cartagena, his ostensible employer, and once he obtained it, marched against Cúcuta, the principal town on the border and currently occupied by the royalists. With Castillo protecting his southern flank, he launched his attack at the end of February. The royalists numbered some eight hundred men. Bolívar had only five hundred; but a furious bayonet charge decided the battle in the patriots' favor.

The Battle of Cúcuta is not one of the more famous engagements of the independence struggle, and the bulk of the royalist army got away. However, like Bolívar's previous campaign along the Magdalena River, it had major psychological impact. It cleared a strategic corner of New Granada of enemy forces and eliminated a base from which they could have threatened Tunja, capital of the United Provinces, and even Santafé, now capital of the State of Cundinamarca, which had meanwhile become bogged down in a civil war with the confederation. In addition, the patriots found merchandise at Cúcuta worth an estimated million pesos that merchants of Spanish-occupied Maracaibo had sent ahead in the expectation that a victorious march of the royalists would soon allow them to sell the goods in interior New Granada.

For Bolívar, the main importance of taking Cúcuta was the fact that it could serve as a launching point for the liberation of Venezuela. Fortunately, too, his thesis of the inseparability of the destinies of Venezuela and New Granada had been making headway, at the same time that his recent successes were winning him the confidence of a wide range of New Granadan leaders. Not all of them, to be sure: Colonel Castillo, for one, regarded as harebrained Bolívar's idea of launching an immediate invasion of Venezuela, in view of the fact that Monteverde had at his disposal on the Venezuelan side of the border forces greatly superior to those the patriots of New Granada could spare for the enterprise. But the government of the United Provinces, which awarded Bolívar the rank of general in its own army, gave at least conditional support. Bolívar was authorized to lead New Granadan forces into Venezuela, though for the moment only as far as Trujillo, roughly halfway between the border and Caracas, and it insisted on the restoration in Venezuela of the First Republic's institutional order that Bolívar had just criticized so bitterly. These conditions went against Bolívar's military ambition and political ideas, but he ostensibly accepted them rather than waste time quibbling.

At bottom, both the skeptics like Castillo and Bolívar's supporters, who included the president of the United Provinces, Camilo Torres, were correct. New Granada had greater population than Venezuela and gold mines too, but its resources were difficult to concentrate because of the extremely mountainous topography and reigning political disunity. Over in Venezuela, Monteverde had between 6,000 and 7,000 men, while the forces available for Bolívar's expedition were a mere two divisions, of approximately 1,000 men between them. Monteverde further maintained permanent contact with the Spanish Antilles. Thus from a purely military standpoint what Bolívar proposed was indubitably rash. But the political and social conditions in Venezuela were rather different—perhaps even more favorable to Bolívar's scheme than he himself recognized.

At the fall of the First Republic, the disillusion of independence supporters in Venezuela, just when a liberal and constitutional government had been established in Spain, naturally should have facilitated the peaceful restoration of Spanish rule.

However, the victorious Monteverde wasted the opportunity that lay before him. He finally proclaimed the new fundamental law in November 1812, but he never conscientiously enforced it, pursuing instead an essentially vengeful and reactionary agenda. He hardened repression against the defeated and quarreled continually with those royal officials who sought to moderate his policies as a way of promoting reconciliation. And though the counterrevolutionary action of *pardos* and slaves had contributed to the royalist triumph, neither was any serious attempt made to satisfy the desire of people of color for greater equality. The result of this combination of factors was growing discontent in all parts of Venezuela. And in fact the new collapse of Spanish power in Venezuela had begun as early as January 1813, when a band of republicans who had taken refuge on the island of Trinidad invaded eastern Venezuela under the leadership of Santiago Mariño and there began carving out a patriot sanctuary. By so doing they would among other things make it impossible to concentrate all available forces in opposition to Bolívar.

The campaign that Bolívar now undertook was the first truly large-scale operation for which he was undisputed supreme commander. He launched it in a condition of distinct numerical inferiority, but he proposed to overcome that problem through rapidity and flexibility of movement, the element of surprise, and tactical improvisation as needed. Such an approach, in addition to making up for quantitative deficiencies, was fully in accord with the personal idiosyncrasy of Bolívar—a man who slept little and in fact appeared to be in almost perpetual motion. As commander, he became known for the custom of dictating orders to two or even more aides simultaneously while he paced the corridor or swung in a hammock. A lover of dancing, he would also attend dances in the towns he passed through on campaign but leave the floor every so often to issue orders on some political or military problem, then return to the ball. At first, to be sure, there was not much time for dancing. Wishing to march on Caracas as soon as possible, Bolívar made his definitive return to Venezuela on 14 May, and in less than ten days, advancing quickly over mountainous terrain and meeting no serious resistance, he was already in Mérida, the most important city of the western Venezuelan Andes. There Bolívar gathered both additional supplies and recruits; Mérida is also the first place where he was acclaimed with the title *Liberator.*

The next objective was Trujillo, another population center of Andean Venezuela, to which Bolívar dispatched his vanguard division while he remained behind to consolidate republican control in the area of Mérida with another part of his army. Such a division of forces was inherently risky, but everything turned out according to plan; after a few minor encounters, Trujillo was also in patriot hands. On 14 June (one month after the campaign began) Bolívar himself entered the city, and on the very next day he issued the proclamation known as the Decree of War to the Death, which from that time on has ranked as one of his most controversial measures.

The decree began with a message of greeting and promise of liberation for the Venezuelan people and went on to speak in forceful language of the atrocities committed by the Spanish oppressors, those "monsters" who "infest" American soil and have "covered it with blood." In retaliation, Bolívar pledged summary execution of any Spaniard who did not actively support the "just cause" of independence, while offering forgiveness to Americans even if guilty of aiding the enemy. According to Bolívar, a war to the death had already been launched by the royalists, so that his measure was in answer to the atrocities committed by the enemy. There was, for example, the Basque officer who supposedly had offered to pay one peso for each ear of a rebel that he received (and how precisely did he propose to distinguish rebel from loyalist or neutral ears?) and even attached the ears to the rim of his hat as adornment. But naturally not all atrocities were committed by soldiers of the king. Another notorious case was that of the Venezuelan Antonio N. Briceño (nicknamed "El Diablo," or "The Devil"), who at the outset of Bolívar's Venezuelan campaign broadcast an offer of freedom to any slave of a Spanish owner who succeeded in killing his master. Next he decapitated two inoffensive Spaniards and sent one of their heads to Bolívar and the other to the New Granadan officer Castillo, together with documents signed in the victims' blood. Bolívar repudiated the words and actions of Briceño, but it was the royalists who administered due punishment: he was captured in a skirmish and summarily executed.

It would be pointless to try to establish who committed the first atrocity and thereby set off the cycle of reprisals, not only because of the frequent impossibility of verifying the facts but also because in the last analysis Bolívar's decree was more than a mere response to actions of the other side. He was also trying consciously to bring about a polarization of attitudes, forcing Spaniards to embrace the republican cause out of fear for their lives, while committing Americans to a struggle without quarter from which they in turn would be unable to desist. Of course, the measure did not necessarily produce the desired effects. Even some supporters of independence considered it too extreme (terrorist, one would say today), and it damaged the image of the patriots abroad. But it must be noted that it was never applied strictly to the letter—and it was scarcely Bolívar's intention that it should be. A babe in arms recently arrived from the parent country would not be shot simply because he did not take up arms against the king. And for male adults of military age, the group of Spanish-born that was mainly targeted, the application of the death penalty was not going to be either continuous or universal. Yet the threat of applying it remained.

After reaching Trujillo, Bolívar did not receive from the New Granadan authorities either authorization to continue his advance or an order to suspend it, with the result that he felt entitled to adopt whatever plan of action he judged best—as indeed he would surely have done no matter what. But in spite of his victories Bolívar found himself in a delicate situation: his forces had not yet fought a major engagement, which meant that he was able to advance with surprising ease but also that the principal enemy forces remained intact. In particular, there was in the province of Barinas, to the south of Trujillo, an important concentration of royalists whose assigned mission had been to invade New Granada from Venezuela. Now that Bolívar had done exactly the same thing in reverse direction, this force became a standing threat to his rear. Consequently, and despite his interest in reaching Caracas as quickly as possible—and before Mariño could get there from the east—Bolívar chose first to double back upon Barinas. Happily for him, the series of easy successes continued. After one part of Bolívar's army completely routed an advance column of royalists, the enemy commander in Barinas, observing that the patriots seemed to be turning up everywhere and at any moment, decided it would be prudent simply to evacuate the province. Abandoning his artillery and other equipment, he withdrew into the plains of the Orinoco Basin. The royalists even left behind some 200,000 pesos in the local office of the state tobacco monopoly, with which Bolívar managed to satisfy a part of the back wages owed to his soldiers; but he let it be known that government officials would not receive salaries until after the campaign ended.

The danger in Barinas having been eliminated, Bolívar turned his attention again to the advance on Caracas. He dispatched José Félix Ribas, who was his cousin as well as military subordinate, from Trujillo to Barquisimeto, which he occupied after a bloody encounter in the outskirts. Ribas then had the Spanish officers duly executed, while the other prisoners, mainly Venezuelans, he incorporated into his own army—a system of recruitment that was becoming standard procedure and of course meant for the common soldier that, in final analysis, it did not much matter which side he was fighting on. Monteverde himself, until recently bogged down opposing Mariño in the east, established headquarters at Valencia to resist the further approach of Bolívar, and near there, on the plain of Taguanes, the contending parties fought the decisive battle of the campaign. This time Bolívar commanded in person, and thanks to the patriots' recent string of victories, he for the first time had gained numerical superiority. The battle was finally decided by one of Bolívar's more inspired improvisations, when he mounted an infantry company on the rump of cavalry horses in order to position this combined force to the rear of the Spanish army. Monteverde's defeat was so complete that he hastened to seek refuge in Puerto Cabello, leaving open the road not only to Valencia but from there to Caracas.

Royal officials and sympathizers in the capital were naturally seized with terror at the approach of the very author of the war to the death and his sanguinary horde. A flotilla of royalist fugitives set sail from La Guaira to take refuge in Curaçao, just as Bolívar had done the year before. However, Bolívar proceeded to accept an offer of peaceful capitulation brought to him from Caracas by another delegation of royalists; its terms were somewhat different from those of the notorious Trujillo decree. Then, on 7 August 1813, he entered once more the city of his birth, amid fervent acclamation. Thus ended what has come to be called the "Campaña Admirable," or "Admirable Campaign," which was of course "admirable" not for the size of the forces involved or number of battles but for the sheer rapidity of Bolívar's movements—a blitzkrieg long before that term was invented—and for the uninterrupted chain of triumphs.

The victorious general was acclaimed more specifically as Liberator, a title he had now unquestionably earned. But the precise nature of the liberation he brought was not wholly clear. The one obvious thing was the elimination of the symbols and professed servants of the Spanish monarchy. While again in Venezuela, Bolívar would also give freedom to those of his own slaves who enlisted in the republican armed forces, though he did not yet call for general emancipation. As a further step, in accordance with the instructions of the New Granadan authorities and in the opinion of a good many Venezuelans, he should have restored the constitutional order first established in 1811. Yet nothing could have been farther from Bolívar's intentions, and neither were the objective conditions that might have permitted such restoration at all present, in the midst of an unfinished military struggle and the social and economic disorder it had unleashed. Bolívar thus exercised power in practice as military dictator, aided by three secretaries of state whom he himself named. At the beginning of 1814, before an assembly of notables in Caracas, he offered to lay down supreme power, in the first of a long series of rhetorical resignations that he would keep presenting until, in April 1830 (in the ultimate decline of his fortunes), one finally was accepted. Bolívar said that he wanted to devote himself purely to the military struggle, but at bottom he was seeking reaffirmation of his dictatorial power. And he obtained it, in part because of the fear already inspired at the start of the new year by a revival of enemy activity.

Yet Bolívar was not dictator even of all the liberated portions of Venezuela. General Mariño, who with his own forces had freed the eastern provinces of Cumaná and Barcelona and whose political power derived from exactly the same source as Bolívar's—military success—was not inclined to recognize the higher authority of the Liberator, who indeed was *not* liberator of eastern Venezuela. Neither was Mariño interested in any scheme of power sharing; he preferred to be the unchallenged military and political chieftain of his own region and leave the adoption of an overall Venezuelan government for later. Although Mariño did not seek permanent separation from the rest of Venezuela, his attitude represented at the very least a rebirth, or rather survival, of the federalist spirit that Bolívar always deplored. Nor were regionalist stirrings slow to reappear even in some of the provinces liberated by Bolívar.

The restored Republic—the *Second* Republic, as it is known in Venezuelan history—also faced serious economic difficulties due to the frequent interruptions of normal production and trade, to say nothing of the lingering effects of the disastrous 1812 earthquake. The result was a sharp fall in government revenue precisely when there was need to cover large military expenditures. Bolívar literally declared another war to the death against any who defrauded the state tobacco monopoly, and he ordered property owners to pay the cost of maintaining one or more patriot soldiers, but the efficacy of such measures was questionable. In reality, of course, the financial crisis was the same that earlier had contributed to sinking the First Republic and no less obviously had undermined the royalist government of Monteverde. In the short term any government, royalist or republican, could survive by raising loans, voluntary or otherwise, receiving "donations" that were voluntary only in name, confiscating enemy assets, and getting further and further behind in the payment of salaries or other obligations, but these were expedients of steadily diminishing utility. One institution grievously affected by forced loans was the tobacco monopoly, which had been an exceptionally lucrative revenue source and whose operating capital was diverted time and again to military expenses. In this way, it was left without sufficient funds either to buy tobacco from the growers or to pay its operating costs, which in turn meant reduced revenue later on.

A more immediate danger was the continued presence of the enemy on Venezuelan soil. The royalist bastions of Maracaibo, Coro, and Guayana held firm, and Monteverde, instead of surrendering after the loss of Valencia and Caracas, had entrenched himself in Puerto Cabello to await a change in fortune. Even in areas nominally under Bolívar's control, though many Spanish-born royalists had fled before the patriot advance, not all had left, and neither could one take for granted the allegiance of the American-born. Many of the latter had greeted the monarchical restoration of 1812 with enthusiasm, and after that they had been continually exposed to royalist propaganda whose most effective spokesmen were the parish priests (who tended to support whatever regime was in power, whether by conviction or from habit). Bolívar was careful to insist that the archbishop of Caracas order his priests to explain to the faithful the benefits and legitimacy of the same republicanism that until recently they had been denouncing. He was careful also to take some preventive measures: there was no exact application of war to the death, but arrests and executions did occur.

Militarily, the first object of Bolívar's attention was Puerto Cabello, where Monteverde rejected all demands for surrender. He trusted not only in the strength of his fortifications but also in his access to the sea, thanks to which in September 1813 he received the first significant reinforcements sent out from Spain since the beginning of the conflict. The royalist garrison was strengthened with the addition of over a thousand veteran troops, whose arrival was at the same time an indication that the collapse of Napoleonic power had begun in Spain itself, under the combined assault of the Spanish resistance and the British expeditionary forces commanded by Wellington. Obviously, more reinforcements would be coming, and meanwhile they gave Monteverde superiority over the units besieging him. Bolívar therefore lifted the siege, and in this sector a stalemate developed.

More serious for the patriots were new outbreaks of social and racial conflict not unlike those that shook the First Republic in its final agony, but this time even more deadly. The revolution did not lack popular support, but that support was neither deep nor, much less, universal. The leadership of the Second Republic, like the First, was primarily in the hands of the creole elite; and it was evident that neither free *pardos* (the largest single element of the Venezuelan population) nor slaves were yet generally convinced of the advantages of independence. The abolition of formal legal discrimination against free people of color, as contained in the constitution of the First Republic, had not been rescinded even if that constitution was not put back in place, but little else had been done to offset longstanding suspicions and resentments; neither did patterns of individual behavior change overnight. Thus the possibility again existed of exploiting ethnic and class hatreds against the republic, and while the professional Spanish military and high royalist civil officials were generally hesitant to adopt such tactics, they were used with devastating effect by certain royalist guerrilla chieftains drawn for the most part themselves from middling social sectors. Also joining the fray were bands of rebellious slaves who had risen up against the government of Miranda in 1812 and were still out marauding, converted now into mere bandits (according to the patriot authorities) or social revolutionaries (according to one later romantic interpretation), and ready for pretty much anything except to serve the whites. The result was a higher level of popular participation in the independence movement than in most parts of Spanish America, but not to the advantage of the patriots. The situation in Mexico during the same years was vaguely comparable, although there the roles were reversed: in Mexico it was Miguel Hidalgo and his successor, José María Morelos, another patriot priest, who stirred up a popular following in the countryside and small towns, while the upper social strata, whether creole or peninsular, rallied to the side of the king.

The most critical threat arose in the llanos, or plains, of the Orinoco Basin, where the efforts of creole great landowners to encroach on open grazing lands were an added complication and one that gave the hard-riding, free-living *llaneros* (a breed roughly comparable to the Argentine gauchos) further reason to distrust the republican cause. Among the royalist guerrilla leaders who worked to rally the populace of the llanos against the patriots, one who clearly stands out is José Tomás Boves, a Spaniard who arrived in Venezuela toward the end of the colonial period with charges of contraband pending against him. He was condemned, spent time in prison, and then was confined to the town of Calabozo, in the central llanos, where he became a small-scale merchant and cattle trader, activities that gave him extensive knowledge of the region and a valuable network of acquaintances. He initially embraced the cause of the revolution, but he changed sides after he came under suspicion of disloyalty and in addition saw the tide of the struggle turn increasingly against the First Republic. As of mid-1813, Boves was becoming a scourge of the Second Republic, at the head of a guerrilla band in the central llanos. He gathered under his command a legion of *llaneros,* mostly *pardos* and mestizos, all with their own horses and unburdened by heavy or complex equipment—the lance was their favorite weapon. Boves's followers lived off the land and general pillaging, so that their capacity for rapid movement was unsurpassed.

At the end of September 1813 Boves seized Calabozo, which had been occupied by Bolívar's forces following the Campaña Admirable, and executed all prisoners. The patriots shortly retook the town, but before the year was out Boves, with several thousand followers, was menacing the rich agricultural zone between Valencia and Caracas in which Bolívar himself was a principal landowner. Boves did not immediately attack either of the two cities, and in January 1814 Bolívar in his private capacity purchased a new sugar mill, a step expressing his unshaken confidence in the future as well as demonstrating that his role of Liberator did not yet wholly eclipse that of landed proprietor. Nevertheless, he knew that his capital city was endangered and with a typical burst of frenetic energy launched an engineering campaign to surround the Caracas urban center with fortifications. Virtually the entire able-bodied population was enlisted to dig ditches, raise parapets, and perform related tasks.

Even in territory apparently under republican control, royalist guerrillas and gangs of marauders without political affiliation harried the countryside, for the brilliant patriot victories of the Campaña Admirable had not led to solid dominion over the area liberated. The numerical balance of forces by early 1814 was also turning against the patriots, and though they had organized some production of military supplies, it was never enough to meet their needs. The resulting shortages could not be overcome by purchasing abroad, both because of the interruption of normal trading and for lack of funds—and for possible international loans or credit sales, Venezuela's Second Republic would have been a client in the very highest risk category.

If one were to pinpoint a single event as the beginning of the end for the Second Republic, it was probably the first battle of La Puerta, won by Boves in February 1814 at a site between Calabozo and Caracas. One immediate consequence of the defeat was an outbreak of terror in Caracas, which led in turn to the execution without delay of some eight hundred royalist prisoners held at Caracas and La Guaira. Bolívar had been trying fruitlessly to arrange an exchange of these prisoners for patriots held by the royalists, and at the end of January he had even formally suspended war to the death. But rather than run the risk that the royalist prisoners, heartened by Boves's victory, might rise up with the aid of secret sympathizers, he gave the order for them to be killed—which was done without excepting even the hospitalized sick and injured. Thus war to the death quickly returned, and indeed the episode represents the extreme example of its application on Bolívar's part.

Despite all fears, the republicans did check the advance of the enemy, which had been temporarily deprived of the leadership of Boves because of a wound he had received in the recent action. And they would still score a few military successes—which, however, failed to reverse the overall decline of their fortunes and inevitably entailed losses of men and equipment ever more difficult to replace. An episode that earned a special place in the lore of patriotic heroism marked the battle of San Mateo, fought in late March at an hacienda owned by Bolívar himself. Boves, recovered from his wound, led the royalists, and Bolívar commanded the patriots, but the battle is chiefly remembered for the action of the New Granadan officer Antonio Ricaurte, who on seeing the enemy about to seize the building where the patriots' munition was stored, chose to blow up the structure with himself and companions still inside rather than see it fall into enemy hands. His sacrifice is immortalized in the Colombian national anthem, whose last stanza includes the words:

> Ricaurte at San Mateo,
> blown into atoms,
> wrote in flames,
> "duty before life."

At the end of the day, the patriots held the battlefield of San Mateo, but it was not due solely to Ricaurte's heroism, for at long last Mariño had stirred from his stronghold in the east and was coming to Bolívar's aid. The relationship between the two was still a difficult one, but clearly Mariño's arrival delayed the final collapse of the Second Republic. Then in mid-June Bolívar and Mariño together faced Boves in the second battle of La Puerta, and this time the patriot defeat was even more disastrous. Both generals escaped, but their army was annihilated. Boves next turned to attack Valencia, commanding a force swollen to 8,000 men—a seemingly incredible number at this stage of the struggle—and, with the city also threatened by other royalist forces, he quickly obtained its capitulation. The Valencians had surrendered in the hope of being treated with mercy, something Boves had no intention of showing. Instead there followed a massacre of patriot leaders and general sacking of the city, with details of refined cruelty, such as the victory ball to which Boves invited the creole women whose husbands and fathers he had just had executed.

In Caracas, even before Valencia's fate was known, the atmosphere of fright was even greater than in February. Bolívar dispatched an urgent mission to Barbados urging the British authorities there to intervene in Venezuela with troops and war supplies, supposedly not to join the fight against Spain—still allied with Great Britain in Europe—but to repress bandits and rebellious slaves and, in case an armistice might be arranged, to serve as guarantors. But even if the British had been disposed to accept the invitation, which they were not, aid could not have arrived in time. Nor did Bolívar have any other way to defend his capital. He accordingly evacuated it, aiming to regroup in Mariño's eastern bailiwick. The fear inspired by the approach of Boves caused a large part of the civilian population to emigrate, too, mostly on foot for lack of sufficient mounts to carry the fugitives. Their number (including women and children) has been conventionally estimated, probably with some exaggeration, as 20,000. The distance from Caracas to Barcelona, the immediate objective, was almost four hundred kilometers, and many of the emigrants never got there. Those who did reach their destination arrived exhausted and in tatters; a few got through only because the commander-in-chief and certain of the other horsemen offered rides on their mounts over the most difficult stretches.

Boves on his part lost no time in sending the bulk of his army eastward in pursuit, and shortly after Bolívar's arrival in Barcelona he suffered another defeat. The patriots renewed their exodus, now to Cumaná, which Bolívar reached with a handful of followers and where things continued going wrong. In particular, an angry dispute arose over the cargo of silver utensils and precious ornaments that Bolívar had seized from churches in Caracas with a view to exchanging them for arms in the British Antilles. Unfortunately, an Italian captain who had been working for the patriots set sail precipitously with the treasure, and though Bolívar and Mariño managed to board his ship before he cast off, they in the end had to share the valuables with him. Worse still, during the two leaders' absence, some of their associates came to suspect them of betrayal, much as Miranda had been suspected two years before when he deposited government funds on a ship ready to sail from La Guaira. Bolívar actually recovered the greatest portion of the ecclesiastical treasure, but he was still arrested and imprisoned by his former companions on returning to the mainland. There was now nothing more he could do: on 8 September he embarked again, together with Mariño, for Cartagena.

Those patriots who stayed behind in the northeast corner of Venezuela maintained a precarious struggle for a few more months, until they suffered total defeat at the battle of Urica, in early December, whose one redeeming feature from the republican standpoint was that in it Boves himself was mortally wounded. Meanwhile in western Venezuela, some patriot soldiers continued resistance as guerrilla fighters, while others retreated into New Granada. A majority of Venezuelans now submitted peacefully to the agents of Fernando VII. Venezuelans were less numerous, however, than they had been in 1810. Battle casualties and the executions carried out by one side or another had taken their toll, but in addition many persons met a premature death through illness or malnutrition, conditions that were aggravated when they had to flee their homes or faced other by-products of military struggle. Still others left

Venezuela, to continue the fight in New Granada or take refuge in the Antilles (royalists in Cuba or Puerto Rico, republicans mainly in Haiti or the British islands); either way, they did not necessarily return when the fighting was over. This combination of factors clearly offset the natural rate of population increase. And neither did Venezuela experience only demographic decline. There are no statistics reliably measuring the fall in gross production, but it must have been substantial because of the physical destruction of crops and installations, constant interruption of domestic and foreign commerce, and military levies that inexorably siphoned manpower (slave and free) away from the economy.

Social deterioration was even more serious, in the view of some contemporaries. The civil patriot Martín Tovar lamented in a private letter, "no one can put this country back together now; I believe *(Confidential)* that we are going to fall into the hands of the blacks." With these words he gave voice to the deep sense of alarm among the creole upper class, which had triggered the revolution in the belief that a weak and distant monarchy was incapable of maintaining social order and that accordingly it was time for them to take control into their own hands. But somehow control had then slipped out of their hands, and really out of anyone's, because neither had the representatives of Spain succeeded at any point in reestablishing colonial tranquility—neither Monteverde nor other top commanders nor, much less, the civil officials of the king. As for the royalist guerrilla chieftains like Boves, they were impervious to control by their own hierarchical superiors, and while they kept the allegiance of their *llanero* lancers through personal charisma and the offer of plunder, they scarcely even tried to reconstruct the administrative or judicial system in the territory they seized.

Yet even though it has been conventionally alleged by republican propagandists during the struggle and some later Venezuelan historians that the havoc wrought by royalists like Boves was primarily responsible for the reigning disorder, this is only part of the story. The misdeeds of royalist irregulars are well documented even in official Spanish sources, but they represented only one expression of certain norms of conduct that could be observed also on the patriot side and were really inevitable. The forces involved were generally small, but the cost of the war far exceeded the resources readily available, so that both sides had constant recourse to arbitrary exactions and pillage. They could not repress the excesses of their soldiers, if only because the latter could seldom be paid in cash. For the rest, hatreds of class and race were latent even before the revolution, ready to burst forth violently when opportunity presented itself. The war to the death thus reflected, among other things, some of the long-standing friction between Spaniards and native Venezuelans, while the excesses of guerrilla fighters who followed Boves and other such leaders expressed the resentment of *llaneros* against creole magnates that also antedated the conflict. All of which is over and above the obvious grievances of free and enslaved blacks: it was reliably asserted that black soldiers, forcible recruits or volunteers, patriots or royalists, would sometimes consciously aim their weapons at the whites in enemy lines rather than the colored soldiers at their side. And racial tensions would continue to mark Venezuela's nineteenth-century civil wars even after independence was won.

If only because of general exhaustion, on this occasion the royalist restoration would last longer than the time before. Bolívar, once described by an adversary as more dangerous in defeat than in victory, had every intention to return and renew the war as soon as possible. But first he had to undertake another detour through New Granada.

IV

New Granadan and Caribbean Interlude (1814–1816)

The Liberator was again in Cartagena by mid-September 1814 and received a hero's welcome despite the catastrophic end of Venezuela's Second Republic. But he had no intention of remaining in the port city. The day after his arrival, he sent a message to the congress of New Granada, gathered at Tunja, with his own explanation of what happened in Venezuela. And in early October he left Cartagena for the interior, to report in person to the New Granadan authorities who had sponsored his campaign for the liberation of Venezuela and try to arouse their enthusiasm for a repeat performance.

The New Granada that Bolívar found in 1814 had not greatly changed since his first arrival. The idea of formal independence from Spain had made progress, having been declared by the State of Cundinamarca (formerly the province of Santafé) in July 1813, as Cartagena had done in 1811; two more provinces followed suit, although there was still no joint declaration by the entire country. The different provinces continued adopting miscellaneous innovations, of which the most noteworthy was a manumission law issued by the province of Antioquia. It established the principle of free birth, leading to the gradual elimination of slavery—a system that would be applied all across northern South America once the war of independence was over. For the rest, educated New Granadans were busily debating questions of political theory and practice in their local assemblies and in the periodical and pamphlet literature that proliferated thanks to relative press freedom and to the importation of new printing presses. Periodicals had few readers, to be sure, because of the overwhelming illiteracy of the population and its no less overwhelming poverty: in the Andean interior, a copy of a weekly paper would have cost more or less the same as the standard daily wage of one or two *reales* (12.5 to 25 U.S. cents).

Unfortunately, the centralists of Cundinamarca still preferred to have their own government, apart from the rest, rather than accept the authority of a confederation, whose weakness they deplored and with which they waged intermittent civil warfare. And various royalist redoubts still held out—Santa Marta, in a continual state of war with Cartagena, and likewise the impoverished and isolated province of Pasto in the far south. The New Granadan "Precursor" Antonio Nariño, temporarily setting aside the quarrel of his Cundinamarca with the confederation, left Santafé with an army to subdue Pasto, and in May 1814, not far from his objective, was taken prisoner by the enemy and eventually shipped to a Spanish dungeon. Then too, triumphant royalists from western Venezuela at one point penetrated as far as Pamplona, halfway between the Venezuelan border and Tunja, the federal capital.

The Liberator passed through Pamplona, which had been meanwhile retaken by the patriots, on his own way to Tunja to report to the confederation authorities. His previous ally Camilo Torres, president of the federal congress, reiterated his confidence in Bolívar, and so did the congress itself, though not simply with a view to helping him launch a new campaign to liberate Venezuela. The representatives meeting in Tunja did not doubt the intimate connection between the fate of Venezuela and that of their own provinces, but their immediate concern was the conflict with Cundinamarca that made it impossible either to properly organize New Granada or to mobilize resources against outside threats. Because no military leader of New Granada was remotely as experienced as Bolívar—with his defeats as well as victories—he was offered command of the confederation army that was being prepared to compel Cundinamarca finally to enter the union. Bolívar recognized the harm done by New Granada's civil war and, in the hope of ending it once and for all, accepted the offer. However much he condemned federalism as a system and to that extent sympathized with Cundinamarca's centralist position, it was under confederation auspices and with the help of such men as Torres that he had undertaken the Campaña Admirable of 1813. The confederation also had, for better or worse, the more realistic chance of achieving the unification of New Granada, even if under a political system that he deplored.

The army that Bolívar led against Santafé was made up of about 2,000 men, both Venezuelan and New Granadan. Cundinamarca had fewer and was also hampered by its own internal dissensions. The forces of the confederation thus met little resistance until they reached the very outskirts of Santafé, where the dominant faction had aroused popular enthusiasm for resistance by exhorting the inhabitants to fight not only for the dignity of the former seat of the viceroyalty but in defense of the holy Catholic faith as well. Bolívar, in effect, was described as a heretical pillager of churches, and the ecclesiastical authorities decreed both his excommunication and that of anyone who aided him. It became necessary to take the city by storm, in a bitter three days' battle that ended only when the defending forces, confined to the main plaza and running out of food and water, finally accepted defeat.

After the battle, the church dignitaries lost no time in lifting the excommunication of the victorious commander, explaining that they had been misinformed about his intentions. Cundinamarca now became a member of the confederation. A new local government was set up, and it invited the general government of the United Provinces to move from Tunja to Santafé, or more precisely Santafé de Bogotá, as it was increasingly known—the incorporation of a place name of native Chibcha origin serving to pay tribute, at least rhetorically, to New Granada's indigenous roots. By the time confederation authorities arrived there, in January 1815, they had been endowed with somewhat greater faculties by a reform adopted the previous September, and a true national executive had been created, where before there had been only the president of congress. But the executive consisted of an unwieldy triumvirate as in the First Republic of Venezuela. Nor was it easy to overcome the separate provinces' habit of independent action. The Liberator, now entitled captain-general of New Granada and given supreme command of all military operations, would soon have direct and bitter experience of that very problem.

Even though New Granada's Andean center had so far faced only civil war, several threats had to be dealt with. The royalists of Pasto struck northward to take possession of Popayán, and reinforcements had to be sent to the Cauca Valley to halt their advance. In the northeast, there was always the possibility of another invasion from Venezuela through the Cúcuta gateway; and along the coast the struggle continued between Cartagena and Santa Marta. More serious still, though for the moment more distant, was the danger arising from the final defeat of Napoleonic forces in Spain and the consequent restoration of Fernando VII to his throne. With a view to restoring absolute monarchy, the king promptly denounced the liberal Constitution of 1812 and unleashed a campaign of persecution against Spanish liberals. His intentions for Spanish America were similar: to restore the colonial regime just as it existed before the revolution and to crush the revolutionaries.

For the recovery of its American colonies, the Spanish monarchy assembled the largest fleet ever to have crossed the Atlantic from Spain: almost fifty ships, carrying over 10,000 men, a majority of them veterans of the war against Napoleon, and commanded by one of Spain's ablest generals, Pablo Morillo. At first it had been thought that the destination of the expedition was the Río de la Plata, which had been almost wholly free of Spanish control since 1810; because of the commercial importance of the port of Buenos Aires and its hinterland, the merchants of Cádiz were eager for that region to be retaken. But in the end it was decided to send the expedition to Venezuela, which happened to be the destination least desired by the expeditionaries themselves, who had heard of the war without quarter being waged there. They were not told where they were going until they were already at sea. However, the distance to Venezuela was shorter, and it was assumed that once Morillo's men extinguished the last embers of revolution there, they could easily reconquer neighboring New Granada and continue on to wherever else they might be needed. So the expedition set sail in February 1815 and reached the Venezuelan coast in early April. It shortly obtained the peaceful capitulation of the island of Margarita, off the northeastern coast, which was the last Venezuelan province in rebel hands, even though some scattered guerrilla bands remained at large on the mainland. Morillo then established himself in Caracas, to prepare the invasion of New Granada.

Even before he had final word of Morillo's destination, Bolívar decided to take charge personally of the fighting against Santa Marta. The royalists had once again advanced up the Magdalena Valley and even reached Ocaña, in the eastern Andes. However, the Liberator now repeated in reverse his brilliantly successful campaign of late 1812 and early 1813; he seized a series of river ports and reopened the main communication route to the coast. Yet for the definitive conquest of Santa Marta he needed the cooperation of Cartagena, where the present commander of its military forces was Manuel del Castillo, a prominent member of the local aristocracy and also a man who had earlier quarreled with Bolívar. Castillo's hostility had not diminished; in an incendiary pamphlet he accused the Liberator of both military ineptitude and lack of courage. The situation was further complicated by the friendly relationship between Bolívar and the political leaders of Mompós, the largest of the river ports and the one in which he temporarily set up headquarters. The dominant faction in Mompós was distrusted by the current government of Cartagena both because of regionalist rivalries and because it was allied to Cartagena's populist party, which had just been driven from power. The end result was that Cartagena not only proved reluctant to offer Bolívar the aid he requested but warned him not to advance beyond Mompós.

Cartagena's authorities did not reject all cooperation; they simply offered it on unacceptable conditions. The primary stumbling block was, of course, their insistence that Castillo play the leading role in any campaign against the royalists—and their refusal to let Cartagena forces serve under Bolívar's orders. The latter was suspected of aiming to establish a military dictatorship and war to the death, unleashing on the coast the same kind of extermination as in Venezuela. Week after week, he sought to negotiate a settlement of differences, without success, and meanwhile sickness and desertion steadily diminished his army. Eventually Bolívar became convinced that he had no choice but to use force against Cartagena; he advanced to the outskirts and laid siege to the city. But as apparently he himself came to recognize later, in this he committed a serious error. Cartagena with its walls eight meters or more in width and its fortress-castle of San Felipe—so massive and so expensive to build that the king of Spain plaintively wondered why he could not see it even from his palace across the ocean—was impregnable except by a siege long enough to overcome the defenders through starvation. And time was precisely what Bolívar lacked, because of the imminent arrival of Morillo in Venezuela and the certainty that his next target was New Granada.

Bolívar had hoped that factions opposed to the present rulers of Cartagena would collaborate with him from within the city walls; instead his sympathizers were arrested and exiled. The situation of the besieging army was made even more difficult by propaganda spread through the surrounding towns insinuating that the Liberator and his army had come to the coast to subject its inhabitants to a hateful tyranny. Many in the countryside refused to supply food to Bolívar's troops, and the defenders of the city tossed dead animals into the besiegers' wells so that neither would they have potable water to drink. It is hardly surprising that the royalists took advantage of this internecine conflict, and of the concentration of republican forces in and around Cartagena, to again occupy the lower Magdalena Valley as far as Mompós. This setback together with the news, received almost simultaneously, of Morillo's landing in Venezuela, convinced Bolívar that there was nothing more he could do in New Granada. He proceeded to resign his command and on 8 May 1815 embarked for the Antilles.

Even if Bolívar had remained in New Granada, it is unlikely that the patriots' final encounter with the army of Morillo would have turned out differently. The Spanish commander lost little time in Venezuela. At the beginning of July, he left Puerto Cabello for Santa Marta with over 5,000 European veterans, and from Santa Marta he continued in mid-August to

Cartagena, which now found itself besieged by the roy
There were bombardments and intermittent attacks o
city's fortifications, but by far the most effective weapons of the
new besiegers were sickness and hunger, which steadily undermined patriot resistance. By the end of November the few foodstuffs still available were being sold by speculators at astro-
nomic prices; those who could not buy were reduced to
devouring rats or strips of leather soaked in water; thousands
had already died. In the end, anyone who could piled onto a
few corsair ships to try to escape to the West Indies, and
around six hundred managed to reach Haiti and Jamaica without either dying at sea or being captured by the enemy. When
the army of Fernando VII finally entered Cartagena on 6 December, it viewed a gruesome cityscape of living skeletons and
unburied corpses. A third of Cartagena's roughly 15,000 inhabitants had died during the siege.

At Cartagena the victorious royalists began the rash of executions of civil and military patriot leaders that was to be a notorious feature of their reconquest of New Granada. In the rest of
New Granada, the expeditionary force met some resistance, but
its advance was rapid: in May 1816, barely a year after Morillo's arrival in Venezuela, the "pacifying" army (as it called itself) pacifically entered Santafé. Among those who were then
shot in the capital city was Bolívar's ally and confidant Camilo
Torres, former president of the United Provinces. Some more
fortunate leaders were merely sent into exile or fined, hid themselves successfully, or escaped to the Antilles or to the eastern
llanos, that is, the New Granadan portion of the vast Orinoco
plains. But for the moment the restoration of colonial rule was
almost total in New Granada, just as in Venezuela. In all Spanish America at this point, only the Río de la Plata, which had the
advantage among other things of geographic distance, remained
free of Spanish control. In Mexico as well as Venezuela and
New Granada, scattered bands of republican guerrilla fighters
survived, but they appeared to represent no serious threat. Under these circumstances, the focus of the independence movement, at least as far as northern South America was concerned,
shifted to the non-Spanish West Indies, where Bolívar had already made his way.

Bolívar's first stop was Jamaica, the British possession that had long been an emporium for trade, mostly illegal, with the Spanish colonies. During the wars of independence, the new Spanish American states did their best to increase that trade, legalizing it, and in addition sought in Jamaica, as in other non-Spanish islands, to purchase needed arms for their struggle. Jamaica was likewise a center of communications, nest of espionage, and refuge for those temporarily displaced by the fortunes of war. For all these reasons it harbored an important community of Spanish Americans as well as merchants and speculators from other parts of the world who were engaged in relations of every sort with the Spanish Americans. Bolívar therefore proposed to accept the hospitality of the island in the hope that he might begin preparing a new stage of the war against Spain.

The Liberator arrived in Jamaica almost penniless and with no way to draw upon his formerly plentiful assets in Venezuela, now either destroyed or embargoed. To live with a minimum of decorum he accepted the financial aid of the English merchant Maxwell Hyslop, a sympathizer with the Spanish American cause who would later serve as Venezuelan agent in London. In addition, Bolívar had been preceded by his fame as a fighter for independence—the best-known of them all thanks to his spectacular defeats as well as victories—so that he was invited to dine with the British governor and had contact with many leading members of local society. He put to good use his talent as a polished conversationalist, exactly as before in the salons of Paris. But there were also enemies on the lookout for him. On one occasion an assailant—according to the traditional though unsubstantiated version, a servant of his who had been bribed with Spanish gold—tried to assassinate Bolívar while asleep in his hammock. That night, however, he decided to sleep somewhere else, whether for one of his amorous escapades or for another reason, and in the darkness the attacker did not realize that he was stabbing instead a third party who lay sleeping in Bolívar's place.

To anyone who would lend an ear, Bolívar insisted that despite all appearances the revolution was not and could not be defeated and that for all sorts of reasons its triumph could only benefit the interests of Great Britain. In a letter to his friend Hyslop, who he hoped would bring it to the attention of others, he even mentioned the possibility that the provinces of Panama and Nicaragua might be given over to Great Britain, "to make of them the center of commerce by building canals which, after the dikes guarding both oceans have been broken, will reduce all distances, however long, and permanently establish British commercial supremacy." As Nicaragua was a dependency of the Viceroyalty of New Spain (i.e., Mexico), it is unclear what authority Bolívar imagined he had for making such an offer; and the same can really be said as to Panama, which, though part of New Granada, so far had simply not taken part in the revolution. What remains beyond doubt is Bolívar's conviction of the absolute importance of British opinion and policy, so that he spared no effort to win the favor of Great Britain for Spanish American independence. In his Jamaica writings he also demonstrated again the fluidity and elegance of style that make him easily the best writer among the leaders of Spanish American independence, a man whose works can still be read with pleasure and profit. Bolívar's private correspondence is enlivened with many sparks of ironic humor that appear less often in his public documents; but the latter do display a notable lucidity even when the author is defending sometimes questionable viewpoints.

The best-known of all Bolivarian texts is without doubt the "Jamaica Letter" of September 1815, in which he reiterates his defense of independence and his conviction—quite unsupported by recent events—that its triumph was already assured. He expressed surprise at the lack of concrete assistance from European countries and the United States, when commercial interests and ideological affinities should have led them to give support. Even so, he expressed confidence that a brilliant future awaited the Spanish Americans precisely because they would enjoy "the guidance of a liberal nation which will lend us her protection." He did not need to point out that here he was referring to Great Britain.

The greatest part of the document, however, and its lasting importance, is found in Bolívar's extended analysis of the past, present, and future state of Spanish America. Here he underscored the paradoxical situation of Spanish Americans like himself, who were "neither Indian nor European, but a species

ly between the legitimate proprietors of this country and
anish usurpers"—and who were now asserting their rights
against those "usurpers" but without actually restoring the
rights of the original possessors. A further complication was
that the colonial regime had kept its subjects in a "purely pas-
sive" role, with no significant share in the political, ecclesiastical, or military government of America. Bolívar exaggerated
somewhat as regards the total lack of political experience, but
he then went on to draw a sweeping conclusion: being un-
schooled in the "science of government," the Spanish Americans
were not prepared to govern themselves and would require firm
guidance by a powerful executive. Above all, they should not
seek to erect perfect institutions but those most in keeping with
their own immediate conditions and idiosyncrasies.

In that last respect, Bolívar was repeating the warning contained in his Cartagena Manifesto against the creation of "ethereal republics" doomed to failure, and he again explicitly condemned federalism. Nevertheless, he insisted that the strong
government that Spanish America required should be republican, rejecting—on grounds of political theory and with the cita-
tion of various classical antecedents—the alternative of constitutional monarchy that did not lack supporters, particularly in
southern South America and Mexico. He further rejected as impractical the idea of forming all Spanish America into a single
great nation, however much some present-day admirers have attributed such an objective to him. He was perfectly aware that,
despite all similarities of language, customs, and religion, there
were distinct local characteristics and interests that separated
one region from another, quite apart from the enormous geographic distances that in an epoch of primitive transport and
communications also stood in the way of strict unification. Bolívar was at all times a proponent of Spanish American solidarity
and in the Jamaica Letter expressed hope for a league of American nations whose representatives would meet on the Isthmus of
Panama, just as the amphyctionic league of the ancient Greeks
held its meetings on the Isthmus of Corinth. He nevertheless
predicted the creation of some seventeen new independent nations. He did not specify whether that number was to include

Brazil and Haiti or just the former Spanish colonies, but it was a remarkably exact forecast: with the separation of Panama from Colombia in 1903, the final number of Latin American nations was twenty.

Some of the prophecies Bolívar made as he passed in review the different regions of Spanish America were also remarkably accurate. For Chile, he foresaw a future of order and republican liberty, due to its manageable size and isolation, the "simple and virtuous character of its people," and the "example of its neighbors, the proud republicans of Arauco [i.e., the still unsubdued Araucanian Indians]." Chile did in fact become a model of moderate liberalism and internal stability during most of the nineteenth century. At an opposite extreme he placed Peru, whose wealth of precious metals and virtually enslaved native Indian population were in conflict with "every just and liberal principle." For obvious reasons, Bolívar lingered longest over the cases of Venezuela and New Granada, whose union under a single central government he had long been advocating and had indeed been putting into practice as he waged war against Spain on either side of the border that separated them and as commander-in-chief of the military forces of one and the other. He stated that the nation thus formed should be called Colombia, a name first suggested by Francisco de Miranda (to whom he failed to give credit for the invention). And he proposed for Colombia a government on the British model, though with the necessary republican trappings. It would have a president serving for life instead of a king, and a hereditary senate similar to the House of Lords—two features that would again appear in future Bolivarian projects. Yet he recognized that New Granada, because of its recent addiction to federalism, might not accept association with Venezuela under a central government, in which case it would "form a separate state which, if it endures, may prosper, because of its great and varied resources." New Granada did eventually form a separate state, though not simply because of its federalist addiction; and despite Bolívar's optimism it became one of the less prosperous Latin American nations.

While Bolívar in Jamaica was thus pondering the future of Spanish America, the separation of New Granada even from the former parent country appeared in grave doubt. The desperation of the patriot defenders of Cartagena who once feared Bolívar as a hateful dictator reached such an extreme that their agents invited him to come take charge of the city's defense. Because he had never intended to abandon the military struggle, Bolívar resolved to accept the invitation and left Kingston in mid-December 1815, almost two weeks after the fall of Cartagena, news of which had not yet reached Jamaica. He learned of the disaster at sea, through a chance encounter with a **corsair** vessel. However, he had not been heading directly for the South American coast but rather was planning a prior stop in Haiti. There he hoped to join forces with Luis Brión, a merchant, soldier, and now also corsair from Curaçao who had joined the fight for Venezuelan independence and at the moment was at Aux Cayes, on Haiti's southern peninsula. He similarly intended to visit the Haitian president, Alexandre Pétion, and plead for his help. Thus the fall of Cartagena did not influence Bolívar's decision to go to Haiti, but it did mean that his next objective would be the coast not of New Granada but of Venezuela, which he judged ready for a new reaction against Spain.

Bolívar reached Aux Cayes on Christmas Eve of 1815. He met Brión, who had with him a corvette acquired in England as well as a supply of munitions originally intended for Cartagena but now available for other uses. Also present were a good many other military and civilian patriots from both Venezuela and New Granada. Not all of them were friends of Bolívar, so that while in Haiti he would have to overcome personal resentments and factional rivalries as well as collect arms and volunteers. But the first requirement was to obtain the good will of Pétion, without which no serious expedition could be launched from Haitian territory. Hence on 31 December Bolívar was already in Port-au-Prince, the Haitian capital; and soon afterward he had his first meeting with Pétion.

Haiti having been the second American—and first Latin American—nation to achieve independence, there existed an obvious bond of sympathy between its people and government and the South American revolutionists. Yet the relationship was not without complications. Haitian independence had been the by-product of a slave rebellion that horrified creole elites of the whole Caribbean Basin, Venezuela included, because of the atrocities committed on both sides and because of the example it set for the slaves elsewhere. President Pétion and his collaborators were naturally aware of the reservations that numerous Spanish American creoles had concerning their country, and while they did not hesitate to offer asylum to patriot refugees, they necessarily had some reservations of their own concerning the Spanish Americans.

Moreover, the government of Pétion faced other serious problems. The president himself—a genuinely liberal and enlightened statesman—had belonged to the group of free colored inhabitants who joined the Haitian revolution and, once it was successful, believed themselves entitled, by their superior education and manners vis-à-vis the mass of former slaves, to have the main voice in running things. Basically, the Pétion regime represented this element. But the country had also split in two, Pétion gaining the center and south while northern Haiti fell to the former slave Henri Christophe, who made himself a crowned monarch as Henri I. There remained the danger of a new outbreak of conflict between the rival Haitian states. Nor was the international situation exactly favorable. France had abandoned the effort to regain her former colony by force but not the hope of winning Haiti back by other means; and as long as France did not recognize Haitian independence, other European powers did not propose to do so either. Much less would the United States give recognition, for the slaveowning southern states fiercely opposed any official dealings with a nation born out of slave rebellion. And until his government obtained international recognition, Pétion did not wish to offend anyone unnecessarily. Hence any intervention on his part in the Spanish American revolution would have to be discreet and preferably sub-rosa.

U.S. and European merchants were perfectly willing to trade with Haiti, but commerce had been falling off and along with it the Haitian government's income. In the area ruled by Pétion, a type of agrarian reform had taken place, through the dividing up of former plantations and their distribution in the form of small peasant plots. But the new owners mainly raised crops for their own consumption, allowing the export agriculture that had once made Haiti the wealthiest of all West Indian colonies to languish. The resources at Pétion's disposal were thus sorely limited at best. Nevertheless, they were not as limited as those otherwise available to the displaced South American revolutionaries, and they consisted not only of hard cash and armaments but of the good will of a community of foreign merchants established in Haiti. Among the latter, the Englishman Robert Sutherland became a particular friend of Bolívar, just as Hyslop had been in Jamaica.

If in the end Pétion accommodated Bolívar's requests as far as possible, it was due in large part to the Liberator's personal magnetism and the Haitian leader's ability to recognize the many-sided talents of his South American guest. He set just one important condition, which Bolívar readily accepted: to abolish slavery in all liberated territory. To preserve appearances, Pétion channeled most of his aid through the firm of Sutherland rather than giving it directly, but it was in any case substantial: several thousand rifles, along with powder and ammunition, plus a free hand to recruit volunteers on Haitian territory. Pétion even supplied a printing press, with which to prepare the ground for the liberating army by means of circulars and proclamations. The Haitian president likewise arbitrated in favor of Bolívar in the various disputes that arose with other military chieftains, backing those like Brión who insisted that the Venezuelan and New Granadan factions must obey a single leader, who in practice could only be the Liberator. Most of the others did in the end accept his leadership, though not always gracefully.

Bolívar's expedition was finally able to set sail from Aux Cayes at the end of March 1816. It consisted of seven or eight schooners but less than three hundred persons, including crew members (mostly Haitian), military (mostly officers coming from Europe, the Antilles, and South America), and women. The Liberator's detractors emphasize the presence of Josefina Machado ("Señorita Pepa" for short), a favorite mistress whom he had met at the time of his triumphal return to Caracas in 1813. She had to come from Puerto Rico to join the flotilla, and her delay in arriving supposedly delayed the departure of everyone else. But she was by no means the only one of her sex, as there were lovers and in some cases wives of other military men, not to mention the mother and a sister of Señorita Pepa. The immediate destination of the expedition was in any case Margarita island, where the independence struggle had broken out again under the leadership of Juan Bautista Arismendi, a figure who initially had accepted an armistice offered by Morillo but had now returned to the fray. Before the fleet's arrival on 3 May, it had to fight a sea battle, with the ladies on board, against two royalist ships; but the patriots were successful, and in recognition for the victory, Bolívar rewarded Brión, who was serving as naval commander, with the rank of admiral.

After a few weeks on Margarita with Arismendi, Bolívar on 1 June set foot once more on the mainland, at Carúpano. The very next day, in line with his pledge to Pétion, he issued his first decree for the abolition of slavery. It declared "the absolute liberty of the slaves who have groaned beneath the Spanish yoke in the past three centuries," but a careful reading shows that for strictly pragmatic reasons Bolívar did not propose to do away with slavery at one stroke. Instead, he offered freedom to any who enrolled in the forces fighting for independence, along with their family members; slaves not disposed to do so remained for now in bondage—and their families with them. This was of course the same thing that both patriots and royalists had done before at specific times and places: the difference now was that Bolívar converted a sporadic practice into a general norm.

Thus far, everything had gone rather well. But before long disaster overtook the expedition. Few slaves, even of those who were aware of Bolívar's decree, came forth to serve, while the mere fact of having allied himself with a republic of rebellious ex-slaves damaged the Liberator's image among those of his own social class and race. Nor did he succeed in consolidating his continental bridgehead. Bolívar had conceived a sound strategic plan, which was to go to the Orinoco River delta and from there move upstream to make contact with republican guerrilla bands scattered here and there in the interior; the Orinoco system might even serve as a back door to New Granada. The success of the plan depended, however, on the support of the small republican fleet, whose crew members were on the point of mutiny over bad rations and related problems. Meanwhile, Bolívar had also dispatched his old rival Santiago Mariño along with General Manuel Piar—the latter, like Brión, from Curaçao and the highest-ranking *pardo* in republican service—to Güiria, just across from the island of Trinidad, to seek recruits and supplies. Unfortunately, they did not obtain, or at any rate did not send, the help Bolívar hoped for. And so, with his original plan appearing ever more problematic, Bolívar abandoned it—in favor of one even more problematic. He decided to make a landing after all on the central coast, between La Guaira and Puerto Cabello, and from there gain entry into a region of much greater population and resources. With one lucky stroke, he might obtain all he needed to repeat the Campaña Admirable of 1813 and return in triumph to Caracas. Bolívar wrote to a comrade that one week after landing he expected to be in the Venezuelan capital. Yet this was an enormously risky undertaking. Enemy forces were better prepared than they had been in 1813, and the sentiment of the population less favorable than what Bolívar expected. He succeeded in landing, with 1,000 men, at the small town of Ocumare on 6 July; everything else was catastrophic failure.

The rash of bad luck began when a majority of Bolívar's ships, instead of remaining just offshore to protect the beachhead, raised sail to engage in something more profitable, trading with Curaçao. Hence part of the Liberator's small force had to stay behind to protect the arms and supplies stacked on shore, while the rest moved inland, only to suffer a decisive defeat on the 13th. With just three ships still available, it was impossible to stage an evacuation of the entire expedition, but one contingent did elude the enemy and escape toward the interior, and initially Bolívar insisted on going with them. However, in the confusion that reigned on the beach at Ocumare—soldiers and officers and frightened women milling about amid scattered piles of war matériel—and with Bolívar mistakenly informed that the town of Ocumare itself had fallen to the royalists—the commander-in-chief climbed aboard one of the three small ships to seek safety as best he could. Most of the ammunition given by Pétion, and also the printing press, were left on shore to be

seized by the enemy. The fugitives even abandoned two cases of
books, which undoubtedly had been brought from Haiti by the
indefatigable reader who was their leader.

The precipitous evacuation of Ocumare ranks obviously as
the nadir of Bolívar's military career. Even so, it does not seem
to have shaken his own faith in the inevitable triumph of his
cause: as was his custom, he chose to view the setback as lamen-
table but transitory. To be sure, in this case the revival of his fortunes would take some time. Bolívar decided to sail first for the
coast of Puerto Rico, hoping to resupply at the enemy's expense,
and he experienced a series of exciting adventures at sea, particularly when his schooner ran aground off the Puerto Rican
shore. There it was boarded by a Dutch captain who agreed to
carry Señorita Pepa and female companions to safety: the ladies
finally reached the Virgin Islands, where they remained while
the rest of the expedition continued on to Güiria, in eastern
Venezuela, to rejoin Mariño and all those who had stayed behind when Bolívar left for Ocumare. But his reception was not
entirely friendly. Mariño and some of the others viewed the
Ocumare fiasco as final proof of Bolívar's unsuitability for command and consequently organized a movement to depose him
and even condemn him as a traitor. Bolívar had partisans of his
own in Güiria, but he recognized that his position was for the
moment unsustainable and, rather than become enmeshed in
another civil war among the patriots themselves, chose to retire
once more to Haitian asylum.

Pétion had not abandoned his faith in the Liberator, who at
least fulfilled his promise concerning slavery. Hence, when
Bolívar reached the island in early September, the events of his
previous visit were repeated almost to the letter. The Haitian
government, again using the British merchant Sutherland as
intermediary, provided weapons and other supplies and allowed the hiring of ships and recruitment of sailors. The new
expedition was smaller than the one before, but the highly
competent Brión once more held naval command. Bolívar left
the port of Jacmel on 18 December 1816, reached Margarita
the 28th, and landed at Barcelona, on the mainland, the last
day of the year. The city had been retaken for the republican
cause the previous September, by some of the members of the

Ocumare expedition who remained on land and reached Barcelona after a 750-kilometer march through the interior plains under the leadership of General Gregor MacGregor, a Scottish officer who had been fighting for Venezuelan independence since 1811 and was married to a cousin of Bolívar. The latter would never again go into exile.

Revolutionary Rebirth and Reorientation (1817–1819)

By the time Bolívar returned to Venezuela at the end of 1816, the forces of the king had consolidated their control much more fully than was the case in mid-1813 at the start of the Campaña Admirable. True, that control was somewhat porous in eastern Venezuela, as shown by the survival of fairly important patriot bands both on Margarita and on the mainland. But in the old province of Caracas, heart of Venezuela, the royalists were solidly in command, backed by that part of Morillo's expeditionary army that did not accompany him to New Granada. Hence the stage that began in 1815 has been characterized by the Venezuelan historian Germán Carrera Damas as one of "foreign military occupation"—for the first time, the royalist forces were not made up predominantly of native Venezuelans.

The restored colonial government had in its favor a climate of weariness and revulsion against armed struggle, the inevitable result of the torrents of death and destruction that had been, so far, the most tangible results of the independence movement. Yet neither the servants of the king nor the king himself—committed as he was to bringing back an obsolete system of absolute monarchy—knew how to take advantage of the opportunity. The Spanish constitution was suppressed, and under the existing military government (just as was the case before with Monteverde) there was little room for the de facto influence in strictly internal affairs that the creole elite had enjoyed before

1810. Morillo even forbade his officers to marry creole women. And although European commanders sought to limit the role of the ferocious royalist guerrilla chieftains who had done so much to destroy the Second Republic, they themselves committed a share of excesses.

While royalist leaders were failing to take advantage of a seemingly promising situation, their republican counterparts demonstrated an ability to learn from experience and make adjustments. This was most certainly true of Simón Bolívar, who clearly grasped the need to give the revolution a more popular image and flavor than it had had during the First and Second Republics. The death or exile of many of the earlier high civil and military officials and the return to colonial obedience of a great part of the *mantuano* elite obviously facilitated such a reorientation. So did the Haitian alliance and Bolívar's adoption of an explicitly antislavery policy. Still another factor was the enlarged role now accorded to patriot leaders of popular origin, such as the *pardo* Manuel Piar, at the very time that the royalist counterparts of such men were increasingly marginalized through the reassertion of conventional military command structures. In the long run, the most important case was that of José Antonio Páez, who before the revolution had been a small-time merchant and ranch hand in the western llanos, ethnically a mestizo and largely untouched by formal education, yet who was now the undisputed leader of a patriot redoubt in the country's far interior. However, before combining forces with Páez, Bolívar had to solidify his latest beachhead and then carry out the strategic plan conceived on his previous return to Venezuela—to enter the delta of the Orinoco and go on from there to take command of the river system—but then discarded in favor of the calamitous Ocumare campaign.

Bolívar still had not wholly abandoned his obsession with Caracas, so that first of all he attempted one more thrust toward the Venezuelan capital—or perhaps it was only a feint to confuse the enemy. Whatever his precise intention, he suffered another defeat in the battle of Clarines, near Barcelona, on 9 January 1817. Bolívar next undertook, in earnest and with greater success, the conquest of Guayana, the province that encompassed both sides of the lower Orinoco. Piar was already there and in early 1817 had laid siege to Angostura (today Ciudad Bolívar), a river port and provincial capital. Bolívar established contact with Piar and also seized the Guayana mission territories of the Capuchin friars, not so much because the friars were Spanish-born royalists—some twenty of them ultimately were shot in an episode never fully explained—as for the foodstuffs and other supplies that could be extracted. A royalist flotilla controlled the river itself and thereby gave protection to Angostura, but Piar defeated an army of reinforcements sent to the region by Morillo, who was now back in Venezuela, and the tide turned decisively in the patriots' favor when admiral Brión reached the Orinoco in early July with a flotilla of schooners and brigantines, to tighten the siege of Angostura and open a supply route from the Atlantic to the patriot camps. Angostura surrendered on 17 July, in what was the greatest success of republican arms since the Campaña Admirable. It was also a victory with more lasting effect, and a personal triumph of Bolívar even if Piar had paved the way and Brión delivered the coup de grace. Yet Bolívar had shared all the privations of his troops, had exposed himself to grave dangers—once spending the night immersed in a small lake to escape enemy pursuers—and he, more than anyone, had orchestrated the campaign.

It was during the Orinoco campaign that the Liberator decisively reestablished his primacy among revolutionary leaders. There were others who had also won many battles, or remained in Venezuela while he was traveling through New Granada and the Antilles, or in still other respects could claim a right to command. Mariño especially had always been disinclined to serve as subordinate to his rival from Caracas and attempted, while Bolívar was in Guayana, to organize a coup against his authority, convoking an assembly in the small town of Cariaco to reform the civil and military government of the nascent republic. The so-called "Congresillo" (or mini-Congress) of Cariaco declared the restoration of federal and representative institutions as they existed under the First Republic, gave supreme military command to Mariño and naval to Brión, and with apparent irony, named Bolívar as one member of a three-man executive. Even some friends of Bolívar took part in the Cariaco meeting, whether tempted by the hope of personal advantage or misled by the organizers, but the affair ended in total failure. Whatever his failures and shortcomings, Bolívar stood out above all the rest for his experience of the world, his political sense, and those hard-to-define personal traits conventionally lumped together under the heading of charisma. He naturally denounced everything that had been done, and a majority of military chiefs, including some who had taken part in the recent plotting, pledged him anew their wholehearted allegiance. Mariño, seeing he lacked sufficient support, retired without a struggle to the island of Margarita.

The most important of the figures who continued in a state of insubordination was Manuel Piar. He had not been present at Cariaco because he was in Guayana at the head of his troops, but it was clear that he enjoyed playing a subordinate role no more than Mariño. Hence the arrival of Bolívar to take personal command of operations along the Orinoco had been hardly to his liking. He further took offense when Bolívar placed someone else in charge of the valuable former Capuchin missions. Piar thus asked to retire from service, ostensibly for reasons of health, even before the end of the campaign. Permission was granted, and rumors soon began to circulate to the effect that he was working to undermine Bolívar's authority—rumors that were doubly worrisome because Piar was not only a military officer of exceptional talent but a *pardo*. The greatest fear was that he aimed to exploit racial tensions against the Liberator and other remnants of the old *mantuano* elite, thus counteracting Bolívar's current effort to give his cause a more popular aura.

What has never been established beyond doubt is whether Piar's personal resentment extended to outright conspiracy. In any case, Bolívar summoned Piar to his headquarters for explanations, and by refusing to come, Piar seemingly confirmed suspicions. For several weeks Bolívar's forces tried to catch up with him as he moved from one point to another of eastern Venezuela, until at the end of September he was finally captured. Piar was then tried by court martial and condemned to death for treason; and once Bolívar approved the sentence, it was quickly carried out. Bolívar himself never doubted Piar's guilt, even though he later recognized that others equally guilty had been allowed to live. The execution of Piar he called a "political necessity," obviously in part because Piar's presumed treason carried with it the threat of unleashing race war but also because it had to be demonstrated that all men without exception, regardless of rank or fame or social background, must obey their supreme commander. That demonstration having been made, Bolívar even saw fit to restore Mariño to a position of command.

Bolívar was not satisfied merely to assert control. He also took the first steps toward creation of a more stable regime, a *Third* Republic of Venezuela. He still did not think conditions ripe for adopting a new constitution, much less for restoring the federal charter of 1811; he retained supreme civil and military power in his own hands. However, Bolívar set up in Angostura a Council of State, as a consultative body and cabinet of ministers. He decreed the creation of a rudimentary court system, and he took special interest in the encouragement of privateering warfare, confident that the distribution of corsair licenses to Venezuelan and foreign seamen and the sale of prizes they seized from enemy commerce—of which one share accrued to the government treasury—would provide a needed source of revenue. This last was particularly important in light of the scarcity of other resources in the land so far liberated.

Privateering inevitably became a source of conflict with foreign governments because of the privateers' frequent failure to distinguish between Spanish goods subject to confiscation and the property of neutrals. In addition, a bitter dispute arose with the United States because of the action of Venezuelan naval vessels in seizing two U.S. ships for violation of a blockade of Angostura decreed while that port was still in royalist hands. An agent sent from Washington reached Angostura early in 1818 to observe the state of the country and to press claims over this and various other incidents of the war at sea. The emissary began by lavishly flattering the Liberator as a worthy imitator of George Washington; but he ended up, when he failed to obtain prompt resolution of the claims, adopting language that Bolívar deemed "extremely abusive and injurious to the government of Venezuela." Although he never rejected outright the possibility of paying some reparations, Bolívar refused to have further contact with the U.S. representative, and the experience no doubt had something to do with the later outburst in which he denounced as an undesirable characteristic of Anglo-Americans their "arithmetical conduct of affairs," that is, excessive concern for financial advantage.

Besides his promotion of privateering, as a source of revenue as well as a weapon against the enemy, Bolívar did what he could to encourage the export of Venezuelan products. This would both help revive a depressed economy and produce customs duties for the republican treasury; and with control of the Orinoco now assured, oceangoing ships (though not those of deepest draft) were reaching Angostura. Unfortunately, the plains of the Orinoco provided little in the way of potential exports, but one traditional line of business in the region was the exporting of live cattle, and despite wartime pillage and the indiscriminate consumption of animals by both warring parties, there were still some available to sell to neighboring West Indian islands. To derive greatest advantage from this resource, Bolívar made the export of mules an official monopoly while allowing anyone to export cattle subject to a steep export duty.

With the funds obtained from both corsair prizes and overseas trade, the Angostura regime imported war matériel, which European and North American dealers were happy to sell despite their countries' theoretical neutrality in the conflict and pertinent neutrality legislation. In some cases they even sold on credit— which was the start of the South Americans' foreign debt. Bolívar was likewise anxious to encourage the recruitment of trained European soldiers and officers, now without military employment since the final defeat of Napoleon and available for new adventures. Some foreign volunteers (or mercenaries, depending on one's point of view), like the Scotsman MacGregor, arrived even earlier. However, the recruitment campaign took off in earnest from Angostura, with lavish offers of salaries, bonuses, and other conditions that were often impossible to fulfill: the results would be seen in 1818, when a major influx took place.

Another objective of the Liberator that was economic in nature and at the same time military and political was to confiscate the property of Spaniards and royalist Americans. The wealthiest and most densely populated part of Venezuela was still in royalist hands, so that in the short run there was little available to confiscate, but Bolívar issued some general regulations on the seizure and administration of enemy property and its eventual distribution to the veterans of independence as a war bonus. His decree of October 1817 stipulated that the highest-ranking generals would receive assets worth 25,000 pesos, with the amounts offered to each rank steadily diminishing until a mere common soldier was to be awarded 500 pesos' worth. The decree has been acclaimed by some twentieth-century admirers of Bolívar (in particular those eager to claim him as a precursor of contemporary social revolutionists) as an early instance of agrarian reform, but it is somewhat doubtful that such was his true intent. After all, the benefits were promised only to one part of the population, the military, and though they were an ever greater part, it is worth noting that the natives of the llanos, for example, were not really much interested in land ownership but in cattle. Also noteworthy is the enormous disparity in the size of bonus offered to different ranks, in which respect Bolívar's decree was a far cry from that of his Uruguayan counterpart, José Artigas, who stipulated that properties seized from the enemies of the revolution should be distributed among all the populace, with preferential treatment given to the poor. Even so, Bolívar did not exclude the lower ranks, and while the full implementation of the measure was left until later—with the result that many soldiers sold their claims to an eventual bonus to speculators for a fraction of face value—the measure did not lack social relevance. It perfectly fitted in with Bolívar's effort to strengthen the popular base of his struggle; that in turn reinforced the effort to attract José Antonio Páez as ally.

Just a few days after his definitive return to Venezuela, Bolívar had sent an emissary to the *llanero* chieftain's camp to discuss collaboration. Even when he gained possession of Guayana, he was still far from Páez's theater of operations, but he remained in almost constant touch with him, seeking to forge a permanent collaboration. On his part, Páez came to accept Bolívar's role as supreme chief of the revolution despite the protests of many of his own men, who had given total allegiance to Páez himself and felt a lack of confidence in Bolívar because of his past defeats as well as his original sin of having been born into the *mantuano* aristocracy of Caracas. Páez nevertheless realized that of all those available Bolívar was the person best qualified to lead the movement for independence, and when he insisted, the forces under his immediate command likewise offered obedience.

Páez by this point wore the title of general, but he was far from being a professional military officer; his fundamental battle tactic was to throw his mounted lancers against the enemy in one disorderly charge after another, always remaining in the midst of them himself and, if anything, excelling his men in exploits of horsemanship and combat. He similarly shared their style of life, existing in the open for days on end, riding as much as a hundred kilometers a day, and subsisting on little more than tough beef cooked without salt. He knew the geographic scene of his operations like the palm of his hand—he could always tell where to ford the rivers when they overflowed their banks in rainy season or how to find water in time of drought. He thus enjoyed ever greater prestige among the general population of the llanos and an unquestioned ascendancy over his men, not a few of whom served earlier under Boves or other royalist guerrilla leaders. They had changed sides in part because of the fame Páez was acquiring and also in part because the very nature of the conflict was changing. The sidelining or disappearance of the former chieftains of royalist irregulars served to dampen enthusiasm for Fernando VII. Moreover, with the government of the king reestablished in the wealthiest and most important part of the country, there were now more opportunities for booty at the expense of the monarchists than the republicans. Páez, of course, did not discourage pillage, particularly as he had no other way of paying or supplying his followers.

It has to be noted that Páez's forces were composed of both Venezuelans and New Granadans, just as his theater of operations covered parts of both former colonies. More precisely, his immediate followers included Venezuelan *llaneros* and patriots from the province of Casanare, in the adjacent llanos of New Granada, which had so far been spared from the Spanish reconquest that subdued the Andean interior. Casanare thus became a sanctuary for fugitives from the collapse of the New Granadan

Llanero lancers on attack. (Author's collection)

confederation, some of whom hoped to create there a formal civil and military organization similar to what had just collapsed in the highlands. But that was not at all what the plainsmen, whether Venezuelan or New Granadan, were interested in. Instead, in September 1816 an assembly of warriors in the town of Arauca, located on what is today the Colombian side of the river of the same name, acclaimed Páez as their one and only leader.

In late 1816 and early 1817 Páez expanded activities in the western llanos of Venezuela, to the point that Morillo concluded Páez was really more dangerous than Bolívar. So as to be in a position to check his advance, the Spanish commander abandoned a costly and so far fruitless royalist campaign to retake the island of Margarita. But Morillo also wanted to prevent the union of Bolívar with Páez, and for that purpose he dispatched an army toward the lower Orinoco to check Bolívar's movements. It routed one of Bolívar's generals in the battle of La Hogaza, which did indeed delay the Liberator's departure to join Páez. However, Bolívar at once set about raising new troops and war supplies, and on the last day of December 1817 he left Angostura for Páez's encampment.

The meeting of the two leaders took place at the end of January 1818, amid the embraces and acclamations of their respective companions. Even then, not all *llaneros* were happy about serving under the supreme command of Bolívar, but he soon won their respect and even affection. Despite his suspiciously elitist origin, he demonstrated that he too could withstand privations and that neither did he lack dexterity in the skills of the llanos. His ability to ride horseback over great distances without complaint earned him the honorary nickname of *"culo de hierro"* or "iron ass." He stood out also for his expertise as a swimmer, another talent of obvious value in the Orinoco region. On one occasion Bolívar challenged another officer to a swimming race, which he proposed to win even with his hands tied; he did not win, but the tale of his bravado was spread and did him no harm. Moreover, Bolívar took pains to treat Páez as his equal, as indeed he was in the environment of the llanos, and their collaboration was crowned with success even sooner than had been feared by Morillo, who until after Bolívar's meeting with Páez believed him to be still in Angostura.

The army that Bolívar brought with him from Angostura numbered about 3,000, although that number was deceptive. Most of the men were barefoot, which in the llanos was natural enough, but they did not have adequate armament either: some of the infantry were armed with bows and arrows. Páez had with him another 1,000, mainly horsemen. The one great advantage that this motley combined force possessed was its capacity for rapid movement and improvisation. A much cited example involved the crossing of the Apure River, when the barges that should have carried the patriots over failed to appear. Páez quickly solved the problem: with a glance at the other side of the Apure, he spied some river craft belonging to the enemy and immediately sent a hundred of his horsemen into the water, holding their lances in their mouths while clinging to the manes of their horses. They crossed the river, seized the royalist boats, and made possible the crossing of the rest.

When the republican forces approached Calabozo, capital of the central llanos and former base of operations of Boves, they had their first encounter with the army of Morillo and were victorious. However, the Spanish commander executed a successful withdrawal toward the central Venezuelan Andes, where the *llanero* cavalry would be at a disadvantage facing veteran Spanish infantry. Bolívar still aimed to continue the pursuit all the way to Caracas, his ultimate goal, but in this he was thwarted by Páez's insistence that his men had other fighting to do first in the llanos. (While Páez's acceptance of Bolívar's leadership had been perfectly sincere, it obviously was not unconditional.) In due course, having lost patience with Páez's delay in sending reinforcements, Bolívar decided to march on Caracas without them, only to be soundly defeated by Morillo's army in mid-March at El Semen, not far from La Puerta (where he had suffered disastrous defeat in 1814 at the hands of Boves). Páez did then come to his aid, in time to cut short pursuit by the royalists; and before long Bolívar was again planning an advance into the highlands in the direction of Caracas.

But instead of advancing triumphantly on his hometown, Bolívar, a month after the battle of El Semen, found himself the victim of a nighttime ambush, at a site in the llanos known as Rincón de los Toros, or "Corner of the Bulls." While he was sleeping in his hammock, a royalist party was admitted to the patriot camp by the New Granadan officer Francisco de Paula Santander, who would later become first a key collaborator and ultimately principal rival of the Liberator. His action was blameless in this case, however, for the enemy had previously obtained the patriot password from a prisoner they seized. The royalist party managed to kill a number of republican officers, and they riddled Bolívar's hammock with bullets—but fortunately for him, he had awakened and got away in time. He did not undertake any more significant campaigning for the rest of 1818. The dry season was coming to an end, and soon the rivers of the llanos would be overflowing. Not only that, but Bolívar's forces had suffered some important losses since the beginning of the year. Yet the balance was not wholly negative. The enemy had suffered losses, too, and the patriots had succeeded in consolidating control over a wide if thinly populated swath of interior Venezuela.

After the mishap at Rincón de los Toros, Bolívar returned to Angostura and generally stayed there until December. He devoted himself to military planning and preparations, to organizing the precarious republican government—whose penury made it necessary among other things to pay soldiers' wages in meat—and to welcoming the ever greater number of European soldiers of fortune who arrived to fight for South American freedom. The man immediately in charge of the recruiting was Luis López Méndez, who had remained in England after forming part of the diplomatic mission that Bolívar took to the British capital in 1810. He was now serving as agent both for the purchase of war supplies, including an array of elegant uniforms that were now surplus with the end of the Napoleonic wars, and for the contracting of soldiers and officers who were likewise surplus and drawing at best half pay.

López Méndez operated to a large extent on credit, thus accumulating ever more foreign debt for the new republic, and he had a taste of debtors' prison at the insistence of certain unhappy creditors. He had to find his way around the restrictions and prohibitions that the British government, in line with its theoretical neutrality in the conflict, placed on arms sales and recruiting. But the Spanish American cause enjoyed considerable sympathy in London commercial and intellectual circles, and the prospect of its eventual success was beginning to seem a bit more realistic: even as Bolívar consolidated his position in Venezuela, his Argentine counterpart, José de San Martín, was successfully leading an army across the southern Andes to overthrow the king's rule in Chile. It was thus not too difficult to evade the restrictions, whose application was in any case erratic.

In the matter of recruitment specifically, European volunteers were offered immediate promotion to one rank higher than the one they held, reimbursement for the cost of travel to Venezuela, wages corresponding to the salary scale of the British army, and the chance to cover themselves anew with glory. Over the entire period of the struggle, more than 4,000 Europeans joined the forces of Bolívar, of whom some had arrived earlier on their own account; but the first substantial number arrived in 1818. They came from Poland, Germany, and various other countries, even though the great majority were from Great Britain (including Ireland, then under British rule). Sometimes all the foreigners have been lumped together under the heading of the "British Legion," and for a time one unit was named just that, but in reality they made up several different units, and not a few were added to native military units to increase their strength and to serve as examples.

The United States was a less important recruiting area, though there too adventurers were ready to enlist, such as those who joined the ill-fated expedition of Gregor MacGregor in 1817 against Spanish-held Florida. General MacGregor occupied Amelia Island, at the far northeast corner of Florida, but soon ceded control to another expedition led by the French corsair Louis Aury, who was evicted in short order by the United States army. MacGregor was, of course, a former collaborator of Bolívar and his relative by marriage—but when the U.S. agent who visited the Liberator in Angostura alleged, with exaggeration, that the so-called República de las Floridas was a nest of pirates, Bolívar was able without technically stretching the truth to deny having authorized it. At the same time, U.S. seamen played a significant role not only in privateering but in the regular Venezuelan navy (a distinction not always clear-cut). Indeed an outright majority of the men who sailed in either the regular or irregular naval forces were foreigners; and while the naval dimension of the conflict was strictly secondary to the land struggle, it did not lack importance. Privateers flying a Venezuelan or New Granadan or Argentine or other Spanish American flag were continually striking blows against Spanish commerce in the Caribbean, while patriot warships (corsair and otherwise) helped protect republican coastal positions, including the vital entrance to the Orinoco River.

The contribution made by foreign volunteers/mercenaries on land and sea to the final victory is often exaggerated, especially by non-Latin American authors: even without them, independence would have been won, at more or less the same time. But its winning would have been slightly more difficult. The accumulated military experience brought by veterans of European wars and their technical proficiency in the handling of arms and military maneuvers were highly valuable, even if the lessons learned in Europe were not always readily applicable to the South American theater. From the standpoint of creole commanders, another advantage of foreign recruits was the greater difficulty they faced in deserting, as compared with native soldiers, due to unfamiliarity with the local language and customs. Eventually, some foreign units did cover themselves with glory, and some individual officers won a place in the very front rank of the liberators. A case in point is the Irishman Daniel F. O'Leary, who arrived in Angostura in March 1818 and in the end would become Bolívar's aide-de-camp, confidant, all-purpose collaborator, and even biographer. Others, however, rendered comparable service, on the battlefield and in the building of new nations.

The other side of such service to Latin American independence was the quantity of headaches that the foreign military also caused. They commonly arrived with unrealistic ideas of the country and type of conflict they were entering, and rapid disillusionment could then produce alcoholism, indiscipline, or even rebellion. Men familiar with the capitals of Europe suffered culture shock at the least on reaching Angostura, which though seat of government and of a bishopric, was a town of roughly 6,000 people and thoroughly lacking in cultural or other amenities. There were a few stone houses, around the central plaza, but far more of thatch and wattle. The new arrivals similarly faced exotic tropical diseases and a monotonous diet of plantains, manioc, and beef. And they soon realized that many of the promises made to them could not be honored. The offered promotions were not usually a problem, but money for their generous salaries was a different matter, and they did not always enjoy having to adapt to the local custom of pillaging to stay alive. Their uniforms meanwhile disintegrated under the tropical rain and sun—or desperate for funds, they would sell the uniforms to Venezuelan officers, who might end up wearing elegant European jackets but no shoes. Finally, some of them were repelled by the seeming barbarity of the war being fought, as exemplified by the execution of prisoners that continued to occur despite periodic suspensions of war to the death. O'Leary noted that executions were generally done by sword or lance, as powder was valuable, and amid the laughter and applause of bystanders.

Although he disapproved of much of what he saw, O'Leary never abandoned service. Some others did return home as soon as they could, and a few became involved in criminal or seditious activities. Colonel Henry Wilson became enmeshed in an obscure intrigue whose apparent purpose was to replace Bolívar with Páez as supreme commander; for this he was tried and expelled from Venezuela. A Colonel Hippisley, annoyed because he did not receive the general's commission promised by López Méndez, went home in a dudgeon and published a memoir that has become a classic reference for the Liberator's detractors and anathema to guardians of the Bolivarian cult. A still greater number died of wounds or disease. But little by little the most sickly or disaffected were eliminated in one way or another, while those who stayed on became socially as well as physically acclimatized.

Not all the foreigners reaching independent Venezuela were military. Because no foreign power yet recognized the country's independence, the only governmental agents were informal, but there were private merchants and entrepreneurs whose mere presence, apart from its possible economic significance, attested (more or less) to the seriousness of the new republic. One of Bolívar's decrees made clear that foreign residents would be subject neither to military conscription nor to the forced loans constantly exacted from native inhabitants. He also saw to it that his government's newspaper, *Correo del Orinoco*, was distributed abroad as well as internally. Its first issue appeared in June 1818, printed on a press brought from Trinidad, and it carried not just official messages and decrees and carefully edited news of the war but articles of analysis and opinion, some of them written by the supreme chief himself, who thus resumed the journalistic vocation he had earlier practiced in Jamaica.

Among the documents published in the *Correo* was the October 1818 regulation calling for election of a new Venezuelan congress, to meet in Angostura the following year. Bolívar had no intention of restoring the earlier federal republic, and he was still distrustful of congresses, but he realized the political advantage that election of a new congress might offer both domestically and in the court of international opinion. It would be a demonstration of liberal principles as well as of institutional consolidation (in the latter case suggesting a rather higher degree of consolidation than as yet truly existed). The call to elections blithely ignored the fact that Caracas and in fact most of Venezuela's population remained under Spanish rule and unable to participate; but as compared to the suffrage legislation of the First Republic, the socioeconomic qualifications for voting were notably more flexible, and for military of the rank of corporal or higher they were waived entirely. Common soldiers were still required to have some property or trade and to be heads of household, but only because—as the measure curiously explained—massive voting by the soldiery in the midst of war was just not practicable. Presumably the voting even of corporals and higher was often subject to pressure from their commanders, but in the last analysis the regulations reflected rather clearly the brand of military populism that characterized this new stage of the independence conflict.

The Congress of Angostura opened its sessions in February 1819 with twenty-six members, a number that later increased with the incorporation of additional deputies, including representatives of the New Granadan province of Casanare, which had accepted de facto the supreme authority of Bolívar. Its mission was both to enact legislation and to endow Venezuela with a new constitution more to Bolívar's liking than the federal charter of 1811. But the most noteworthy event of its existence was neither any law passed nor the second Venezuelan constitution that it duly adopted but the address Bolívar himself delivered at the inaugural session.

The Angostura Address is another of the Liberator's basic political texts. Its analysis of the state of Spanish America is the same as that already set forth in the Jamaica Letter, though this time the author did not dwell at speculative length on the future of the continent but presented his own recommendations in more detail. These once again were based in considerable part on a deeply negative assessment of the colonial heritage: "Enslaved by the triple yoke of ignorance, tyranny, and vice, we [Spanish] American people have never experienced knowledge, power, or virtue." He therefore reiterated the lesson he had expressed so often before, that the institutions of the First Republic, supposedly inspired by those of the United States, were wholly inapplicable to Spanish America—and he even hinted that U.S. institutions might in the end prove too perfect for the North Americans themselves:

Although that country is a singular model of political and moral virtue; and though freedom was its cradle and its nursery, and though it is nourished on pure freedom . . . it is a miracle, I repeat, that a system as weak and complex as federalism ever managed to guide it through circumstances as difficult and delicate as those of its recent past. But I should say that however successful this form of government proved for North America, it never entered my mind to compare the situation and nature of two States as diametrically different as English America and Spanish America. Would it not be difficult to apply to Spain England's political, civil, and religious Charter of Liberties? Well, it is even more difficult to adapt the laws of North America to Venezuela. Do we not read in [Montesquieu's] *Spirit of the Laws* that they must be suitable to the country for which they are written? That it is an astonishing coincidence for the laws of one nation to be applicable to another? That they must take into account the physical aspect of the country, its climate, the nature of its terrain, its location, size, and the way of life of its people? . . . This then is the code we should consult, not the one written for Washington!!!

Bolívar cited an array of historical examples in support of his views, yet time and again he showed particular admiration for the British style of constitutional monarchy, which seemed to combine a reasonable degree of civil liberty with great institutional stability and an executive power that was subject to the necessary checks and balances yet strong and effective in its operations. Nevertheless he again ruled out a strictly monarchical solution for his own country, on grounds both theoretical and practical. Although he did not dwell on the matter, he doubtless realized not only that monarchy had been discredited among his compatriots by the bad example of Fernando VII but also that there was a lack of suitable candidates for the throne. After all, a British prince would be Protestant, which was unthinkable; a Frenchman would presumably be vetoed by the British; and a member of the Spanish royal family, even if acceptable to Venezuelans, would be forbidden to take the job by the intransigent Fernando. Nor is there the least indication that he considered a crown for himself.

Certain of Bolívar's constitutional prescriptions did reflect the concrete influence of the British model, despite all he kept saying about the inadvisability of imitating foreign institutions. The most obvious example is his recommendation of a hereditary senate, in which the heroes of independence and their descendants would fulfill the role of a Venezuelan House of Lords, alongside a lower chamber to be chosen by popular (but not *too* popular) election and thus comparable to the House of Commons in London. Elsewhere in his address Bolívar turned to an even older model, the Areopagus of ancient Athens, as one of the antecedents for his novel proposal of a "Moral Power" as a fourth branch of government. It would function on the one hand as ministry of education, while on the other it was to use persuasion and moral influence to correct customs and foment civic spirit. Nevertheless, his primary focus, as always, was on the need for a strong central executive.

After he had presented his ideas for a new constitution, Bolívar in the last part of his address turned to three topics that in his view required the legislators' special attention. Two of these fitted in closely with his aim of placing the independence movement on a more popular footing, while the third reflected his continental vision. He implored the deputies to confirm the freedom of slaves in accordance with his Carúpano decree of 1816 and subsequent proclamations. Secondly, he implored them to confirm his measure for the distribution of confiscated assets among the soldiers of independence. And finally, he called for "the union of New Granada and Venezuela into a single great state," in which respect he did not fail to note that in reality "the fortunes of war" had already "authenticated this union." In the end, the Congress of Angostura broke no new ground with regard to either abolition of slavery or the distribution of confiscated property; it instead left the definitive treatment of both matters to be determined at a later time. It did adopt for Venezuela the Constitution of 1819, centralist in structure as Bolívar wished but without inclusion of the "Moral Power," merely ordering that his proposal on the latter point be printed and circulated for wider study. The constitution was in any case short-lived, for while the deputies were busy with constitution making, Simón Bolívar was already heading westward to New Granada, to complete the creation of the "great state" that he also had just recommended.

VI

The Invention of Colombia (1819–1821)

In New Granada in 1816 the collapse of what an older school of Colombian historians liked to call "La Patria Boba"—"The Foolish Fatherland"—had been as complete as that of Venezuela's Second Republic but was not the result of a similarly hard fought and bloody struggle. Instead, it was accomplished by a series of strokes launched into the interior, following Pablo Morillo's conquest of Cartagena at the end of 1815, in the course of which a population, tired of civil and foreign warfare and generally disillusioned with the independence movement, all too frequently acclaimed the invaders. But if the fighting was less intense than in Venezuela, the same could not be said of the repression that followed, which took the lives of almost the entire top command of New Granada's revolution and in effect prepared the ground for Bolívar to create a new *patria* in place of the former one, foolish or not.

The execution of patriot leaders and even a good many followers in New Granada was sometimes the work of summary war tribunals set up by Morillo, sometimes carried out with no semblance of trial and without even recording the names of the victims. At times the cadavers were disassembled so as to display arms and heads in public places as a warning of what could happen to traitors. Those who escaped execution, thanks to the intercession of a royalist friend, by sheer luck, or because their errors were deemed of lesser importance, might well be banished to some unhealthy spot and probably still suffered confiscation of property. Nor did women escape: whether for alleged implication in the crimes of their men or for subversive actions of their own, some of them also were condemned to death or exile, or in the case of lower-class women, to serve as cooks for units of the victorious army. But forced labor was not required only of people accused of disloyalty; for public works, especially the building or repair of roads of strategic value, laborers were peremptorily drafted from any nearby village. And confiscations were just one aspect of the intensified extraction of financial resources, including subsidies for the war in Venezuela to which Morillo himself returned in late 1816. The New Granadan officer Francisco de Paula Santander bitterly commented that the creation of over five hundred patriot martyrs aroused less hostility toward the Spanish than the various tax increases that they imposed.

The combination of fiscal and physical repression inevitably engendered resistance. Guerrilla bands rose up in different places, and the effort of the authorities to combat them led to more repression—and more martyrs, including Policarpa Salvarrieta, the most famous heroine of Colombian independence and perhaps of all that nation's history, who was arrested in Santafé as a covert agent of rebel forces and duly executed. Such punitive measures did not affect the province of Casanare, on New Granada's eastern plains, which remained a pro-independence sanctuary; however, though generally free of royalists, Casanare was no island of tranquility. It was a scene of bitter disputes between rival local factions and between these and still others arriving from the highlands. At the same time, Casanare had considerable strategic importance. It protected the rear of patriot forces on the Venezuelan llanos and was a possible starting point for a campaign against Santafé and the heart of the viceroyalty.

In the hope of bringing some order to the province, Simón Bolívar named Santander governor of Casanare in mid-1818, promoting him to general at the same time. Santander accepted the position, though he made clear that his accepting it from the supreme chief of Venezuela did not imply that Casanare was an integral part of Venezuela. He did not reject the Liberator's vision of a single "great state" but maintained that the formal incorporation of New Granadan provinces could only be agreed to by their own representatives. The specification of this detail undoubtedly reflected the legalistic mentality of Santander, a former law student who left his studies in 1810 to join the revolutionary armed forces. Yet even Santander's detractors, who have been many in his own day and down to the present, have agreed that Bolívar's choice was a sound one. An improvised military officer like so many others, Santander never stood out as a field commander but was a conscientious and talented administrator, both as military staff officer and in the organization of liberated territories. He lived up to Bolívar's full expectations, so that by the middle of 1819 Casanare was ready to play a role in the definitive liberation of New Granada.

It is not known exactly when Bolívar conceived the plan of the campaign that would carry him again to Santafé. The possibility of using Casanare as gateway to the heart of New Granada had naturally occurred to him as to others, but not necessarily as the key element in his overall strategy. In the first months of 1819, with time out for his appearance at the Congress of Angostura, he was preparing new operations against Morillo in Venezuela. Morillo, on his part, did not doubt that to defeat the revolution he had to regain control of the Orinoco Basin and accordingly advanced into the llanos with a reinforced royalist army. However, Bolívar and Páez avoided a frontal encounter with Morillo's Spanish infantry, which was still superior to theirs even with the addition of British and other European veterans. They instead adopted scorched-earth tactics, burning fields and carrying away whatever they could, with the result that, as the enemy forces advanced farther into the llanos, they suffered ever greater hardships and desertions. In the end, the Spanish general returned to his base in the central Venezuelan highlands without achieving his objective. But neither did Bolívar find the opportunity to strike a telling blow against the forces of the king. When the onset of the rainy season brought a relative pause in hostilities, Bolívar remained in possession of the greater part of the llanos, but he never got around to carrying out his own offensive plans.

As inactivity was never agreeable to Bolívar, around the middle of May 1819 he definitively embraced the option of a campaign to liberate New Granada. What finally seems to have convinced him of its feasibility was the news he had from Santander, who informed him of the readiness of Casanare province and of the patriots' success in turning back (with tactics mainly of evasion and harassment) no less than two royalist invasions sent down from the highlands. It was still a risky enterprise, for the army would first have to cross the llanos in rainy season, fording rivers that overflowed their banks, then climb the Andes to Santafé, through frigid mountain passes with soldiers habituated to the heat of the tropical plains. There was also the danger of bad behavior on the part of the military chieftains, still not wholly reliable, whom Bolívar would have to leave behind in Venezuela. Yet for him the risks were almost an incentive, and they were offset by the possibility—assuming victory was won—of taking possession of a region with far greater resources than the llanos had to offer and relatively unprotected besides, thanks to the concentration of royalist forces in Venezuela precisely for the purpose of holding Bolívar in check.

The New Granadan option also had in its favor the surprise factor, provided it could be quickly carried out. Morillo, an experienced strategist himself, correctly foresaw that Bolívar might strike westward from the llanos to Santafé. However, Bolívar prepared and executed the campaign before the Spanish general could properly react—so rapidly, indeed, that it brings to mind the lightning campaign of 1813 from the New Granadan border to Caracas, though with the difference that unlike that campaign it owed little to improvisation. While never wholly overcoming his characteristic impulsiveness, Bolívar was beginning to master, by experience, the elements of military science. He was thus careful, among other things, to instruct General José Franciso Bermúdez in the east to continue threatening Morillo in his bastion of central Venezuela, and Páez to strike toward Cúcuta at the border between New Granada and Venezuela, to distract the enemy and prevent the sending of royalist reinforcements from Venezuela while Bolívar advanced over a more direct route toward the viceregal capital.

Even though he had made his decision, Bolívar submitted the plan to a war council meeting in a primitive hut of the llanos, where other officers used the skulls of cattle as stools to sit on. Despite any reservations, all but one voted agreement. A few days more were spent gathering animals and equipment, including boats for river transport, but by the end of May the expedition had already left—for Cúcuta, Bolívar announced initially. In effect, he hoped to keep his true objective secret as long as possible, to deceive both the enemy and his own troops, who would not necessarily relish the idea of climbing the Andes to the New Granadan heartland and might well desert. The army of liberation was further accompanied by an indeterminate number of women and children. The women (or "Juanas," i.e., "Janes," as they were called) performed a variety of services: they were of course wives and lovers, cooks and nurses, but it was not unheard of for them at times to take up arms and fight. Some were pregnant, and at least one would give birth on the march, to continue the very next day with infant in her arms.

On 4 June Bolívar crossed the Arauca River into New Granada, and a week later he met up with Santander. The latter, as a native of New Granada and familiar with the terrain, was given command of the army's vanguard, and with the incorporation of still other New Granadans the total invasion force numbered over 3,000 men, a majority of them infantry. All of them (plus the women), from commander-in-chief on down, shared the same discomforts: permanently wet and covered with mud, assailed by plagues of mosquitoes, eating almost nothing but meat and not always enough of that. Additional boats had to be improvised out of cattle hides to carry supplies and, in deeper waters, those people who could not swim. On occasion Bolívar personally plunged on horseback into the water to rescue someone in danger of drowning. But the expedition moved forward. On 27 June Santander and the vanguard occupied Paya, in the foothills of the Andes, after defeating a detachment of royalist defenders in the campaign's first armed encounter.

The hardest part was still to come. From Casanare to the high plain where Santafé was located there were several different routes, any one of which could be torture for the traveler in the best season of the year and far worse at the particular time of Bolívar's crossing. Moreover, on Santander's recommendation, Bolívar had chosen the route that was shortest but also most difficult, rising to an altitude of almost 4,000 meters before finally reaching Socha, in one of the temperate highland valleys. The trail was primitive in the extreme, with tree trunks as bridges over some of the mountain streams; at times the only way to tell the direction of travel was by observing the bones of men and animals strewn along the way or the crosses set up in memory of victims who died in previous attempts. At least part of Santander's vanguard was made up of New Granadan highlanders accustomed to the cold mountain air, though not necessarily provided with adequate clothing after crossing the flooded llanos. Somewhat the same could be said of the British legionnaires, who came with the main corps of the army, chiefly composed of Venezuelans. But the Venezuelans were natives either of the llanos or of lower Andean ranges of warmer climate, and they were cruelly punished by the cold breezes of the high passes. However, no one escaped suffering. There came a moment when the extent of discontent in the ranks led Bolívar to convoke still another council of officers, to discuss the possibility of abandoning the effort. It is unlikely that he was prepared to give up under any circumstances, but he felt it expedient to invite the presentation of other views. Fortunately for him, Santander came back from his advanced position to attend the session and insist on going ahead as planned: he vowed that he and the vanguard would do so no matter what the rest decided to do—and in the end, the decision was to proceed.

Before the army finally emerged from its crossing at Socha, located a mere 2,700 meters above sea level, it had lost a great part of its equipment and all its horses. Coming from the llanos, the horses too were accustomed to other climates and terrains; they destroyed their hooves on the rocky paths and grew weak for lack of adequate fodder. A considerable number of humans likewise perished, including roughly a fourth of the British, due to the combined effects of cold, exhaustion, and the rarified air at high altitude. It is therefore easy to imagine the joy of the survivors when they reached their immediate destination—a first installment of the vanguard on 1 July, the rest in stages—and

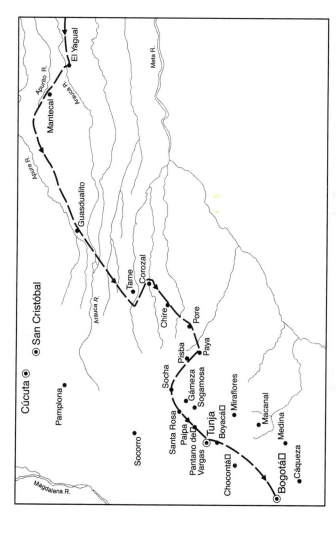

The Campaign to Liberate New Granada in 1819. (Adapted with permission from Juan Friede, *La Batalla de Boyacá—7 de agosto de 1819—a través de los archivos españoles* [Bogotá: Banco de la República, 1969])

were greeted with shelter and hot food by the people of the region. There were bread and potatoes and naturally a large amount of *chicha,* the fermented maize drink that was the beer of the Andes. With the mayors and parish priests of the surrounding country generally rallying to the patriots' side, almost the entire population seemed anxious to show support; recruits, horses, and other kinds of help were soon flowing in.

If a good detachment of royalists had been waiting for the successive groups of exhausted soldiers as they emerged from the mountain passage, it would no doubt have been possible to annihilate them. But while the Spanish colonel José María Barreiro, whose mission it was to guard the approach to Santafé, was always aware of the possibility of invasion from the llanos, he was convinced that the Paya-Socha route was impassable for an army. And he was caught unawares not only by the choice of route but by the size of Bolívar's force. Convinced in any event that what he faced was more like a band of ragged beggars than a true army, he was content to take his time, guarding the access to the capital while concentrating his own forces and hoping to wear down his foe. Whether this choice of strategy was due to overconfidence or to incompetence, it had disastrous consequences.

The first few armed encounters were indecisive, and the same can be said of the battle of Pantano de Vargas, fought on 25 July, as far as its immediate effects are concerned (though not its psychological impact). During the morning hours Bolívar's army, in its progress toward Santafé, crossed the Chicamocha River to occupy a soggy field surrounded by a semicircle of hills. There the patriots were exposed in a highly unfavorable position to possible enemy attack, unless Bolívar quickly occupied the surrounding heights—which by a grave oversight he did not do. It is one of the errors cited by Bolívar's detractors to suggest that he was not quite as great a commander as his admirers allege, but it definitely would not be repeated on this campaign. It is just unfortunate that on the present occasion Barreiro reacted with more promptness than usual and did seize the heights to the right of the field. Combat began around noon and continued for several hours, until the royalists seemed on the point of gaining a sweeping victory. But just then the patriot colonel José Félix Rondón, one of the *llaneros* who had once fought under the royalist Boves, gathered fourteen other mounted lancers and in the best *llanero* fashion led a furious charge against the enemy infantry. Taken by surprise, and fearing that Rondón's men were only the first installment of a major wave of patriot reinforcements, the royalists fell prey to sudden consternation and were spared a humiliating defeat only by the sun's setting, which forced an end to hostilities. On the patriot side, one of the more notable casualties was James Rooke, head of the British contingent, who died, after the battle, from the amputation, naturally without anesthesia, of a wounded arm. But both armies suffered important losses, quantitatively more or less equivalent, and in that sense the combat may be considered a tie. In terms of morale, however, it was a victory for the patriots, who had clearly demonstrated their fighting capacity and henceforth would have to be taken seriously.

Bolívar hastened to replace his losses and even add to his total strength by summoning all male adults to take arms, under penalty of summary execution if they did not present themselves. And thanks to the generally favorable attitude of the local population, new recruits continued to arrive. They did not necessarily arrive armed, much less with any sort of military training. Bolívar nevertheless wasted little time in renewing his advance, and at the beginning of August he executed one of the most brilliant maneuvers of his career, leaving camp under cover of darkness and taking his troops on a rapid march behind the back of the royalist army to fall upon Tunja, the provincial capital and site of an important deposit of arms and other supplies. In addition, and of critical importance, Tunja was a point on the main road to Santafé, situated in between Barreiro's army and the viceregal capital.

In an effort to place himself once again between Bolívar and the capital, Barreiro undertook a forced march of his own in the early morning of 7 August, over a difficult route somewhat to the west of Tunja. He achieved his objective, reaching the main road close to a narrow bridge over the Teatinos River (today Boyacá River, actually more brook than river). His soldiers, worn out and soaked by steady rainfall, stopped to rest and take refreshment; but they did not rest long, because the patriot army, after a night's sleep in Tunja and a good breakfast served by that

Battlefield of Boyacá, partly paved over for holding commemorative events; the bridge in lower left. (Author's collection)

city's patriot ladies, was already on the way to intercept them. Bolívar had a slight numerical advantage, of roughly 2,850 men against 2,700, but this was not a significant difference. About two in the afternoon, what has come to be known as the Battle of Boyacá got underway. The royalist vanguard seized control of the far (or southern) side of the small stream, gaining a favorable strategic position but in the process dividing Barreiro's forces. After that, the battle broke down into two separate engagements, one around the bridge and the other on the slope to the north of the river; both ended badly for the royalists, who were not only tired but increasingly demoralized. In less than two hours Barreiro had surrendered, along with most of his officers and some 1,600 men. One of the prisoners turned out to be the same officer whose betrayal led to Bolívar's embarrassing loss of Puerto Cabello in 1812, and no sooner had the Liberator spied him in the crowd of prisoners than a gallows was set up to hang him. A few royalists escaped, but between casualties and prisoners, the main royalist army in New Granada simply disappeared.

With its small number of combatants and short duration, the Battle of Boyacá would hardly figure as more than a skirmish in the wars of Napoleon, but it is no exaggeration to say that it was the most important of all Bolívar's victories. Prior to Boyacá, he had lost about as many battles as he had won; from now on, he would go from triumph to triumph, with only occasional and transitory reverses. Moreover, the campaign to liberate New Granada, overcoming extreme obstacles of climate and terrain, has no exact parallel in the struggles for independence elsewhere in the hemisphere and could only make a profound impression in both America and Europe, with predictably opposite effects on royalist and patriot morale. The final victory in Spanish South America, at Ayacucho in Peru five years later, was a military engagement on a larger scale but in last analysis a corollary of Boyacá. Even if the date of that final encounter was still not known, there could no longer be much doubt as to the result.

The importance of Boyacá lay not only in the destruction of the enemy army and the psychological impact but in the fact that it opened the path to Santafé and to the human and material resources of the surrounding provinces. Although New Granada was far from the wealthiest of Spain's colonies, it was, after Mexico, the most populous and thus a potentially valuable source of recruits. It had craft industries to produce cloth for uniforms, leather goods, and other necessities. Metalworking was almost nonexistent, but there were gold mines, and even if the total output of precious metal was less than that of either Mexico or Peru, which specialized in silver, there were government mints in Popayán and Santafé and a stock of coin in circulation. Moreover, such was the speed of Viceroy Juan Sámano to abandon his capital on receiving the unexpected news of Barreiro's defeat that he not only left behind a personal cache of gold but some 700,000 pesos of gold, silver, and coin in the royal mint. Sámano did not take the time to mount a holding action that might have delayed Bolívar's advance; he simply fled the capital disguised in a green ruana (or poncho) and did not stop until safely ensconced behind the walls of Cartagena. The high court judges and other top royal officials fled, too, not to mention a substantial number of merchants and other local inhabitants (Spanish or creole) of monarchist persuasion. Most of the royalist garrison that remained in Santafé withdrew to the southwest, to Popayán, to be joined there or on the way by at least some of the defeated royalists who had fought at Boyacá.

The victor of Boyacá, Simón Bolívar, entered Santafé on 10 August. Having learned there was no more resistance, he had hurried ahead of his troops, accompanied by only a few aides. He was joyously received by the inhabitants, but he had to repeat the entry, with triumphal arches and all the ceremony called for by Spanish tradition, a few weeks later. On that second occasion, a detail whose significance would have been missed by the general public, was the presence—among twenty young ladies ("nymphs," they used to say) who paid him homage in the central plaza, today Plaza Bolívar—of Bernardina Ibáñez, a native of Ocaña in whose home he had stayed during his Magdalena River campaign of 1813. Now seventeen years old, Bernardina quickly became one of the great loves of Bolívar's romantic career. A curious detail of the relationship was the fact that her sister Nicolasa became the lover of Santander, despite being married to a mid-level royalist bureaucrat, who conveniently had fled the city after Boyacá.

Just as Bolívar and Santander were courting two women who happened to be sisters, they also shared the task of completing the liberation of New Granada and organizing the liberated provinces. Bolívar retained supreme command, civil and military, of both Venezuela and New Granada, but he named Santander vice president of New Granada, with functions similar to those of the vice president of Venezuela who was named in Angostura the previous February and who was left in charge of Venezuela when Bolívar embarked on his latest campaign. In the same way Santander, at age twenty-seven, was to be left in charge of New Granada after Bolívar's other responsibilities took him away from the former viceregal capital, now called once again Santafé de Bogotá to emphasize the break with the colonial past. And when shortly afterward the Republic of Colombia, comprising all northern South America, was formally constituted, 'Santafé' was dropped altogether.

In strictly military matters, Bolívar, even before Boyacá dispatched some of his forces to spark uprisings elsewhere in New Granada or to work with existing guerrilla bands. Most of the eastern cordillera was soon in patriot hands, and by year's end, the royalists held only the Caribbean coast and part of the southwest, where fighting flowed back and forth. In civil affairs, besides naming Santander as vice president, Bolívar appointed provincial officials, established a high court, and adopted various measures designed to squeeze the greatest possible amount of money and other resources out of New Granada. He slashed the salaries of civil servants and ordered *donativos* that were in fact forced contributions. He also called for massive recruitment of slaves, who were offered freedom in return for military service. This last measure, though its immediate purpose may have been military, was in line with Bolívar's political and philosophical convictions and further had in his view a critical demographic importance. As he explained to Santander,

> We need robust, vigorous men who are accustomed to hardship and fatigue, men who will embrace the cause and the service with enthusiasm, men who will identify their interest with the public interest, and men for whom death can have little less meaning than life. The political considerations are even stronger. . . . It is . . . borne out by the maxims of politics and derived from the examples of history that any free government which commits the folly of maintaining slavery is repaid with rebellion and sometimes with collapse. . . . [And i]s it not proper that the slaves should acquire their rights on the battlefield and that their dangerous numbers should be lessened by a process both just and effective? In Venezuela we have seen the free population die and the slave survive. I know not whether or not this is prudent, but I do know that, unless we use the slaves in [New Granada], they will outlive us again.

By freeing slaves Bolívar would thus dispel the danger of Haitian-style slave rebellion and, by sending them into battle, maintain the balance between the races. On the latter point Bolívar was guided, in part, by the obsessive fear of "pardocracy," or growing protagonism of the *pardo* element that was as much a constant of his thinking (as expressed in private correspondence if not public statements) as was his opposition to slavery as such. Among others of his race and class, the same fear was if anything more pronounced than opposition to slavery, and it parallels the reluctance of so many supporters of abolition in the United States, not least Abraham Lincoln, to accept blacks as equal citizens. There is no evidence, however, that Bolívar regarded nonwhites as inherently inferior: he once described differences of color as a mere "accident of skin." What he feared was that the *pardos* would reach, *as pardos,* for more power than they were yet prepared to handle.

Because Bolívar was not fond of administrative detail, the implementation of his measures for New Granada was generally up to Santander, before as well as after the Liberator left the capital, which he did, actually, not long after his official entry in triumph. It was therefore Santander who had to face the protests of all those who were happy to be liberated but not to pay the cost of liberation. In some cases, Bolívar's measures seemed unduly rigorous even to Santander, whether because he was the immediate target of the complaints or because he recognized that these did not wholly lack foundation. A case in point was the recruitment of slaves, bitterly protested by the gold miners of western New Granada who were heavily dependent on slave labor. Santander did not defend slavery as such (in Spanish South America, almost no one did), but he pointed out the contradiction between taking the slaves used in mining for military service and the pressing need for gold with which to pay the costs of the war. He thus questioned Bolívar's February 1820 order for the enlistment of 5,000 slaves in the western provinces, though in the end he carried it out as far as possible. And despite occasional friction over matters such as this, Bolívar had to declare himself well satisfied with Santander's performance. He likewise accepted, though at bottom he disapproved, the execution by Santander's order of Barreiro and thirty-eight other Spanish officers captured at Boyacá on charges of conspiring from their place of imprisonment. The evidence against them was notoriously weak, but they were executed in the same central plaza that had previously witnessed the creation of so many patriot martyrs, with Santander personally coming forth to observe the execution. The episode represented a return to the practices of war to the death that Bolívar hoped had been finally left behind, but in this instance he preferred not to antagonize the man who had become his principal collaborator.

Bolívar's attention in any case was mainly directed to the conduct of the war itself—and to consolidating union between Venezuela and New Granada. When no new threat from the direction of Morillo in Venezuela materialized, he doubled back to the llanos and retraced much the same route he had taken to victory earlier in the year. By mid-December he was in Angostura, where he first had to resolve a political crisis. The vice president of Venezuela whom Bolívar had left in charge when he embarked on the Boyacá campaign was Francisco Antonio Zea, a distinguished man of science and letters and faithful ally of the Liberator. But Zea was a civilian and a New Granadan, and on both counts he faced the suspicion if not hostility of the military chieftains and political factions of Venezuela; nor did he show much tact in his dealings with them. Eventually Zea was induced to resign his post and, adding insult to injury, was replaced by a Venezuelan general whom not long before he had ordered put in jail. However, the mere presence of Bolívar, crowned with military success and interested not in imposing punishments but in gaining support for his future projects, was enough to restore due obedience and order in Angostura.

Bolívar's presence was also enough to formalize his cherished objective of union between Venezuela and New Granada. After hearing Bolívar's report on his achievements, the Congress of Angostura—representing basically the liberated portions of Venezuela plus a handful of New Granadans—adopted what was grandly called the Fundamental Law of the Republic of Colombia. This was not a true constitution, whose adoption was left for later, but it did establish a concise frame of organization, with an overall government headed by a president and vice president for the conduct of the war and matters of general interest. Bolívar was naturally given the office of president, and he made sure that the unfortunate Zea was chosen Colombian vice president, which both salved his injured pride and removed him from direct involvement in Venezuelan affairs. The immediate administration of Venezuela and New Granada was entrusted to separate regional vice presidents, and for Venezuela one of the surviving statesmen of the First Republic was named, while Santander was the obvious choice for New Granada, in effect to continue what he was already doing. The Fundamental Law called for creation of a third regional vice presidency in the former **Presidency** of Quito, or modern Ecuador, which was at least tentatively included in the union without its consent, for it had no representatives in Angostura and in fact still lay wholly under Spanish control. But because it had loosely formed part of the Viceroyalty of New Granada, its incorporation was a necessary step toward Bolívar's aim of preserving the territorial integrity of the viceroyalty even after independence.

Bolívar did not linger long in Angostura, as there remained the war to be fought; before the end of the year, he was on the move again. Although Morillo remained entrenched in central Venezuela, Bolívar did not propose to seek a definitive encounter just yet, but rather to complete the liberation of the New Granadan coast, for which purpose he next returned to the interior of New Granada in order to mobilize support. (While there, he also gave orders for the payment of pensions to war widows and orphans out of his own salary.) And in March 1820 the coastal campaign got off to a good start when a force, carried by sea from eastern Venezuela, occupied Ríohacha on the Goajira Peninsula. This should have been a first step toward the liberation of Santa Marta and Cartagena. Unfortunately, the force was made up in large part of Irish legionnaires who mutinied in protest over their poor conditions of service and in a drunken brawl set fire to the town. The Irish then seized one of the ships that had taken them to Ríohacha and sailed off to Jamaica, which was no doubt good riddance but allowed the royalists to regain what was left of the place and disrupted Bolívar's strategic plan.

By happy coincidence, the fiasco on the Caribbean coast came at the same time that news arrived of an upheaval in the parent country that could bode only good for the Spanish American cause. In Spain not everyone, of course, had been happy with the return to absolutism engineered by Fernando VII on his return from French captivity in 1814. And among the disaffected were not only liberal men of letters but a significant part of the military officer corps, among whom the Masonic lodges, also of generally liberal ideology, had been gaining followers. The common soldiers were neither Masons nor men of letters, but neither were they eager to serve in colonial wars. Thus on 1 January 1820 a rebellion broke out at the port of Cádiz among troops assembled for shipment overseas, and from there the movement spread until Fernando felt compelled to give up not his throne but at least his absolute power and to revive the liberal Constitution of 1812 that a few years earlier he had overthrown. Spain's restored constitutional monarchy had no intention of recognizing the colonies' independence, among other reasons because of the influence of the Cádiz merchants who were last-ditch defenders of the Spanish monopoly of colonial trade. The new Spanish regime nevertheless imagined that, by restoring constitutional guarantees and limited American representation in the government of the empire, it would be possible to reach a negotiated settlement. It therefore instructed royalist commanders in America not only to swear allegiance to the constitution but to enter talks with the insurgents. Morillo in Venezuela expected nothing positive to come of this, but as a disciplined officer he reinstated the constitution and invited his adversaries to discuss a peaceful end to the conflict, meanwhile proposing that both sides agree to an armistice.

In the view of Bolívar and other American leaders, the Spanish events were promising in the extreme, not just because they prevented the sending out of a new expeditionary force and raised a slight possibility of peaceful settlement but also because of the probability, indeed near certainty, that they would produce confusion and wrangling in the enemy camp. Bolívar accordingly agreed to negotiations, even while making clear that independence per se was not negotiable. He did not immediately accept the proposed armistice, and while he still delayed launching any decisive action against Morillo, hostilities continued amid the exchange of messages and proposals. On the Caribbean coast of New Granada, the patriots advanced toward Cartagena and placed the city again under siege, though its final surrender by the royalists did not occur for another year. More important was a new advance by Bolívar from Cúcuta into western Venezuela, which took him as far as Mérida and Trujillo. By this time, few if any royalist leaders believed in the possibility of outright victory, and their forces were suffering ever more desertions. On 25 November, therefore, Morillo was only too happy to agree to a half-year armistice, plus a treaty to "regularize" the conflict by setting standards for the exchange of prisoners, humane treatment of the civilian population, and similar details. Two days later he met personally with Bolívar near Trujillo for the formal signing. Morillo arrived for the meeting in gala uniform and with full military escort, whereas Bolívar offered a strikingly different impression: simply dressed, he came riding on a mule and accompanied by a handful of officers. Yet according to all accounts, Bolívar charmed his Spanish counterpart; the following toasts and embraces were perfectly sincere, and the two men then passed the night under the same roof.

Of symbolic importance was the mere fact that the two sides had met and treated each other as equals, meaning at least in practice that Spain recognized the existence of the new Republic of Colombia. However, the war was only suspended, and Bolívar's efforts to follow up the armistice with the negotiation of a permanent peace—even sending a cordial letter to Fernando VII—came to nothing. In fact hostilities resumed even before the end of the stipulated six-month period, thanks to a series of disagreements over and violations of the armistice terms. In the lack of fast and reliable means of communication, different war fronts found out about the armistice at different times, a circumstance that easily lent itself to misunderstandings and deceptions. Bolívar himself suggested to Santander that he delay promulgation of the agreement until additional territory was first brought under republican control. But the thorniest question concerned Maracaibo, in western Venezuela, which had been a royalist bulwark but suddenly rose up and declared itself part of Colombia. This was an eventuality not contemplated in the terms of the armistice, which in any case the people of Maracaibo had never promised to obey. But the prime mover behind the Maracaibo uprising was one of Bolívar's generals, Rafael Urdaneta, himself a Maracaibo native. Bolívar had no part in hatching the scheme, yet Maracaibo was simply too valuable an acquisition, and the Liberator rejected all demands for its return. The royalists consequently declared the armistice broken, and by the end of April 1821 fighting formally began again. It began without the presence of Morillo, for shortly after his meeting with Bolívar the Spanish general resigned his command

and returned home, leaving the royalist forces in the hands of Marshal Miguel de la Torre, an able officer but less so than his predecessor and actually married to a relative of Bolívar.

At last the moment had arrived for an advance on Caracas, and it was even more meticulously planned than the New Granadan campaign of 1819. Urdaneta coming from Maracaibo and Bolívar himself from the western Andes were to join forces with Páez, who would advance from the llanos, while still another patriot army threatened Caracas from the east. La Torre still had an impressive number of troops guarding the central core of Venezuela, plus the advantage of interior lines of communication and supply, but his army was at a serious disadvantage in terms of morale; the king's soldiers were deserting daily. Bolívar's plan, in any event, functioned perfectly. In mid-May, the patriots' eastern army actually entered Caracas, and though the royalists soon retook the city, they had to divide their forces in the process. The following month, the other patriot contingents successfully assembled at San Carlos, southwest of Valencia. La Torre proposed to give them battle more for reasons of military honor and discipline than from any hope of victory.

The battle took place on 24 June, at Carabobo, not far from Valencia. La Torre had positioned his men in a favorable location on a mesa overlooking the Valencia road, but he had slightly inferior numbers: less than 5,000 men as against 6,500 for Bolívar, who had never before gone into battle with so large an army under his command. Because a frontal attack on the enemy position was not practical, Bolívar ordered a flanking movement to scale one side of the height where the royalists were situated. In this movement the British infantry performed outstanding service, and suffered heavy casualties, but once the operation was completed and the first patriot cavalry appeared on the mesa, royalist resistance crumbled. The battle lasted under two hours, about as long as Boyacá, and another royal army was destroyed; approximately four hundred men succeeded in taking refuge in Puerto Cabello, which once more became a royalist bastion under republican siege. Five days later Bolívar entered Caracas, liberated one last time.

Even while the battle of Carabobo was being fought, the constituent congress of the Republic of Colombia was meeting at

Cúcuta, a central point chosen because it was about as hard or as easy to get to for either Venezuelans or New Granadans. The Congress of Angostura, in summoning the new congress, unrealistically set 1 January 1821 as its opening date, but by the time elections were held and a quorum of deputies managed to get to Cúcuta, it was already May. Even then, Caracas and its immediate hinterland were still under royalist control and unable to participate, as well as all the Presidency of Quito except the port of Guayaquil, which in October 1820 staged its own uprising for independence. But Guayaquil had not yet voted to join Colombia, much less sent deputies to Cúcuta. The gathering was thus far from fully representative, but it was more so at least than the Angostura body, and with only one dissenting vote it proceeded to ratify the union proclaimed at Angostura. After all, union already existed de facto, as far as Venezuela and New Granada were concerned, and it would have been rash to dissolve it in the midst of a war for existence. That was quite apart from the adamant support of union on the part of Bolívar, who felt that it not only was needed for winning the war but was eminently desirable in the long run because of the historical and cultural ties of the peoples involved, their supposedly complementary resources—and because a large state would simply be taken more seriously in the concert of nations than a number of small ones.

What had just been done, at least on paper, had no exact parallel elsewhere in Spanish America, for this original Colombia—*'Gran,'* or "Great," *Colombia,* as it is conventionally termed in retrospect—was the one independent nation whose territory took in all of a former Spanish viceroyalty. In North America the Mexican Empire of Agustín de Iturbide (which he established on assuming leadership of the independence movement there), as well as its successor republic, briefly incorporated Central America but never the Spanish Antilles or Philippine Islands, which had also belonged to the Viceroyalty of New Spain; in southern South America, the Viceroyalty of Río de la Plata was fragmented into Argentina, Bolivia, Paraguay, and Uruguay; and when Peru finally became independent, it lacked its former viceroy's tenuous jurisdiction over Chile. But the impressive Colombian union was not exactly an "imagined community," in the now familiar terminology used by Benedict Anderson in describing the emergence of modern nation-states, or at least it was truly "imagined" only by a select minority of citizens. It rested less on any natural affinity of peoples from Cumaná to Quito, who typically thought of themselves as members of some local or subregional community, than on the precise manner in which independence had come about, under the overall leadership of Simón Bolívar, and on his personal will and vision.

Of course, even though the desirability of maintaining union while the war lasted was broadly accepted, this did not necessarily mean that it would prove workable in future years; and there was the questionable representativeness of the congress itself. Hence even many who voted in favor did so with mental reservations. But voting for union was only a first step: it next had to be decided what kind of union to form, whether a strictly centralized state or a federation. In the debate that followed, many of the same arguments were heard as earlier in the United States constitutional convention, although the question to be resolved was not quite identical, for in the United States some sort of federal union had been taken for granted and debate revolved simply around the proper sharing of powers between state and federal authorities. In the Colombian case, the deputies from Venezuela mostly rejected outright a federalist solution, whether from doctrinal conviction or out of solidarity with Bolívar, whose views on the issue were well-known. Among New Granadans, however, there was an appreciable current of federalism. In some cases those who had been federalists in the days of the United Provinces had not changed their convictions despite the calamitous end of that particular federation, and some also believed that federalism would somehow protect their region against domination by the Venezuelan military chiefs who, thanks to the execution of so many of their New Granadan counterparts during the Spanish reconquest, held virtually all top commands.

But the most important military officer of New Granada, Santander, had already been put in charge of regional administration by Bolívar and was clearly destined to play an important role in any future Colombian government. He himself had been a federalist in the earlier civil strife, but it was now to his advantage to embrace the centralist cause as championed by Bolívar. The same was true of the young professional men of generally liberal orientation—many of them from the outer provinces of New Granada like Santander (whose home town happened to be Cúcuta)—who were already gravitating to his political circle and expected to collaborate with him in future. Hence the constitution finally adopted was centralist. As a concession to federalists, one article provided that after a trial period of ten years a new convention should meet for possible constitutional reform: this might be termed the "Great Compromise" of the Colombian constitutional convention, comparable to the agreement in the earlier U.S. convention that overcame the fears of the small states by granting them equal representation in the Senate. But in the meantime Colombia's constitution was made unamendable, and the degree of centralization that it established was in fact rather extreme. The three traditional entities of Venezuela, New Granada, and Quito were simply dissolved, and the entire country was divided into provinces and departments that had no meaningful local autonomy and whose top officials were all named from Bogotá, which became the national capital despite some Venezuelan reluctance, in view of its location, roughly equidistant between Caracas and Quito.

It would almost appear that the deputies at Cúcuta, seeking to avoid the excesses of federalism, had fallen into the opposite extreme. At least in so doing they believed they had properly interpreted the desires of Bolívar. However, they ignored such schemes of his as a hereditary senate and "moral power," drafting a fairly conventional liberal document in whose articles could be detected the influence of both the U.S. constitution and the Spanish liberal charter of 1812. Bolívar in any case did not object to the degree of centralization. What did bother him was the division of powers between the executive branch and the legislative, which he considered too favorable to the latter, especially as he imagined that any future congress was bound to be a nest of impractical theorists and hairsplitting lawyers, incapable of understanding the iron necessity of strong government for Latin America's new nations. Despite his private reservations, however, and despite another in his line of public avowals that he wished no longer to bear the responsibility of government, Bolívar accepted both the new constitution and election, by the constituent congress itself, as first chief executive to serve under it. He was elected without opposition.

Selection of a vice president proved more difficult, as well as highly important, because it was Bolívar's intention to concentrate on his military role and completion of the war of independence, meanwhile leaving the immediate conduct of governmental affairs in the vice president's hands. Bolívar being Venezuelan, the second highest position obviously had to go to a New Granadan, and two names principally suggested themselves: the New Granadan "Precursor" Antonio Nariño, and Santander. The former, recently returned from Spanish imprisonment, did not lack illustrious credentials, but he was saddled with the enmities he had created in the civil conflicts of the first years of independence. Santander's credentials were less numerous but more recent, and he had the backing of his own coterie of enthusiastic young followers over and above that of Nariño's enemies. He was elected, though it took more than one round of voting to produce a majority.

In addition to its constitution making, the Congress of Cúcuta adopted legislation on matters that it felt could not be left until the first regular congress. Some measures provided only the necessary detailed regulation of specific articles contained in the constitution. Others comprised a package of liberal institutional reforms, one of which was the definitive response to Bolívar's call for the abolition of slavery. It established the rule of free birth, whereby any child of a slave mother was henceforth born free, and also a special fund to buy the liberty of those born too soon to benefit from the law. The adoption of the law occurred amid an outpouring of emotion in the hall, with deputies shedding tears of pride and joy and in some cases declaring the freedom of their own slaves on the spot. The measure was similar to that adopted in the province of Antioquia in 1814 as well as to the treatment accorded the institution of slavery in several parts of the early United States (e.g., New Jersey). But it had several limitations, for it not only failed to free outright any existing slaves, but provided that even the children born free in the future would have to work for their mothers' owners until age eighteen, to repay the cost of their early up-bringing; and the special taxes earmarked for the manumission fund were far from the most productive.

Some other reforms touched on taxes and ecclesiastical af-fairs. The *alcabala,* or colonial sales-tax, was replaced by a di-rect tax on personal income, which would prove notably hard to collect. The Indian tribute was abolished, as a degrading legacy of colonialism, and Indians instead became subject to all the regular taxes from which they had previously been exempt in return for paying tribute. Customs duties were simplified, in a generally downward direction. And a few blows were struck against the power and privileges of the church. The congress or-dered the suppression of all male convents that did not have at least eight members and earmarked the income and property of suppressed houses for the support of secondary education. The Inquisition, reestablished during the Spanish reconquest, was re-abolished; and although the deputies stopped short of declaring religious toleration, in a law concerning freedom of the press they eliminated all prior religious censorship save for editions of Holy Scripture. This entire series of innovations closely resem-bled the work of early reformers in other parts of Latin America during and just after the independence movement; it was cer-tainly not unique or extremist. But the reforms did go against some traditional prejudices and vested interests, so that Bolívar, who hardly disagreed with the ultimate objectives, considered some of the measures at least premature. He correctly foresaw that they would generate discontent and to that extent get in the way of the most essential task, which was the consolidation of national independence and internal order: it was one more sign of the lack of practical common sense that he attributed to civil-ian lawmakers in general. Yet there was nothing to be done about it for the moment, and he still had fighting to do.

VII

South to Quito
(1821–1823)

Bolívar did not stay long in Cúcuta after taking the oath of presidential office. He continued to Bogotá, where he busied himself with assorted official duties and briefly renewed his romance with Bernardina Ibáñez. He also arranged for the widow of Camilo Torres, who had been a loyal friend as head of the United Provinces of New Granada and then had become a patriot martyr, to receive a generous annual pension of 1,000 pesos (roughly equivalent to the salary of a provincial governor), payable from his own salary. In close collaboration with Vice President Santander, he immersed himself in logistical arrangements—organizing the production of munitions, cloth for uniforms, and much else. He drew up orders for troop movements, and he sketched strategic plans whose ultimate objective was Peru, the most solid bulwark of Spanish power in South America.

The liberation of Peru was important not only for reasons of American solidarity but because the royalist armies stationed there were a constant threat to the patriots of neighboring states, as those of Quito and **Upper Peru** (modern Bolivia) knew all too well, having been the targets of very effective counterrevolutionary forces sent out by the viceroy of Peru in Lima. For a long time, therefore, Bolívar had his sight fixed on Peru: as early as January 1817 he had urged on his soldiers with the proclamation, "You will fly with me to rich Peru!" For similar reasons, the Argentine Liberator, José de San Martín, after crossing the Andes to liberate Chile in alliance with the Chilean national hero Bernardo O'Higgins (son of an Irishman in Spanish service), had already led an expedition to Peru, landing on its shore in September 1820. San Martín's arrival set off spontaneous uprisings along the coast, and he gradually expanded his beachhead until he occupied Lima itself, where on 28 July 1821 he formally proclaimed Peruvian independence. The highlands remained in royalist hands, but the presence of San Martín naturally changed the equation of forces. It also posed a challenge for Bolívar, who could not waste time if he hoped to reap his own share of glory in what promised to be the culminating phase of Spanish American independence.

Before seeking fame in Peru, however, Bolívar needed to complete the liberation of the Presidency of Quito, where so far only Guayaquil had gained independence. In a region otherwise characterized by social and economic stagnation, Guayaquil stood out as the notable exception, chiefly on the basis of cacao exporting, in which during the late colonial period it had become a serious competitor of Venezuela. The Napoleonic wars of Europe and the Spanish American wars of independence brought frequent interruptions of Guayaquil's maritime commerce, but it was also spared the immense damage being done to Venezuelan plantations by physical destruction and by the drafting of workers, slave or free, into military service. With good reason the people of Guayaquil foresaw a promising future for their province, and some members of the incipient commercial bourgeoisie dreamed of prolonging indefinitely the status of autonomous city-state that Guayaquil had assumed following its successful October 1820 rebellion against Spanish rule. Others looked to future union with Peru, with which Guayaquil was linked by traditional economic ties as well as a network of personal and family connections, because in fact Lima was more easily reached from Guayaquil by ship than was the city of Quito overland (to say nothing of far-off Bogotá).

Although for many in Guayaquil, union with Colombia was the least desirable alternative, it had already been legislated at Angostura and again at Cúcuta, and Bolívar had no intention of permitting anything else. On hearing news of the Guayaquil uprising, he had accordingly dispatched General Antonio José de Sucre to bring military assistance to the local revolutionary junta and at the same time promote Colombian political interests. Born in Cumaná to a military family, Sucre had left university studies at an early age to fight for independence, and though his introverted personality won him limited personal popularity among fellow officers, Bolívar was fully convinced of his professional superiority. Certainly the choice turned out to be a good one. Sucre reached Guayaquil in time to help repel a punitive expedition sent from Quito in the Andean highlands and then to lead an expedition sent in reverse direction by Guayaquil that ended in disaster when a subordinate officer went into action prematurely. Although the setback was not Sucre's fault, it stands as the only defeat he suffered in his entire career as general in the independence struggle.

Bolívar meanwhile was getting ready to play his own part in the liberation of Quito. He left Bogotá in mid-December 1821 and established temporary headquarters at Cali, in the Cauca Valley. He proposed initially to go by ship to Guayaquil but soon abandoned the idea in order to go south by land. Impatience may have been a factor in his change of plan, for this way he would not have to wait for the necessary flotilla to be assembled. Furthermore, the land route to Quito was more direct, even if it did entail other difficulties. From Cali to Popayán there were no special problems, but then came the valley of the Patía River, dreaded for its torrid climate and festering diseases, not to mention a human environment that had proved equally unhealthy for the New Granadan patriots. Its people were mostly of African or part-African descent, and they harbored deep resentments against the creole planting and mine-owning aristocracy of Popayán: many were either fugitive slaves or descended from fugitives. Royalist leaders had taken advantage of these social tensions to organize local guerrilla bands, much as in Venezuela during the early stages of the conflict there.

After the Patía came the canyon of the Juanambú, beyond which lay the steep slopes of the geologic "knot" of Pasto, guarded by some of the most fanatical of all the king's defenders. The *pastusos,* as the inhabitants were called, mostly Indians or mestizos, had cut short the military career of Nariño in 1814 and, more recently, destroyed a patriot army that was trying to maximize republican-held territory before the armistice signed by Bolívar with Morillo could take effect. Between Pasto and Quito there were more geographic obstacles to overcome. The city of Quito itself had in 1809 been the scene of one of the very first rebellions of the independence period, even if still aiming only for local autonomy; promptly suppressed by an army from Lima, the *quiteños* rose up again in 1810 but were suppressed again in 1812.

Since then, Quito had returned to monarchical obedience. The top of Quito's social pyramid was occupied by an aristocracy notorious for its pretensions to nobility and lack of true solidarity with the popular majority, which was basically a depressed mass of Indians and mestizos, whether living in separate native communities, or on creole haciendas, or in the towns and cities where they provided labor for the numerous workhouses devoted to production of coarse woollens. To be sure, the Quito elite did not oppose all political change—provided it received its share of power and privilege. Some members of the professional middle sectors were more resolutely inclined toward independence, and the urban lower class had earned a certain fame for rebelliousness even before 1809. However, few signs of active disaffection could be detected at the moment, both because of the relative moderation of recent Spanish administrators and because of the arrival of an army of reinforcements late in 1821 under the command of Juan de la Cruz Murgeón, who reached South America with an appointment as viceroy of New Granada after the battle of Carabobo and quickly realized that the principal loyalist stronghold still remaining within his jurisdiction was Quito. Happily for him, he succeeded in crossing the Isthmus of Panama on his way there just before a local revolution of November 1821 separated Panama from Spain and led to its peacefully joining Colombia.

Another problem for Bolívar was the physical impossibility encountered by Santander—now left in charge of government at Bogotá—in trying to gather and send on to the Liberator all the troops and supplies he urgently requested. But Santander did his best, and meanwhile Bolívar had recourse to any trick of psychological warfare that he thought could conceivably weaken enemy resolve. He falsified documents and newspaper articles with the report that Spain had recognized Colombian independence and sent them to Pasto, specially marked for the attention of the Spanish commander, Colonel Basilio García. A shrewd and capable officer, García did not fall for the stratagem. Nor, in the short run, did Bolívar succeed in his attempt to woo the royalist bishop of Popayán, a Spanish-born cleric famous for his wine cellar who was currently a fugitive in Pasto. Bolívar put great emphasis in his letter to the bishop on the anticlerical measures adopted by the restored liberal regime in Spain, a factor which earlier helped convert the bishop of Mérida, in western Venezuela, from convinced royalist to deputy in the Colombian constituent congress. Later on, the bishop of Popayán would let himself be charmed by Bolivarian charisma, but for the moment he did not answer the letter.

Even without all the supplies requested or the hoped-for replies to his correspondence, Bolívar began his move southward in March 1822, bringing an army of some 3,000 men. Commander of the vanguard was Colonel José María Obando, a man related by extramarital ties to the cream of Popayán society but never accepted as equal and who, in some part for reasons of social resentment, had become a royalist guerrilla fighter; only recently had he switched sides, and it was hoped that his previous influence among the people of the Patía region would favor the Colombian advance. Moreover, the army did manage to cross the Juanambú and reach the vicinity of Pasto without meeting military resistance other than sporadic harassment by royalist irregulars. Harassment by the forces of nature was more serious, with the result that illness and desertion had already decreased Bolívar's army by roughly a third.

Bolívar still had a numerical advantage of two to one over García's forces, but the Spaniard had the advantage of the terrain and the firm backing of the *pastusos*. Bolívar therefore decided to avoid a frontal attack and took a detour around Pasto to a point southwest of the city, on the Guáitira River, from which he could either turn back suddenly and fall on Pasto from a different direction or go on to Quito, leaving Pasto to be conquered later. García disrupted this plan by destroying the one bridge over the Guáitira River and moving his own troops over a path known only by the local inhabitants to a position from which they dominated the republican camp. Bolívar then had no choice but to accept the challenge and attack, and he was furious when his second-in-command, General Pedro León Torres, by a misunderstanding, offered his men a chance to eat before the battle. For this apparent insubordination that delayed the start of the action, Bolívar stripped Torres of his command on the spot. The other man proceeded to break his officer's sword in two and declare his resolve to fight as simple grenadier—whereupon Bolívar, no less overcome with emotion, embraced Torres and gave him back his command. Unfortunately, Torres was one of many who would die that day.

The fighting in what is known as the Battle of Bomboná, 7 April 1822, was long and bloody. The republicans succeeded at heavy cost in climbing up to the heights where the enemy was positioned, but even when Bolívar threw in his reserves they were unable to take control of them. What saved the Colombian army from serious defeat was a flanking movement by one division whose men thrust bayonets into the mountainside and used them to pull themselves up, finally emerging behind the royalists and sowing enough uncertainty to cause their dispersal. The military result was nevertheless indecisive: at the end of the day, Bolívar had possession of the field but with losses six times greater than the enemy's. Over a quarter of his men were dead or wounded, and the army needed time to recover before it could continue toward Quito. So Bolívar withdrew temporarily to the other side of the Juanambú; sick himself, he had to be carried by stretcher.

Bomboná has probably earned Bolívar more criticism than any of his other major battles, both for the strategy and prior maneuvering that brought him to the battlefield and for his management of forces in the fighting itself, hurling so many men against a nearly impregnable position. However, it was only part of the larger campaign for the liberation of Quito, because at the same time Sucre was again advancing toward Quito with an army from Guayaquil, and Bolívar's approach at least had the effect of diverting some enemy forces that otherwise might have been used against Sucre. The latter had left Guayaquil early in the year and was reinforced en route by an army of 1,000 men—Peruvians, Chileans, Argentines—sent from Peru by order of San Martín. By mid-May Sucre was drawing near his destination, and by a rapid movement on the early morning of 24 May, he occupied a position on the slope of Mount Pichincha, the volcano that dominates the city of Quito. Marshal Melchor Aymerich, who had succeeded to leadership of the royalists at the death of Murgeón, decided precipitously to give battle, and with disastrous results. The following day he signed a capitulation with Sucre that entailed the formal surrender of all forces under his command and recognized that the former Presidency of Quito now formed part of the Republic of Colombia.

The terms of Aymerich's surrender made no explicit reference to Pasto, but there Colonel García quickly realized that his position was untenable. First making sure to intercept the news of Pichincha before it could reach Bolívar's camp, the Spanish commander expressed willingness to accept an honorable surrender, and Bolívar did not hesitate to offer it. Even when he learned of Sucre's victory, he did not want to believe that it was the reason why Pasto surrendered and wrote to Santander instructing him to make clear in the government newspaper that the fall of the royalist stronghold was due to his efforts rather than Sucre's. Yet this attack of petty jealousy was quite out of character in Bolívar, whose supreme self-confidence immunized him against fear of being overshadowed; before long he was heaping deserved praise on his lieutenant. Bolívar also refused to let the bishop of Popayán, who was still in Pasto when it surrendered, go through with an offer of resignation and instead flattered him astutely in such a way as to gain his adherence to the new political order. The bishop's conversion seems to have been sincere; that of the *pastusos,* who watched the arrival of their liberators more with resignation than enthusiasm, was not.

Now that the road to Quito was finally open, Bolívar entered the city on 16 June amid the acclamation of pretty much everyone from counts and marquises to artisans and day laborers. The municipal government had already voted to ratify union with Colombia, giving the appearance of spontaneous choice to what was in reality a fait accompli. Most *quiteños* do appear to have welcomed independence in the way that it came—as part of a greater Colombia—out of sheer relief that the fighting was over and because they were truly impressed with the aura of providential hero that surrounded Bolívar. But of course no opinion polls were taken, and it is not clear to what extent they truly thought of themselves as forming along with other Colombians an Andersonian "imagined community." There was reason in any case to question the strength of Quito's commitment. Between Quito and New Granada few ties of ethnic or sentimental affinity existed, and there was little economic complementarity. Ties with Venezuela were even weaker. Since the previous century, moreover, the regional economy had suffered a series of plagues and other natural calamities in addition to the competition of European textiles that more and more were displacing Quito manufacturers from neighboring markets. Economic malaise thus ran deeper than political loyalty. And the textile crisis, in particular, would make of Quito, throughout the period of its annexation to Colombia, a center of constant agitation for tariff protectionism, something that conflicted with the economic interest of Venezuela as an agroexporting region and with the ideological tendency of the New Granadan liberals grouped around Vice President Santander.

Guayaquil, of course, was something else again, and one bit of unfinished business was to make it effectively part of Colombia, which Bolívar certainly did not mean to leave to chance. Indeed the control of Guayaquil was more important than ever, now that Colombian dominion was established in Quito, for Guayaquil was its gateway to the outside world. Bolívar also felt the need to bury once and for all Peru's pretensions to the port city and its immediate hinterland. The auxiliary expedition earlier sent by San Martín, under the command of Andrés Santa Cruz, had as one of its objectives to promote Peruvian territorial claims; and though Sucre, having got to Guayaquil first, was able to keep Santa Cruz in a strictly supportive role, the threat was not altogether dispelled.

In actual fact the negotiating position of the Peruvian government, headed by San Martín with the title of "Protector," was not very strong. It was based on economic and other unofficial ties as well as on the history of political subordination to Lima prior to the creation in the eighteenth century of the Viceroyalty of New Granada and again during much of the independence period itself, when Viceroy José Fernando de Abascal assumed direct control over the city and province of Guayaquil. But Guayaquil returned to the jurisdiction of the Presidency of Quito (and through it, that of New Granada) before the October 1820 rebellion that gave Guayaquil autonomous status. Even more important, while Bolívar had just been crowned with another major victory, thanks in large part to the work of his lieutenant Sucre, San Martín in Peru was bogged down in ever more frustrating circumstances. Since his arrival in 1820 he had consolidated control of the coastal plain, and he had occupied Lima without resistance—but only because the current Peruvian viceroy, José de La Serna, saw fit to concentrate his forces in the Peruvian Andes, where most of the population lived. The Andes were home in particular to the great majority of Peruvian Indians, whose real preference would have been to avoid involvement in the struggle but who probably on the whole considered the distant king of Spain a lesser evil than the nearby creole patriots. The highlands further contained the silver mines that were the principal source of government revenue. In final analysis, the largely self-sufficient Peruvian Andes had little need of Lima, whereas Lima without the Andes was almost more a millstone than an asset. Yet San Martín failed to invade the highlands, both because he realized the military difficulty of the task and because he hoped he might attain a negotiated settlement on the basis of creating in Peru a constitutional monarchy under a European prince. He entered negotiations with the royalists to see if they might be amenable, but they were not authorized to accept independence in any form, nor San Martín to accept anything less.

San Martín's relative inactivity brought him criticism and created discouragement and unrest among the military. To complicate matters, there was also increasing discontent with his political initiatives. San Martín's monarchism pleased many members of the Lima elite, including those who held titles of nobility and fancied for themselves a fine future in some Peruvian royal court. This prospect was less to the liking of doctrinaire liberals. However, with the help of his chief minister, Bernardo de Monteagudo, a man thoroughly imbued with Enlightenment notions, San Martín introduced a controversial package of progressive measures that included abolition of the Indian tribute and forced labor and a free-birth law for gradual elimination of slavery. Simultaneously, Monteagudo unleashed a persecution of the influential community of European Spaniards, who had close personal and economic ties to the creole elite. The liberal reforms of San Martín in Peru were even more moderate than those of the Congress of Cúcuta in Colombia, but instead of conciliating extremes with his particular combination of policies, San Martín managed to alienate a broad swath of Peruvian opinion. He thus had ample reason to look northward for possible assistance and in early 1822 had taken the first steps toward a meeting with his Colombian counterpart, only to desist when he learned that Bolívar had not yet left New Granada. But in July 1822 conditions seemed right, and San Martín set sail for Guayaquil, sending the Peruvian navy on ahead. He hoped to get to Guayaquil before Bolívar and welcome him to a city already in the process of becoming Peruvian; what happened was exactly the opposite.

After taking care of the most pressing details in Quito, Bolívar, too, had set out for Guayaquil, sending some Colombian troops before him and making sure that those of Santa Cruz remained in the highlands a while longer. He entered Guayaquil under triumphal arches on 11 July. Bolívar promised the inhabitants an opportunity to express their preference freely as to the future of the province, but meanwhile his supporters agitated noisily for union with Colombia. The disturbances and uncertainty they created then served as pretext for Bolívar to assume direct control of the province, the better to avoid greater ills. When San Martín landed in Guayaquil on the 26th, no vote had yet been taken, but the result was not in question. Therefore the possession of Guayaquil no longer figured in the possible agenda for discussions between the two liberators, which began the day of San Martín's arrival and ended the next.

Seeing that Bolívar—who greeted him effusively as "first friend of my heart and of my country"—had beaten him to the prize was a first source of disillusionment for San Martín. Others followed, even though the substance of the conversations is not exactly known. The two men conferred behind closed doors, with no advisers or stenographers present, much less recording devices, which had not been invented, and the versions of what happened differ in important respects. One version is contained in an official report drawn up by José Gabriel Pérez, Bolívar's secretary, obviously based on what his leader told him. The other principal account is a letter purportedly written by San Martín to Bolívar a month after the meeting and known only by a copy printed in 1844 by the French traveler Gabriel Lafond de Lurcy. It was published in the lifetime of San Martín, who neither confirmed nor denied its contents, and its authenticity has been regularly denied by Venezuelan historians. Its authenticity has even been questioned by some scholars who nevertheless accept as accurate most of what it says; the resulting historiographical controversy, though no longer waged at white heat, has on more than one occasion damaged cultural relations between Argentina and Venezuela.

One topic that everyone agrees came up for discussion is the replacement by Colombia of losses suffered by the Santa Cruz expedition while serving on Colombian soil. Because royalist prisoners were routinely incorporated into patriot ranks and vice versa, there was nothing unusual about adding Colombian recruits to the army of a neighboring country and ally, so on this point Bolívar had no trouble in agreeing to San Martín's wishes. Neither is there doubt that the two men discussed military strategies and requirements of men and supplies for the unfinished business of Peruvian liberation. But there are serious differences concerning the help that San Martín asked Bolívar to provide. According to the Pérez report, the Argentine was not overly concerned about the strength of royalist forces still entrenched in the Peruvian highlands and therefore sought only modest military collaboration. In contrast, the so-called "Lafond letter," which is the principal basis of Argentine interpretations, suggests that San Martín sought major reinforcements for the final stage of the conflict and that Bolívar carefully avoided promising what was needed even when San Martín urged him to come in person to Peru and offered to serve under his command.

If San Martín really made the offer to serve under Bolívar, it is doubtful that it was intended in any literal sense: he would have known that such an arrangement was impractical, because of the wide differences in experience and approach between the two generals and because his own subordinates would be sure to object. But in view of his previous caution in confronting the royalists in Peru, it is also hard to believe that San Martín was uninterested in receiving substantial reinforcements. At any rate, according to the San Martinian version of events, what Bolívar offered was wholly inadequate, and the Bolivarians do not deny that the immediate help he offered was not great, among other reasons because the Pasto region was not wholly pacified and royalists were still offering resistance at Puerto Cabello and a few other points of Colombian territory. Neither, of course, did Bolívar accept San Martín's offer to serve under him, if indeed it was made. In the end, San Martín gained the impression that Bolívar did not want to make a serious contribution to the struggle in Peru unless he had the glory to himself. Most likely that assessment by San Martín was more correct than otherwise; but it is also true that in the last analysis there was simply no room for two such commanders in a single military theater.

A final disagreement had to do with the future political status of Spanish America. Both Bolívar and San Martín had amply demonstrated a continentwide outlook and support for close alliance among the newly independent nations. Both also admired the British system of constitutional monarchy, which San Martín hoped to see established in America, preferably by importing bona fide European princes rather than crowning a native son as in the recently established (and ephemeral) Mexican Empire of Iturbide. Monarchy to San Martín offered the best hope of internal stability and at the same time a possible basis for peaceful settlement with the parent country. But Bolívar, much as he recognized the intrinsic merits of the system, did not consider it a feasible solution for Spanish America. The diversity of races, classes, and cultural traditions, which monarchists believed could be held together only through the traditional reverence for a crowned head, was in his view an obstacle: the egalitarian aspirations of the *pardos* and mestizos and other colored castes who made up a majority of the population could only be satisfied under a republican system based on at least formal legal equality of all inhabitants. Republican equality in other words, rather than the mystical figure of the king, was the best guarantee of stability. Whether nonwhites more concerned with their own daily circumstances than with governmental structure would really have seen in monarchy the threat of personal discrimination is perhaps doubtful; after all, not a few had in fact embraced the cause of the king at different stages of the struggle. Yet Bolívar was certainly correct in doubting the feasibility of monarchy in Spanish America, even if he still dreamed of implanting some sort of constitutional monarchy in republican trappings—an idea he would fully develop in his 1826 draft constitution for Bolivia. Outright monarchy is what he rejected.

The two leaders were separated also by obvious differences of temperament. A cautious and methodical professional officer, with military experience not only in America but in Europe, San Martín was psychologically ill-prepared for an easy understanding with the charismatic and extroverted leader from Caracas, a man largely self-taught as a soldier but capable of sudden strokes of genius as well as impulsive moves that courted (and at times produced) disaster. So agree they did not. On the evening of 27 July, Bolívar offered a festive banquet at which he gave full rein to his passion for dancing but which for San Martín could hardly offset a deep feeling of disappointment. Some time after midnight the Argentine slipped away to his ship and set sail for Lima—where, in his absence, Chief Minister Monteagudo had been overthrown. San Martín briefly resumed command, but on 20 September he presented his irrevocable resignation to the Peruvian congress. In a message to the legislators, he underscored the danger posed in Spanish America by the rise to supreme power of the "successful soldier." He then quietly withdrew to the port of Callao and began the journey that through various stages and further renunciations led him finally to self-imposed exile in Europe.

Only after San Martín's departure was the promised vote finally held on the future of Guayaquil. It was a vote not of the general electorate but of the provincial electoral college, and though preceded by vigorous debate, it ratified what was already ordained: incorporation into the Republic of Colombia. This one step formally completed the creation of the "single state" that Bolívar had dreamed of, stretching from Angostura to Guayaquil and taking in all of the former Viceroyalty of New Granada. The vast edifice was not destined to be permanent. Yet for a few years, at least, Colombia did appear to enjoy a greater weight within the concert of nations than the mere sum of its parts. In 1822 it had already been the first Spanish American nation to receive diplomatic recognition from the United States; three years later it was likewise first to be recognized by Great Britain. It even obtained a loan in 1824 in the London financial market for the nominal sum of 30 million pesos, an enormous amount for the period even if representing in part the mere refinancing of earlier obligations—and even if, as time would prove, quite impossible to pay back.

Technically, it has to be noted that certain loose ends still remained even after the incorporation of Guayaquil: Puerto Cabello would not finally surrender until the following year, and Pasto was a constant source of worry, with a series of local uprisings due not just to the *pastusos'* fanatical love for Fernando VII but to the brutal treatment inflicted on them by republican commanders. Venezuelan officers, who had the least in common with the *pastusos,* were the worst offenders in this respect. Worrisome news reached Bolívar even from Caracas, where the municipal government questioned the legitimacy of the Colombian constitutional order and called for a constitutional reform convention without waiting for the end of the trial period decreed by the Congress of Cúcuta. The protest was made on the not unreasonable ground that the people of Caracas, and indeed a good many other places, had not been duly represented in the constituent congress. But neither was it hard to detect in the Caracas complaint an undercurrent of dissatisfaction with the unitary structure of the Colombian constitution that in principle subordinated all parts of the nation strictly to Bogotá; and this in turn suggested a rebirth or persistence of the federalist sentiment Bolívar always decried. The Liberator therefore reacted by sending to Congress a message in which he emphasized the inviolability of the constitutional waiting period. He showed himself something less of a stickler for legality in a letter he wrote at the same time to Santander in which he asserted that only with "absolute power" was it possible to rule Colombia, adding for good measure that he could not do his own job properly unless endowed with "unlimited faculties." Those faculties he currently possessed were not literally "unlimited," of course, but they still were extensive. The constitution stipulated that the executive might have emergency powers—"extraordinary faculties" was the operative term—in times of crisis, and these had been formally granted to him by the Congress of Cúcuta for use in any theater of war or recently liberated territory.

Bolívar remained in Colombia's southern departments (present-day Ecuador) until August 1823 and while there made use of his special powers to suspend any of the institutional reforms adopted in Bogotá (or earlier by the constituent congress) that he considered inappropriate. These included the new customs system and, likewise of particular importance in the south, the abolition of Indian tribute. Because of the relatively greater concentration of Indians in the region, tribute provided a larger proportion of fiscal resources than in New Granada or Venezuela, and as military expenses also weighed heavily on that part of the country, it seemed unwise to get rid of it. In place of tribute the Indians were supposed to pay all the other taxes from which previously they were exempt, but the tribute had the advantage of collecting everything they owed in one lump sum, and it further had tradition in its favor, so that there were cases in which the Indians themselves asked that it be retained. Quite apart from its importance as revenue, moreover, the tribute was important as an incentive to the Indians to accept work offered to them by whites and mestizos, so as to earn cash for the annual tribute payment. Hence landowners and other employers, emphasizing the supposed natural indolence of the natives, predicted a grave shortage of workers in case the tribute was abolished, and this argument undoubtedly carried weight, as well.

It goes without saying that Bolívar did not spend all his time issuing military orders or attending to matters of civil government. While in Quito and Guayaquil and places in between, he was also socializing with members of the local aristocracy and establishing a relationship of mutual confidence that was to last: regional notables warmly approved such measures as nonabolition of the tribute and the delay in implementing the new tariff regime. Other Venezuelan and New Granadan officers were similarly forging personal ties with the southern elite. Here an obvious example is Sucre, who fell in love with a wealthy Quito marchioness and later married her by correspondence from Chuquisaca, the city that today bears Sucre's name in Upper Peru (modern Bolivia), to which service in the war of independence eventually took him; it was Sucre's intention to settle permanently in Quito when the war was over. Another example is Juan José Flores, a Venezuelan of middling social origins who arrived in Quito as officer in the triumphant army, married another aristocratic lady, and in 1830, when greater Colombia finally broke up, became first president of an independent Ecuador.

Bolívar on his part remained true to the oath he had taken at the death of his wife in 1803, never to marry again. Nevertheless, on the very day of his arrival in Quito, there occurred an event that is another landmark in his romantic career: his meeting with the young *quiteña* Manuela Sáenz. Manuela was already married to the English businessman James Thorne, who had come to Latin America for reasons not entirely clear and who, though apparently a worthy man, was almost twice her age—and boring to boot, utterly unlike Simón Bolívar. Manuela herself was as much an extrovert as the Liberator, and she did not hesitate to defy the norms of her social environment and historical era; it was she who abandoned her husband, not vice versa. She had lived with Mr. Thorne for a time in Lima (where she witnessed the arrival of San Martín and forged a friendship with the latter's mistress), but she was now back in Quito and before long had become the greatest love of Bolívar's entire life, with the possible exception of his deceased wife. Their relationship was passionate but was more than just physical, so that in due course she would become a confidante and even, it seems, political adviser, however much in general he shared the prejudice of other men of his period against women taking an interest in politics. As he once wrote to his capable sister María Antonia, who managed his business interests while he was away from Caracas, "It is very improper for ladies to involve themselves in political affairs." Yet he made an apparent exception in the case of Manuela, even if not at the outset in Quito but later in Lima and Bogotá, to which she would follow in his footsteps.

For Bolívar himself to get to Lima, there were still some pre-liminary details to be taken care of. San Martín took care of one of these with his resignation, thus clearing the way for his northern rival to occupy his position. Another requirement was a formal invitation from Peru, lest it appear that Bolívar was intervening for motives of personal ambition or Colombian ag-gression. There was no lack of Peruvians urging him to come, but he needed some kind of official invitation, which was not easy to obtain because of the confusion reigning in Lima since San Martín's departure. The executive power had been en-trusted to a triumvirate, which could not get along with the congress; the Argentine-Chilean forces left behind by San Martín were increasingly demoralized in the absence of their leader; and one of the Argentine generals suffered a major de-feat on the southern Peruvian coast early in 1823. At that point a military movement in Lima compelled the appointment of a one-man executive, who turned out to be José de la Riva-Agüero, an intriguing aristocrat who with no evident military credentials assumed the rank of marshal. Riva-Agüero at least realized the need to summon Bolívar and whatever forces he could bring, both to combat the royalists and, ideally, to serve as a counterweight to the influence of Riva-Agüero's rival An-drés Santa Cruz. The necessary invitation soon materialized.

Then there was the need to come adequately accompanied by Colombian troops and equipment. A significant number of troops had already been sent to Peru in advance of Bolívar's anticipated departure from Guayaquil. And the preparation of further military assistance to Peru naturally figured among the key responsibilities of the Santander administration in Bogotá, although the greatest contribution was actually that made by the southern provinces, because of their proximity to the war theater: it has been calculated that three-fourths of the total cost of Colombian participation in the independence of Peru was borne by inhabitants of what today is Ecuador. However, under the Colombian constitutional system the Peruvian enterprise also called for the prior authorization of the national congress before the Liberator as president could personally lead an army to fight a war beyond the nation's boundaries, even though it was the same war that up to now he had been fighting within those boundaries. There could be no real objection to the granting of such authorization, despite the complaints over cost of the war that were now being heard on every side. But the meeting of the first regular congress, which should have taken place in January 1823, was delayed until April by a lack of quorum due principally to the difficulties of travel. From the far south, or present Ecuador, whose legislators had to face not only abysmally bad roads but the hostility of the *pastusos,* only two out of seventeen elected representatives managed to arrive for the opening session. However, once Congress opened, Santander saw to it that the authorization was approved routinely.

Bolívar was meanwhile following Peruvian developments with close attention and felt increasingly frustrated as he observed the squabbling of rival factions and stagnation of military operations against Spain. In mid-April 1823 he therefore sent Sucre on ahead to take command of the Colombian troops already in Peru or on the way, as well as to prepare the ground for his own eventual arrival. Sucre was in Lima when, in June, a royalist army came down from the mountains and again threatened Lima. This enemy incursion convinced the Peruvian congress to name Sucre general-in-chief, but the congressmen did not care to offer battle for their capital—which fell to the enemy. The royalists did not stay long, but the episode increased Bolívar's impatience to go, so that he decided he would depart for Lima even without receiving formal permission from congress. Happily, before he could do so, the legislators' decision reached him. On 7 August he sailed from Guayaquil, and on the first day of September he was in Callao, the port of Lima.

VIII

Apogee: Peru and Bolivia (1823–1826)

The Peru to which Bolívar's continental mission finally took him in 1823 consisted basically of two separate nations, though closely interconnected and both feeling they had seen better days. One was what in Spanish colonial terminology was known as the "republic of Indians," a population whose principal language was Quechua and that had once been the nucleus of the Inca empire that extended from northern Chile to the south of Colombia. At present it was a depressed caste, but it formed a majority of the total population and was not unconditionally submissive. Opposite it stood the "republic of Spaniards," consisting not only of European and American-born whites but in practice also mestizos and acculturated Afro-Peruvians, the latter an important ethnic category along the Pacific Coast.

The peak of society was occupied by the Lima nobility, a group of families even more pretentious than the nobility of Quito; an upper bureaucracy; and a merchant class that deplored the recent loss of its monopolistic privileges. The political importance of Lima and, directly or indirectly, of the groups just mentioned had suffered a blow when in the eighteenth century the two new Viceroyalties of New Granada and Río de la Plata were carved out of the original Viceroyalty of Peru. The economic role of Lima had declined, too, thanks to Spain's introduction of the so-called policy of "free trade," which did not mean that trade was free of duties but allowed direct trading between Spanish ports and colonial cities formerly supplied either by way of Lima or by contraband. Even the mineral wealth of Peru, though still impressive, had been eclipsed during the past century by the silver bonanza of Mexico, which became by far the most important of Spain's overseas possessions.

For various reasons, then, and just as the natives might nostalgically recall the Inca past, the upper and middle strata of the "republic of Spaniards" could well repeat the famous line of the Spanish poet Jorge Manrique: *"Todo tiempo pasado fue mejor"*—"Every past time was better." This did not mean that everything in future time, such as independence, would necessarily be worse. Nevertheless, a certain caution in the face of change was understandable. Moreover, the caution of the creole population was increased by its fear of the Indian majority, particularly since the great Indian rebellion of Túpac Amaru in 1780–1781: some persons who otherwise might have embraced independence held back out of fear that the struggle would degenerate into a massive racial uprising. Just as Cuban planters did not want to lose the protection of parent Spain in case of a Haitian-style slave revolt, many Peruvian whites relied on the arms of the king and the traditional mystique surrounding the institution of monarchy to maintain order among the "republic of Indians."

Assorted disturbances and conspiracies nevertheless appeared, and there was one fairly serious armed uprising in 1814, led by the Indian cacique Mateo Pumacahua. But all these threats were defeated, and they occurred mainly in the highlands—the city of Lima remaining generally faithful to the king until the arrival of San Martín. When Bolívar in turn reached Peru, the royalists had consolidated their control over most of Andean Peru, led by a group of professional Spanish officers but with the rank and file overwhelmingly made up of Peruvians. Along the coast, the forces of independence held sway and could cut off most contact between the highlands and the outside world. It had been assumed that this blockade would necessarily undermine the enemy's position, but that did not happen: the highlands needed little if anything from the outside, whereas Lima was used to consuming wheat from Chile as well as a share of the wealth produced by highland silver mines. Hence Bolívar came to Peru firmly convinced of the necessity to climb up into the sierra and root out Spanish control there. At the very moment of his arrival, moreover, Andrés Santa Cruz was leading an invasion of the southern Peruvian Andes. Unhappily, the Santa Cruz expedition, though it penetrated as far as La Paz in modern Bolivia (which happened to be the commander's birthplace), ended in disaster and in the virtual dissolution of what pro-independence military forces Peru itself had so far been able to muster.

Lima, in any case, made a favorable impression on Bolívar when he arrived. It had twice the population and far more amenities than Bogotá, which was by comparison an isolated provincial village. There was an active social life, both elegant and decadent, with fiestas and balls for the Colombians and other foreign liberators; Lima likewise had regular theatrical performances, of less than stellar artistic quality in Bolívar's opinion but at least with beautiful women in attendance. He thought highly, too, of Peruvian cuisine, a detail that he could appreciate, for even if he readily adapted himself to the rudimentary fare available on campaign, his past experience in Paris and Madrid made him something of a connoisseur of good food and wine. (Unlike many fellow officers, though, he drank with moderation and seldom touched hard liquor.) Finally, the arrival of Manuela Sáenz not long after his own arrival further contributed to Bolívar's enjoyment of the Peruvian capital.

Less enjoyable was the continual squabbling among factions. Just before Bolívar came on the scene, a bitter conflict broke out between President Riva-Agüero and congress, which proceeded to depose him and name in his place the marquis of Torre Tagle, another intriguing aristocrat. But Riva-Agüero refused to accept deposition and set up shop instead in the north coastal city of Trujillo, with his own schismatic congress. Bolívar had no choice but to align himself with Torre Tagle, who controlled the capital city and had acclaimed the Liberator effusively at his arrival; in addition, the congress in Lima voted Bolívar supreme military authority, in effect reducing Torre Tagle to a purely civilian role that was not exactly to his liking. Before long, the quarrel between the opposing Peruvian presidents and congresses led Riva-Agüero to enter negotiations with Viceroy José de La Serna. This in itself was not treasonous, if the aim was to seek a peaceful settlement that included some form of independence (as San Martín had done) or to propose an armistice (such as Bolívar negotiated with Morillo). But the fact that he made his overtures at the very moment when he felt hemmed in by the combined forces of Torre Tagle and Colombia leads one to suspect that he was seeking the help of the royalists at almost any price against his local political rivals. Certainly Bolívar did not doubt that this was treason. He assembled an army and went north, intending to use force against Riva-Agüero if he did not submit peaceably. In the end force was not needed, as some of Riva-Agüero's own officers, also convinced that he was dealing treacherously, overthrew him. Bolívar did not mind letting him simply go into exile, while he himself stayed on in Trujillo, because it seemed a better place than Lima in which to prepare for the final battle.

One advantage of a base in northern Peru was its distance from the intrigues and distractions of Lima; another was greater proximity to Colombia, from which Bolívar eagerly awaited reinforcements. His correspondence with Santander in Bogotá was full of the usual pleadings for men and supplies—and complaints at not receiving what he wanted when he wanted it. Ultimately Bolívar was asking for 12,000 men in the hope (he frankly explained elsewhere) of getting at least 6,000. Santander at one point was led to exclaim, "The Liberator thinks I am God and can say 'Let it be done,' and it will be done. Thus he asks me without pity for arms and men, and the worst of it is that Don Simón receives all the acclamations and the Peruvians fail to recognize the efforts of the Colombian government." Neither did Bolívar always recognize "the efforts of the Colombian government," and he did not conceal his annoyance over Santander's insistence on obtaining congressional authorization for everything done on Peru's behalf.

Bolívar was relying all the more on help from Colombia in light of disappointments and unexpected problems that he experienced elsewhere. The Peruvian authorities seemed unable to rebuild their military forces after the Santa Cruz debacle; promised reinforcements from Chile arrived but went right home because of a dispute over their assignment; the Peruvian navy, commanded by an English officer, paid no attention to directives from Bolívar; and to cap it all off, the garrison of the coastal fortress at Callao mutinied early in February 1824. The mutineers were justifiably unhappy over arrears of pay and other such problems, but when they received no satisfaction, they freed the royalist prisoners in the fortress and raised the Spanish flag. The Peruvian congress, caught in Lima between the Callao mutineers and another royalist army coming down from the Andes, in desperation named Bolívar dictator of Peru. But it was too late to save Lima from still another enemy occupation.

At the time of the Callao uprising, Bolívar was actually close by, in the small port of Pativilca, about 50 kilometers north of Lima. He had arrived late the previous year, when his concerns over dissension and rumored treason in Lima caused him to come south from his Trujillo headquarters. But before he could reach the capital, he fell gravely ill and had to interrupt his trip at Pativilca. For a week he was afflicted with high fever, at times delirious; his very life seemed in danger. The nature of the illness is unclear, and probably it was due to a combination of causes. Bolívar may even have suffered an attack of food poisoning, but whatever else contributed to his condition, it was aggravated by overwork and by his pattern of constant movement from one point to another. While immobilized at Pativilca, he gave clear signs of psychic depression, evidenced not so much in still another formal resignation dispatched to Bogotá as in a personal letter to Santander in which he included the dramatic lament: "Since death does not wish to take me under her protecting wings, I must go hide my head amid the shadows of forgetfulness and silence, before one of the strokes of lightning that heaven is hurling upon the earth touches me and converts me into dust, into ashes, into nothing." After reviewing a list of fallen kingdoms and heroes, he concluded by saying, "finally everything is brought down, by either infamy or misfortune: and I am still standing? It cannot be, I must fall."

Bolívar remained in Pativilca for two months, refusing medical treatment yet gradually regaining strength. Even during the recuperation, he had bouts of frantic activity during which he dictated letters not of resignation but of orders and instructions.

There were more messages to Bogotá pleading for reinforcements and one to Torre Tagle warning him against the talks with the Spanish that he appeared determined to undertake. On this last point Bolívar's fear was well-founded, as the unreliable marquis proceeded to join the royalists after the Callao mutiny. But the Liberator's stay in Pativilca was also marked by a memorable encounter with the Colombian agent Joaquín Mosquera, who stopped on his way back from the diplomatic mission to southern South America on which Bolívar had sent him. Mosquera found Bolívar still ailing and emaciated, but when asked what he proposed to do next, Bolívar gave the one-word answer, "Triumph!" He supposedly added that in three months he would have the army he needed to climb the Andes and attack the royalists in their own stronghold.

It took Bolívar more like four months, but he did get ready for the campaign. Once back in Trujillo, he plunged into preparations, ably seconded by Sucre as head of his general staff and, as secretary general, by José Sánchez Carrión, one of the few Peruvians who enjoyed Bolívar's total confidence. No detail was too small for Bolívar's personal attention. Another standard anecdote concerns the time when on getting up from a chair he tore his pants on a protruding tin nail. It immediately occurred to him that here was the solution to the shortage of tin for soldering purposes, and the next day nails were disappearing from furniture all over Trujillo. The silver vessels of the churches were disappearing too, as forced contributions were mercilessly imposed on ecclesiastical as well as lay persons and institutions. Taxes were raised and salaries cut, so that the army could be paid punctually even if at a reduced rate, and the indispensable supplies were accumulated.

The army in preparation consisted of holdovers from that of San Martín, new Peruvian recruits, and Colombian expeditionary forces. The Colombians either had left Guayaquil ahead of Bolívar or were arriving from the southern provinces, where Bolívar, at his own departure, had delegated his "extraordinary faculties" to General Bartolomé Salom, to be used primarily in support of the Peruvian campaign; troops sent by Santander under the special authorization he obtained from congress actually arrived too late to participate in the decisive battles. The Liberator still had under his command forces numerically inferior to the royalists, but fortunately he did not have to repel any enemy attacks during the weeks when he was engaged in gathering and equipping them. The viceroy had underestimated Bolívar's capacity to quickly assemble an army and in addition was distracted by an outbreak of insubordination behind his own lines in Upper Peru. There the royalist commander on the spot, Pedro Olañeta, had taken advantage of the restoration of absolutism that occurred in Spain in 1823 (with the help of French intervention) to deny the viceroy's authority, accusing him among other things of liberal sympathies. The resulting division among the royalists was naturally cause for rejoicing in Trujillo: the extra time that it gave Bolívar was put to good use.

The army of independence finally commenced its march, by stages, in late May and early June 1824. It had to traverse high Andean valleys and primitive trails where for long stretches men and beasts could advance only Indian file, but at least for the first part of the march, through the northern Andes, Peruvian patriot guerrillas had already prepared the way. Indeed royalist control was essentially nominal to the north of Cerro de Pasco, the great geologic mass that separates the northern from the southern highlands and up to a point also concealed Bolívar's movements from the eyes of his adversary. At the beginning of August, with the army already camped before Cerro de Pasco, Bolívar reviewed the largest and best-prepared military force he had ever commanded, comprising some 4,000 Colombians, 3,000 Peruvians, and additional troops of various other nationalities. On just the other side of Cerro de Pasco, the Spanish general José de Canterac was calmly waiting with an army that was well equipped and fully experienced though slightly inferior in numbers, because not all royalist forces had been gathered in that one spot. When at length Canterac began to move, he miscalculated the probable route of the patriots, who after skirting the Cerro were soon to the south of Canterac and threatening to cut him off from the concentration of royalists in the Cuzco area under Viceroy La Serna. Canterac, however, quickly turned back to face Bolívar on 6 August at the plain of Junín. When the first patriot horsemen began to reach the field, Canterac ordered a cavalry charge with the intention of crushing them before they were assembled and ready for combat. The royalists initially enjoyed superior numbers on the battleground itself and were able to push back their opponents. Yet the tide turned again, and the fighting broke up into a confused scene of separate encounters between cavalry units, until finally a charge by one of the patriot units turned the battle into a general rout.

The Battle of Junín lasted a little over two hours and was waged without a shot fired. It was strictly a cavalry engagement, fought with lances and swords. Neither side suffered heavy losses, and the bulk of the defeated royalist army remained intact. It is even hard to understand why the royalists withdrew as soon as they did, and without ever using their infantry or artillery—perhaps in part that last was because Canterac himself was a cavalry officer. Neither is it easy to understand why Bolívar allowed the enemy to withdraw peacefully instead of setting off in immediate pursuit. Most likely, he could not quite believe that the Spanish general would so easily accept defeat and did not want to risk the fruit of his victory in a chase through territory that until the day before had been solidly royalist and against an enemy still known to be powerful. In fact, however, the royalists' morale had received a blow that was probably irreparable, and in retreat they abandoned arms and luggage as well as the stragglers among their troops. Desertions multiplied. And as the patriots advanced through the territory evacuated by the foe, they consolidated their own control over an ever greater part of Peru.

During that same triumphal progress Bolívar had to face the distant echo of an event in Bogotá that caused great unpleasantness and sorely strained his relations with Vice President Santander. What triggered this minicrisis was the adoption in July 1824 by the Colombian congress and the signing by Santander of a law designed to regulate the emergency powers or "extraordinary faculties" provided for in the nation's constitution and currently exercised by Bolívar. The powers in question represented a legal device routinely included in early Latin American constitutions, but the lack of detailed stipulations as to how they should be used (and the obvious possibilities of abuse) worried many legislators, in particular the more doctrinaire liberals who in the Colombian context were generally followers of Santander. The vice president himself therefore urged congress to clarify the scope of "extraordinary faculties" and, among other things, to determine whether those exercised by General Salom in the far south by delegation from Bolívar were still valid, now that Bolívar was in Peru. When congress finished dealing with the issue, one of the things it made clear was that the grant originally made to Bolívar was only valid within Colombia–legally, therefore, he no longer had any right to the powers in question. Santander in his own capacity as acting chief executive in Bogotá lost no time in renewing the faculties delegated to Salom, but Bolívar was highly offended both at congress and at the vice president for having accepted its interpretation. Santander, he wrote to another correspondent, had been "generous at my expense," and for a time he suspended personal correspondence with the vice president.

The Liberator was hardly left powerless, for in Peru he still had his rank as Colombian general, not to mention his appointment as Peruvian dictator. He nevertheless gave further vent to his displeasure by ostentatiously resigning supreme military command in favor of Sucre, who along with other Colombian officers signed a protest against the "atrocious" conduct of Santander in having accepted the notorious piece of legislation. Their indignation was heightened by the fear—unfounded but real—that in some way the law undermined the legality of their recent military promotions. In order to reassure his comrades, Sucre handed out a new round of promotions. And of course the outburst of agitation among Colombian officers in no way affected the military situation in Peru, where the patriots' advance through the Andean highlands was making untenable the position of the royalists still in control of Lima. Once the Peruvian capital was evacuated by the king's forces for the very last time, Bolívar entered it himself on 5 December.

Even before transferring command of military operations to Sucre, Bolívar had put him in charge of the main body of republican forces in the Peruvian Andes. He knew that Sucre was the best of his generals—in strictly military terms, really a better general than Bolívar—and he was therefore content to stay behind in Lima, practicing his own superior political skills, while Sucre conducted the last major campaign of the independence struggle. The culmination came sooner than the patriots anticipated, because Viceroy La Serna decided to force the issue. Gathering an army of approximately 9,000 men, he set off in pursuit of Sucre, and over several weeks the armies maneuvered back and forth through the southern Andes until they finally met on 9 December on the plain of Ayacucho, some 3,400 meters above sea level. The royalists occupied the best field positions, and Sucre had with him slightly under 6,000 armed men, but the momentum of the war was now clearly in the patriots' favor. Sucre thus had full confidence in the outcome, and thanks to his own tactical skill as well as the reckless courage of the Colombian officer José María Córdova, who led the final charge, the royalists were soundly beaten. Taken prisoner on the field of battle, La Serna signed a capitulation that recognized the loss of Spanish dominion throughout Peru. Olañeta in Upper Peru did not recognize the surrender, nor did the band of royalists who still held out in the fortress of Callao, so that the struggle dragged on a bit longer. Even so, after Ayacucho the military history of independence becomes of purely secondary importance.

While the Ayacucho campaign was coming to its climax, Bolívar in Lima was working on his plan for a future system of Hispanic American nations. For a good many years he had been aiming to call a congress of the newly independent peoples, to strengthen fraternal ties already existing, adopt programs of mutual cooperation, and create a permanent alliance. With the war now coming to a close, he felt the time had arrived to make the dream a reality and on 7 December sent out invitations to the governments of Mexico, the Central American federation, Colombia, Chile, and Río de la Plata (i.e., Argentina), for a congress to meet at Panama City early in 1826. This project is routinely cited by speakers for the Organization of American States and U.S. State Department as a precedent for the current inter-American system, and technically it is; but the present system differs in important respects from that conceived by Bolívar. In particular, his was less inclusive, as it did not even take in all the American nations existing as of the 1820s: conspicuously absent from the invitees were not only the United States but Haiti and Brazil.

Bolívar's omission of the United States has naturally attracted the most attention, and in the view of some Latin American commentators it reflects his farsighted fear of Yankee imperialism—

allegedly he was planning a Latin American defensive alliance precisely against the Colossus of the North. Nor is there reason to doubt his distrust of that northern neighbor. In his view, the very virtues of the North American people made their country a dangerous neighbor, because they promised a rapid national development that would most likely foster expansionist tendencies. Yet if he had in mind an anti–North American defensive alliance when he convoked the congress, he did not frankly express the idea in his correspondence. He instead stressed the difference in customs and traditions that would make understanding more difficult: the North Americans, he said, are "foreigners to us, if only because they are heterogeneous in character." A second reason in Bolívar's opinion for leaving out the United States was its political and commercial rivalry at that time with the British in the Western Hemisphere. He wished at all costs to have British goodwill and did not want to risk it by too close a relationship with the United States. Bolívar had always trusted primarily in British influence to block any scheme by other European powers to help Spain regain its American colonies, and for that reason never assigned much importance to the warning against such intervention in the Monroe Doctrine of 1823; he also believed that Great Britain was not only about to give diplomatic recognition to the Latin American nations (as the United States had already done) but would use its influence to get other European governments to do the same. Indeed, Bolívar hoped that the British—whose Latin American interests he saw as basically geared to commerce and investment—would extend some kind of protectorate over Latin America, and it was obvious that any U.S. delegation to his proposed congress would fight tooth and nail against anything of the sort. Although Bolívar did not want to invite the government in Washington, he hoped that London would send at least an observer.

The omission of Haiti from the list of invitees has drawn less attention but is striking nonetheless, in view of the aid given by President Pétion to Bolívar in time of need. It did not reflect any change in his thinking about slavery or race relations, for he hoped that the participating nations would formally commit themselves to a policy of racial equality. In a list of things Bolívar hoped his Spanish American alliance would accomplish, he included the notation, "Differences of origin and color would lose their influence and power." Yet the difference in customs and traditions was even starker in the Haitian case than in that of the United States, so that in the same sentence where he referred to the "heterogeneity" of the North Americans he also included the Haitians. It further went without saying that any invitation to a republic born out of slave rebellion would be viewed with alarm in many places: not so much in England but certainly in France, which had not yet recognized its former colony, to say nothing of the southern United States or, in Caracas and Popayán, the slaveowners of Colombia itself, a social group relatively few in numbers but influential. In part because of the concerns of those slaveowners, the Colombian government had so far failed to establish diplomatic relations with Haiti.

The omission of Brazil has likewise attracted little attention. Bolívar did not lump the Brazilians under the heading of "heterogeneous" or culturally "foreign," but in the immediate international context there was a problem in that Brazil had become independent from Portugal as a constitutional monarchy headed by a son of the Portuguese king. This conflicted with Bolívar's view that monarchy was not suitable for Latin America, and in addition the new Brazilian empire had worrisome dynastic and diplomatic ties with the European powers of the so-called Holy Alliance that at least rhetorically were still giving support to Spain's colonial pretensions. One other complicating factor was the conflict between Brazil and Argentina over the eastern shore of the Río de la Plata. The conflict had not yet degenerated into the open warfare that was ultimately settled by establishing Uruguay as an independent buffer state, but it was brewing, and as a Spanish American and advocate of republicanism, Bolívar had to support the Argentine claim—despite his distrust of the government currently in power at Buenos Aires.

In the end the United States and Brazil—but not Haiti—were invited to Panama by the decision of Vice President Santander and his foreign minister in Bogotá. When he heard that the United States had accepted the invitation, Bolívar declared himself "pleased," but *reconciled* might have better expressed his true feeling. It made little difference in practice, because one of the U.S. delegates died on the way and the other arrived after the meeting was over. Neither did the Brazilians or Argentines attend. And though the Congress of Panama did finally take place in June–July 1826, with the hoped-for British observer present, it did not accomplish much, adopting agreements that were ratified only by Colombia. Its importance thus lies basically in what the original proposal reveals about Bolívar's thinking on international relations—and in the agenda of *Latin* American integration that it left for future generations to wrestle with.

A major reason for the difficulty in carrying out Bolívar's dream was, of course, the internal fragility of the new nations that were to make up the proposed alliance, and in this respect Peru was clearly no exception. While he remained in Lima, therefore, Bolívar worked closely with Sánchez Carrión and other Peruvian associates, trying to create a national government that could both maintain order and promote development. He showed special interest in education, decreeing the foundation of new schools and welcoming to Peru his former tutor, Simón Rodríguez, who after years spent wandering about the world one day turned up again in South America: Bolívar no sooner heard the news than he instructed Santander to provide Rodríguez with the means of continuing to Peru. Bolívar likewise helped bring the English pedagogue Joseph Lancaster, promoter of the system of "mutual education," not to Lima but to his own hometown, Caracas, assigning for that purpose part of a million-peso bonus voted to him by the Peruvian congress. Bolívar had accepted the grant in question with unfeigned reluctance, in keeping with his disdain for strictly monetary advantage, and on condition that the sum be spent for projects beneficial to Caracas and other parts of Colombia. As things turned out, the million pesos never fully materialized, and it would even seem that the money earmarked for Lancaster's expenses eventually had to be paid from Bolívar's personal resources. But if there was less to congress's material largesse than met the eye, the motions of thanks and praise from an array of persons and institutions in Peru were impressive. Typical of these was the Bolivarian *Te Deum* that came to be sung in Peruvian churches:

> From you, Lord,
> Comes all that is good:
> You gave us Bolívar.
> Glory to you, great God!

Where Simón Rodríguez finally ended up was not in Peru proper but Upper Peru, or modern Bolivia, whose liberation was the next task undertaken by Sucre after Ayacucho. The royalists in the ancient capital of the Incas, Cuzco, and in the rest of southern Peru followed the example of Viceroy La Serna and surrendered peacefully, and when Sucre crossed into Upper Peru in early 1825, royalist troops and officers there began deserting in great numbers. The die-hard Olañeta did not desert, but abandoned by almost all followers, he fought one last battle in April 1825. He lost the battle and in it was mortally wounded as well. In this way, another of the major subdivisions of the Spanish American empire finally achieved independence, seemingly at the hands of the Venezuelan general Sucre and as an aftereffect of his previous defeat of the Peruvian viceroy. Such an interpretation would not, however, quite do justice to La Paz and other regional centers that had raised the standard of rebellion as far back as 1809, even before Caracas. Upper Peru had then for several years become a theater of battle between counterrevolutionary forces dispatched from Lima and patriot armies coming up from Buenos Aires, with the former eventually gaining the upper hand, despite the persistence of patriot guerrillas. Sucre thus did not so much bring liberation to a new part of Spanish America as restore freedom to a people who had earlier won it at least partway and then lost it.

A complicating factor was that Upper Peru had previously formed part of the Viceroyalty of Río de la Plata, whose capital was Buenos Aires. As Bolívar and the government of Colombia had insisted on the validity of the former colonial divisions in opposing Peru's pretension to Guayaquil, it was impossible to ignore Argentine rights in Upper Peru. But neither was it conceivable that the region could join an independent Argentina, not only because the final victory over Spain had come from the opposite direction but because the would-be liberating armies from Buenos Aires during the struggle itself had made themselves thoroughly unpopular, alarming the creole elite by loudly proclaiming the equality of the native Indians yet antagonizing the common people by their lack of respect for traditional religion. Possible union with Peru had more supporters than union with Argentina, due to cultural and historic ties going back before the creation of the Platine viceroyalty. But a clear majority of those who had an opinion on the matter favored becoming a separate nation, an outcome that Bolívar recognized both as desirable and as inevitable. Yet he did not have absolute independence in mind, because he had conceived the idea of combining both Upper and Lower Peru with Colombia in a grand Federation of the Andes, of which each member state would have its own government for domestic affairs while joining with the others for the management of common interests in an association somewhat closer than the general Hispanic American league that he hoped would emerge from the Congress of Panama. He was determined, moreover, that any decision on the future of Upper Peru must receive the consent of Buenos Aires and of Peru. When Sucre on his own initiative convoked an assembly to freely settle the future of the region, he received a strong reprimand from the Liberator, who felt Sucre had exceeded his faculties and that the call was premature. But in practice it was irrevocable; in due course Bolívar confirmed it.

When the assembly called by Sucre finally met in Chuquisaca, the city that now bears Sucre's name, it lost little time in formally declaring sovereign independence under the title *República Bolívar,* shortly changed to *Bolivia.* Bolívar himself, meanwhile, was gradually making his way in that same direction through the southern Peruvian Andes. He found time to send a letter from Cuzco to the Ecuadoran poet José Joaquín de Olmedo, thanking him for the ode he had written in honor of the victory of Junín and at the same time making some learned comments on matters of poetic style: it is hard to imagine either George Washington or José de San Martín doing anything of the sort. Bolívar was also increasingly distressed by the state of the native population as he observed it along his path, and in an effort to improve the Indians' situation he reiterated certain decrees already issued by San Martín though not necessarily enforced, such as abolition of the tribute and of Indian forced labor. To these reforms he added measures of his own, the best known being a Cuzco decree calling for division and distribution of the Indians' common lands in the form of private property. This in most respects repeated a decree he had earlier issued at Trujillo, and like similar measures adopted in Colombia, it remained for a time a virtual dead letter, for lack of interest among most of the supposed beneficiaries and lack of the administrative machinery to carry it out. It had ideological significance, however, as a sign of adherence to liberal notions of legal equality, that is, to give the natives the same rights (such as private land ownership) and of course the same obligations as everyone else.

The Liberator crossed into Bolivian territory in mid-September. He received still more honors and gifts, and the latter he distributed among his deserving comrades-in-arms: he presented the gold crown given to him by the city of La Paz to Sucre, who in turn handed it to Córdova in recognition of his exceptional conduct at Ayacucho. Eventually Bolívar reached Chuquisaca, where the national assembly entrusted to him—and he accepted—the task of writing the new republic's first constitution. He issued decrees on a wide variety of topics, from abolition of the Indian tribute (a reform that, as also in Peru and even Colombia, would soon be suspended) to the creation of public cemeteries in order to end the unsanitary custom of burying cadavers inside churches. The latter was not strictly an anticlerical measure, but it was one dear to the hearts of the dubiously orthodox eighteenth-century philosophers of whom Bolívar was a voracious reader. He in addition invited his old teacher Rodríguez to Bolivia, and in the silver-mining center of Potosí, he met with a delegation sent by the Argentine government, which had peacefully accepted the independence of Bolivia in part because it was eager for Bolívar's help in its quarrel with Brazil over Uruguay. Bolívar was at least tempted, for he had run out of Spaniards to fight and the empire of Brazil might have taken their place; but he could not commit himself without the concurrence of Peru and Colombia, and the firm opposition of Vice President Santander would have been an insuperable obstacle even in the absence of other difficulties.

By February 1826 Bolívar was back in Lima, dedicated again to Peruvian affairs and enjoying the city's social and cultural attractions. Not least, he enjoyed the presence of his beloved Manuela Sáenz, with whom he shared a suburban villa. Manuela as always generated scandal and was frankly detested by many of the Liberator's close collaborators, not for the mere fact of being his lover but for her persistent defiance of conventions—for example, her delight in riding horseback dressed as a man. To

Manuela Sáenz in Lima, wearing a Peruvian sash. (From postcard in author's collection)

Bolívar she was simply an indispensable companion. But he himself was showing ever more clearly the physical impact of his lifestyle of frenetic activity: the vigorous young officer of abundant dark sideburns and moustache painted in Bogotá shortly after the victory of Boyacá, with allegorical Indian princess at his side to symbolize redemption of the oppressed natives, had given way to the wan, clean-shaven face and close-cropped hair that can be seen in certain portraits of his Peruvian period. His loyal aide Daniel F. O'Leary would explain that the change in hairstyles was due to the fact that Bolívar was visibly greying, and even he was subject to human vanity about appearance.

Bolívar also felt some vanity about his skill as constitution maker, which he had been exercising in fulfillment of the commission received from the Bolivian assembly. He put final touches on his proposal in Lima before submitting it to the Bolivians, and he had no doubt that it was his masterpiece, containing all the key ideas that he had been maturing for years. The centerpiece was a president serving for a life term and authorized to name his own successor, who in the meantime would serve as vice president and prime minister. The specific functions assigned to the president were limited, but his permanence in power and control of the succession were calculated to give him influence going well beyond the stipulated powers. As Bolívar stated in the message with which he submitted the project:

> The President of the Republic, in our constitution, becomes the sun which, fixed in its orbit, imparts life to the universe. This supreme authority must be perpetual, for in non-hierarchical systems, more than in others, a fixed point is needed about which leaders and citizens, men and affairs can revolve. "Give me a point where I may stand," said an ancient sage, "and I will move the earth." For Bolivia this point is the life-term president. Upon him rests our entire order, notwithstanding his lack of powers.

The resemblance of all this to constitutional monarchy was obvious enough.

The legislative branch designed by Bolívar consisted not of two houses but three, the third—that of "Censors"—being really a new version of the "Moral Power" proposed at Angostura but never adopted. Another seeming novelty was the creation of a separate "Electoral Power," as an additional branch of government, but it was novel mainly in terminology, for the election system itself was not unlike that of Colombia or other early Latin American republics. Elections were indirect and the suffrage strictly limited; only literates could vote, a requirement that automatically excluded the great majority of the population, including virtually all Indians. Of course, with a life-term president and a successor he himself named, presidential elections at least would not be required. That in itself was a distinct advantage as far as Bolívar was concerned: "By means of this device we shall avoid elections, which result in that great scourge of republics—anarchy, which is the handmaiden of tyranny, the most imminent and terrible peril of popular government." And finally, Bolívar included in his project two rather notable concrete reforms: the immediate abolition of slavery and the introduction of religious toleration. There were few slaves in Bolivia, where forms of Indian forced labor (legal or otherwise) took the place of slavery, but toleration was a rather more daring proposition, even though put forward with impeccable logic: "Religion is the law of conscience. Any law that imposes it negates it, because to apply compulsion to conscience is to destroy the value of faith, which is the very essence of religion."

The Bolivian assembly, which voted to adopt the rest of Bolívar's text with only minor revisions, omitted freedom of religion and delayed the effective date of abolition. However, those two details provided some justification for the Liberator's boast that his proposed Bolivian constitution was an eminently liberal document. Even the life presidency was "liberal" in his view, because of the president's carefully limited functions. Curiously, too, in support of the president's right to name his successor, Bolívar could not resist citing the example of the United States, despite his myriad warnings elsewhere against copying the U.S. model. What he pointed out was the recent tendency for a president to be succeeded by the man he himself had appointed as secretary of state (starting with Madison and culminating with John Quincy Adams). Yet few were convinced by Bolívar's professions of liberalism, because the parallel that most often came to mind was the regime established by Napoleon once he had betrayed the political ideals of the French Revolution. In reality, a more exact parallel was to be found in the pages of ancient history, in the example of Augustus Caesar, first Roman emperor, whose specific powers were unimpressive but who enjoyed vast moral and personal influence thanks to his personal military and political accomplishments and his indefinite tenure in office. It is even noteworthy that Augustus—like Bolívar, lacking a legitimate heir—chose Tiberius as his successor, meanwhile adopting him as son. To complete the parallel, Bolívar's constitution was decked out with Roman terminology, of which the house of "Censors" was only one instance.

Even if the life presidency, seemingly a monarchy in disguise, was the target principally singled out by critics of Bolívar's constitutional invention, certain other details were criticized as overly complicated, in particular the three-house legislature. A further source of controversy was not an article of the constitution itself but Bolívar's frank desire for it to serve as the institutional framework for another of his projects, the Federation of the Andes. Although the latter was to consist of all the territory he had liberated, the exact number of potential member states was negotiable: Colombia as a whole might become a member, or each of its component parts (Venezuela, New Granada, Quito) separately, and there was the additional possibility of dividing Peru into two states, one Northern and one Southern. But whatever the precise number, it was assumed that each member state would adopt for itself some form of the Bolivian constitution, while for the federation as a whole there would be an overall government headed by its own life president, who naturally would be Bolívar.

The Federation of the Andes aroused more skepticism than enthusiasm, both because of its potential unwieldiness and because of the very real socioeconomic, ethnic, and cultural differences among the proposed member states: if Quito had little truly in common with Venezuela, Bolivia had less. However, the adoption of Bolívar's text in Bolivia served as a first step, and Sucre agreed to become the first president under it even though with the condition that it not be for life, as he was determined to return to Quito and live there in happy marriage to his Ecuadoran marchioness. The necessary second step would be adoption of the same constitution in Peru, where its acceptance would further give some guarantee of permanence to everything else Bolívar had accomplished there. And Peru did adopt it, though not without reservations and not for very long. In Peru, critics of the constitution raised the same doctrinal objections as elsewhere, and simply because of its authorship it faced the opposition generated by an emerging nativist reaction against the foreign military presence that had begun with San Martín and now consisted mainly of Bolívar and his Colombians. Bolívar still headed the Peruvian government with dictatorial powers, and he did not lack Peruvian supporters, yet he faced increasing political opposition. The royalist garrison at Callao surrendered finally in January 1826, but former royalists as well as disaffected republicans maintained a disturbing atmosphere of intrigue and agitation. It was expected that the Peruvian congress would nevertheless vote to adopt the Bolivian constitution, but its opening was delayed by disputes over credentials, so that ultimately Bolívar dissolved it and convoked the nation's electoral colleges to decide the matter. Their decision was favorable, indeed almost unanimous—the margin of victory naturally raising suspicions of manipulation by Bolívar's allies. He in any case expressed satisfaction with the result—and soon afterward left the country to return to Colombia.

Bolívar had just won another election in Colombia, for a second term as president. But it was for another four-year term, in accordance with the existing Colombian constitution. The adoption in Colombia of his Bolivian handiwork and possible Colombian adherence to the Andean Federation were more problematic objectives, as he would shortly discover.

IX

The Beginnings of the End: Colombia Coming Undone (1826–1828)

The adoption of the Bolivian constitution in Peru was a triumph for the Liberator but an ephemeral one, and virtually his last. Even before the victory of Bolívar's party in Lima, two events occurred that attested to the fragility of much of his handiwork: the failure of the Congress of Panama and the revolt of José Antonio Páez in Venezuela. To be sure, the lack of major accomplishments at Panama was less of a blow to Bolívar's spirit than might be imagined, because he had been shifting his enthusiasm from broad continental unity to a type of integration more limited geographically but (he hoped) more meaningful, namely, his project for a Federation of the Andes. And for this project, Páez's revolt had its positive as well as negative aspects. The troubling part was the current of Venezuelan separatism that lay behind it. But insofar as it entailed a rejection of the existing Colombian constitutional order, it opened the possibility of reform in line with Bolívar's latest ideas.

Although it was Páez who headed the Venezuelan rebellion, which began at Valencia at the end of April 1826, the movement gave expression to a regional discontent that had been festering ever since the creation of the Colombian union. For Caracas especially, whose subordination to the former viceroy of New

Granada had been largely nominal and which received orders (not necessarily carried out) directly from Madrid, the requirement of obedience to a Colombian government located in the heart of the New Granadan Andes was an affront to its dignity. Venezuelans also had some concrete complaints, not always justified, against the Colombian regime. One concerned a supposed lack of equitable representation in the central administration, even though, at national cabinet level, parity between Venezuela and New Granada was carefully maintained. A relative shortage of Venezuelans in other top positions was basically due to their disinclination to undertake the long and tiresome journey to the Colombian capital, a factor that likewise explains the fact that Venezuela never had a full delegation of elected representatives present in Congress. And if Venezuelans did not exercise their proportionate share of civil authority, they more than made up for it in the military. Because of the almost continual fighting in Venezuela, its soldiers had more opportunity to accumulate experience and promotions, so that the men holding the highest rank of all, that of 'general-in-chief,' were without exception Venezuelans. The execution of so many New Granadan patriots during the Spanish reconquest had also eliminated a good many officers who might otherwise have competed for top command positions.

Other grievances had to do with specific national policies that went against the interests or prejudices of important social groups in Venezuela. Caracas slaveowners objected to the quite moderate law of manumission adopted by the Colombian constituent congress, while doctrinaire liberals—relatively more numerous in Venezuela than New Granada—complained of the excessive moderation of efforts by the same constituent congress and subsequent legislatures to curb the power and privileges of the clergy. The general lowering of customs duties should have drawn thanks from Venezuela as an important agroexporting region, but generally it did not. Finally, Venezuelan opinion was all too ready to believe any accusations of corruption or arbitrary action leveled against the administration of Vice President Santander, of which the most notorious instance was alleged mismanagement of the 30-million-peso loan Colombia obtained in London in 1824.

The 1824 loan was contracted on terms that for the period were rather favorable, but still it gave rise to a storm of opposition. Interest and discount rates were called into question, and so too (with more justice) were the commissions paid to the Colombian loan negotiators. But the main criticisms concerned the seemingly rapid disappearance of the loan funds. Not everyone realized that a third of the face amount represented only refinancing of earlier obligations incurred by patriot agents of Venezuela and New Granada, and there was also a line item earmarked for agricultural reconstruction and development, to be spent above all in Venezuela. Yet it is clear enough that much of the loan money was poorly used. A considerable amount went for purchase of war matériel, when the conflict was already drawing to a close, including the acquisition of two beautiful frigates in the United States that turned out to be almost useless for lack of qualified sailors in Colombia to sail them. Even more widely assailed was the use of the foreign loan to pay internal debts, including some undoubtedly false or inflated. Inevitably there were allegations that high members of the government, including Santander, were profiteering by this means. As far as Santander was concerned, there was no real evidence that he used the loan for personal benefit—but those who opposed his government for any reason did not hesitate to accept all charges as true.

Not all Venezuelans, of course, looked on the central government with equal distaste. Most were too busy trying to survive day by day to spend time worrying about national politics, and in the outlying provinces some people actually looked to Bogotá as a helpful counterweight to the local preponderance of Caracas. In the election of 1826, when Bolívar was reelected almost unanimously as president, there was a keen struggle over the vice presidency, even though in the end Santander won reelection too. But it turns out that, while he garnered not a single vote in the electoral college of Caracas, he had an absolute majority in the eastern Venezuelan provinces of Cumaná and Guayana. Nor were Venezuela's representatives in congress uniformly oppositionist. Thus friends of the vice president insisted on attributing any Venezuelan hostility to the intrigues of a so-called "Caracas Club" made up typically of professional men—

lawyers, merchants, publicists. The military in Venezuela, however, were also disaffected, and like military men elsewhere they had some concrete complaints against the Santander administration and its supporters in congress for gradually whittling away at such military privileges as their colonial-era exemption from the jurisdiction of civilian courts. There was likewise a storm of indignation among the Venezuelan military when one of their own, Colonel Leonardo Infante, was executed in the central square of Bogotá for a murder he may or may not have committed. He had been duly sentenced by court martial, but by a split decision and amid a climate of anti-military and implicitly anti-Venezuelan agitation on the part of New Granadan journalists and politicians, including some close to the vice president. To make matters worse, Santander himself turned up to harangue the soldiers who had been brought to witness the execution, taking the occasion to exalt the majesty of law and the sacred obligation of the military to obey it. The gesture rankled among Infante's former companions and was exploited as one more sign of the injustice inflicted on Venezuela and Venezuelans by the vice president and his coterie.

The situation in Venezuela remained manageable as long as Páez placed his personal prestige on the side of constitutional legality. While the independence struggle in Venezuela still lasted, Páez's feelings were hurt by the fact that General Carlos Soublette was given a special command with authority over all Venezuela and even relative autonomy vis-à-vis Bogotá. Páez felt unjustly passed over, but it would seem that Bolívar, who made the choice, wanted to leave his part of Colombia in the hands of an educated aristocrat (Soublette being a *mantuano* of French descent). Páez clearly did not meet that description, however much he was now rubbing shoulders with British military officers and making himself rich through the accumulation of formerly royalist properties. But he accepted the Liberator's decision. After 1824 there was no longer one superior officer with jurisdiction in Venezuela as a whole, Páez serving only as military commandant of the Caracas area. Yet he was the one Venezuelan of greatest prestige after Bolívar; all those engaged in agitation against Santander and Bogotá realized they must win his confidence, and through flattery and helpful advice they gradually were gaining it.

Páez's first misstep was a proposal made to Bolívar in October 1825 that he crown himself monarch. Painting a somber picture of the country generally, Páez placed special emphasis on the plight of the military, whom scornful "lawyers and merchants" sought to "reduce to the condition of slaves"; Bolívar should therefore imitate the example of Napoleon, in order to save the country. It would seem that this plan was hatched in discussions between Páez and other Venezuelan officers, not all of whom were close supporters of Bolívar but who felt that by crowning Bolívar they would at least get out from under the control of Santander and his particular circle of New Granadan "lawyers and merchants." The same reasoning would explain why members of the "Caracas Club," who tended to be "lawyers and merchants" themselves, took up the idea; and one of their number, Antonio Leocadio Guzmán, was commissioned to carry the proposal to Bolívar in Lima.

One who did not take up the idea was Bolívar's sister María Antonia, a woman of considerable common sense who in a letter to her brother called the proposal "infamous," insisting that his one glory was the title of Liberator. When Bolívar got around to answering Páez the following March, he agreed with María Antonia. "Colombia is not France," he wrote, "nor am I Napoleon. . . . Colombia [unlike France] has never been a kingdom. By its elevation as by its splendor, a throne would inspire terror. Equality would end, and the men of color would lose their rights to a new aristocracy." Bolívar thus once again cited the aspirations of *pardos* and mestizos as a barrier to the establishment of monarchies in Spanish America. But he did not deny the need for institutional reform, and he recommended that Páez carefully study his plan of a constitution for Bolivia, of which he was sending a copy.

Even before Páez received Bolívar's answer, he committed another misstep, at least from the standpoint of constitutional legality, by defying a summons to appear before congress in Bogotá and answer charges that he was responsible for abuses in the recruitment of citizens for militia duty. There was no doubt some truth in the charges, but nothing extraordinary about the alleged abuses. However, civilian politicians in congress, fed up with all sorts of military misconduct, decided that the time was come to take a stand for once and all and see who was in charge of Colombia, whether the generals or the civil authorities—and by choosing to force the issue precisely with Páez, they committed a grievous miscalculation. At first he apparently decided to go to Bogotá and defend himself in person, but the summons to Páez provided the sworn opponents of the central administration with simply too great an opportunity to do mischief. Predictably, they lost no time in spreading the notion that Santander was behind the accusation, whereas in reality the vice president was guilty at most of not doing all he could have to head it off in congress. The result in Venezuela, in any case, was a growing atmosphere of uncertainty and unrest. The municipal government of Valencia implored Páez to remain in Venezuela and take full charge of affairs in the region so as to preserve tranquility; and on 30 April 1826 he agreed to do so, in effect declaring himself in rebellion. The objectives of the movement were far from clear, however. There was much talk of reforming Colombian institutions in a way that would satisfy Venezuelan aspirations, but at the same time leaders of the revolt, including Páez, implored Bolívar to come back from Peru and take charge of the reform process; Páez further pledged not to innovate before Bolívar did return.

Páez's defiance was quickly hailed by most of his military comrades and the civilian enemies of the central administration. Other municipalities of central Venezuela, including Caracas, imitated Valencia's move. Yet on the Venezuelan periphery, where Caracas was as much an object of distrust as Bogotá, the movement gained less support. Even some who initially backed it had second thoughts as its nature became clearer. Opposition to the people in Bogotá was one thing, but the undercurrent of federalism and even Venezuelan separatism among Páez's adherents was something else and not to the liking of those who were above all else friends and supporters of Bolívar. Bona fide Bolivarians also disliked the growing prominence around Páez of the agitators of the "Caracas Club," in particular Dr. Miguel

Peña, a man who had been suspended from the national Supreme Court for a procedural fault and who enriched himself on the way home to Venezuela by accepting in Cartagena a sum of money to carry to Caracas and then delivering an equal number of pesos—but in depreciated coinage. He was in Valencia at the end of April to urge Páez on in his defiance and soon became one of the closest collaborators.

In Vice President Santander's view, the way to solve the Venezuelan problem was for Bolívar to hasten home from Peru and place his vast personal influence on the side of the law. For Bolívar, however, the events in Venezuela represented both a problem and a possibility, so that his reaction was not quite what was hoped for in Bogotá. When he first heard of the accusation against Páez, he wrote to the latter suggesting that perhaps he should feign illness to avoid going to Bogotá, but thanks to the slowness of the mails Páez had rebelled before Bolívar even wrote the letter. When he finally learned of the rebellion, Bolívar wrote back in disapproval but not in very strong terms. He seemed to accept the version that it was somehow the fault of Santander and was pleased with Páez's promise to await his return before making changes.

Bolívar's failure to condemn the Venezuelan rebellion forthrightly was due in part to his conviction that the original accusation against Páez had been unwise, and in part to his desire to promote his own reform agenda. He was even beginning to think that it might not be necessary to observe the constitutional article that prohibited amendments during a ten-year trial period. Not only had the Venezuelan rebellion brought matters to a head sooner than anticipated, but he was increasingly convinced that Colombia had problems too serious for the cure to be delayed by technicalities. In this belief he was not, of course, alone. Improvised assemblies at Guayaquil and elsewhere in the southern provinces had been imitating the example of Venezuela in calling for constitutional changes without delay and calling on Bolívar to direct the process. In personal letters and in the press, he also read from other parts of Colombia complaints similar to those raised in Venezuela concerning both military abuses and civilian prejudice against the military, the use and misuse of the loan funds, and much else besides. Bolívar did not necessarily accept all complaints at face value, but for some time he had felt that dogmatic liberals in the administration and congress were pushing ahead too fast with reforms that were at least premature and thus a source of political and social instability. He now gave vent to this feeling in a letter to Páez:

> The executive, guided by this deceitful tribune [the press] and by the disconcerted assembly of those legislators, has gone in search of a premature perfection and has drowned us in a sea of laws and institutions that are good, but for now superfluous. The spirit of the military has suffered more from our civilians than from our enemies; there has been a wish even to destroy their pride.

Bolívar's sense of duty therefore indicated the need to return to Colombia as soon as possible, and though it has been suggested that he was immobilized in Lima by the city's attractions and amenities—the presence of Manuela not least among them—he lingered a bit longer, above all, because he wanted to leave Peruvian affairs in good order. This was certainly reasonable; his error was in the belief that doing so meant imposing the Bolivian constitution in Peru, as he eventually did but at some political cost.

While attending to final details in Lima, Bolívar sent Antonio Leocadio Guzmán, the same who earlier brought him Páez's proposal that he become a crowned head of state, back to Colombia as his personal emissary. Guzmán carried with him a summary of Bolívar's constitutional panacea, which he was to explain in detail wherever he went. He landed first in Guayaquil at the end of August 1826, and though the people of the port city were more interested in greater local autonomy than in life presidencies, the highest official on the spot, the New Granadan colonel Tomás C. de Mosquera, was a hyperbolic Bolivarian in whose view the Bolivian constitution was nothing less than "a gift from heaven." According to Mosquera, "the sun in the center of the universe, Mount Chimborazo there in its celestial elevation, and the firmament surrounding the works of nature are less, physically, than what Simón Bolívar is in the society of mortals." Mosquera accordingly saw to it that Guayaquil produced a manifesto calling for adoption of the Bolivian constitution and offering the Liberator dictatorial powers to "save the republic."

As he continued his journey through Panama and Cartagena, Guzmán extracted additional declarations urging Bolívar to come home and solve the country's problems, although without explicit support for the Bolivian constitution or dictatorship. He did not pass through Quito, but he really did not need to, for there both military chiefs and the local aristocracy were more than willing to offer Bolívar anything he might want, for they felt intense dissatisfaction with the current state of affairs. Regional grievances in what is now Ecuador were in fact more truly justified than those aired in Venezuela. Since the end of the war, or 1825, to be more precise, the national legislation previously suspended in the south by Bolívar had gone into effect, including the new tariff system that diminished protection for highland textile manufacturers and the abolition of Indian tribute, which had been bitterly opposed by most whites without apparently being seen as a godsend by the native population itself. Quite apart from specific governmental policies, moreover, Ecuador's interests were never fully taken into account at Bogotá, where its representation in Congress was limited not only by its lesser population base but by the extreme difficulty of travel to the capital, and where there was never an Ecuadoran appointed to the national cabinet or raised to the rank of general in the Colombian army. Such problems would not be automatically solved by adopting the Bolivian constitution or giving the Liberator dictatorial powers, but people of wealth and social standing had more confidence in a strong government headed by Bolívar than in the liberal constitutionalism whose results had been so disappointing.

Bolívar himself finally landed in Guayaquil in mid-September 1826. After arrival he repudiated talk of dictatorship and promised to uphold the legal order, all of which reassured Santander and his friends, who were increasingly worried about the Liberator's intentions. However, his conduct as he progressed through the southern provinces aroused suspicions once again. Bolívar may have rejected the title of dictator but acted as though still invested with the "extraordinary faculties" that he had enjoyed when last on Colombian soil but that had by now technically expired. He used them to give military promotions to officers who had been calling for dictatorship, while listening attentively to anyone with a complaint against the existing laws of Colombia. In a letter to Santander, he contradicted his own public statements about dictatorship:

> In this confusion, dictatorship composes everything, because we will take time to prepare opinion for the great convention of the year '31, and meanwhile we calm the parties of the extremes. With constitutional laws we can do nothing more in the Páez business than punish the rebellion, but if I am authorized by the nation I can do everything.

The fact that in this case Bolívar stopped short of suggesting that the "great convention" for constitutional reform be held before the end of the fixed ten-year trial period can hardly have reassured the vice president.

Bolívar reached Popayán, in western New Granada, at the end of October and for the first time encountered a strong current of opinion that questioned his latest political ideas. However, Bolívar's military companions showed few inhibitions in openly mocking the constitutional order, and Bolívar on his part wrote to the vice president from his next stop, Neiva, that he was "confirmed in the fear that Colombia is lost forever"—that "the constitution and laws have reduced Colombia to a Satan's palace which is ablaze at every corner." Not knowing quite what to make of Bolívar's words and actions, Santander wisely decided to go meet Bolívar before he undertook the final climb up to the plain of Bogotá, both to ascertain his intentions and, if possible, to disabuse him of false charges against the government. And the encounter went well. The two men agreed that on reaching Bogotá Bolívar would resume the presidency and, despite his skepticism concerning the Colombian constitution, would govern under its terms, though once again invested with the "extraordinary faculties" that the constitution itself provided in cases of grave necessity.

The budding rapprochement between Bolívar and Santander was almost ruined when the Liberator finally made his triumphal entry into the capital and was greeted by the vice president's friends and associates with a few too many *"vivas"* for the constitution, not to mention an address of welcome by the local intendant that made pointed reference to laws having been violated, apparently by Bolívar's military allies. In high anger, Bolívar interrupted the harangue and stated that on such a day it was proper "to celebrate the glories of the army and not to speak of the violation of laws, caused by the iniquity of the latter." He then left the ceremony and continued into the city with a few companions, through a rain that further dampened good feelings, to the government palace where Santander and his ministers had prepared still another reception. Happily this one went better, with Bolívar uttering his own *"viva"* to the constitution and Santander heaping praise on the heroic army.

The next day, Bolívar demonstrated in a letter to Páez that he had not wholly recovered from the initial bad impression received on his return to Bogotá, for he complained of being surrounded on all sides by enemies and slander; and it is true that the prevailing opinion in the capital even among many of the Liberator's friends—at least among his civilian friends, who tended to be drawn from traditional upper-class families—was skeptical of the Bolivian constitution and hostile to talk of dictatorship. But something of the earlier close relationship with Santander did reappear, to the point that Bolívar even imagined that Santander was looking favorably on the proposed Federation of the Andes. He may not have been entirely mistaken in that regard, for assuming that greater Colombia was divided into three separate states on joining the federation, Santander was by far the obvious candidate for president (whether for a life term or something less) of New Granada.

Because Bolívar was intent on continuing to Venezuela and dealing in person with the Páez rebellion, he did not stay long in Bogotá. However, while there he put on a display of whirlwind activity. He devoted special attention to financial affairs, which in truth were in bad shape: as of the previous June, it had consequently been necessary to suspend service on the foreign debt. That service was all the more impossible to maintain in that the annual interest and amortization between them amounted to one-third the treasury's normal income. Bolívar at any rate now decreed a modest increase in customs duties, suppressed various military and civilian positions, and took additional belt-tightening measures, most of which were accepted as necessary by nearly everyone. Among Bolívar's other decrees, one reestablished a distinct system of administration for Quito and the far south, under a single supreme chief, whereby he hoped to satisfy regional aspirations and perhaps at the same time take a first step toward the conversion of that region into another member of the Andean Federation.

The improvement in relations between president and vice president did not last long. Bolívar left Bogotá at the end of November and the second night out sat down to play cards with Santander and some others who had accompanied him thus far; having won some money, he indiscreetly exclaimed that he at last had received a share of the loan funds. Though meant as a jest, the remark touched what for Santander was a very sensitive point. Moreover, as he continued toward Venezuela, Bolívar listened attentively to all manner of complaints anyone had against the Santander administration and summarized them in messages to Bogotá. He disclaimed any intention of casting blame, but Santander was further annoyed. Then, too, Bolívar kept taking money from provincial treasuries and ordering the concentration of troops and supplies, just in case he finally had to subdue Páez by force of arms. All this again aroused the suspicion of Santander and his friends, who feared the preparations might be aimed not at Páez but at them.

Recent developments in Venezuela provided some justification for Bolívar's measures. The movement led by Páez had undergone a steady process of radicalization, to the point that an assembly he convoked for the consideration of future options recommended holding a Venezuelan constituent convention, to reorganize the government of Venezuela alone and without excluding the possibility of outright separation from Colombia. Such developments served to alarm both moderates and the close friends of Bolívar, who objected to the way Páez had seemingly forgotten his promise not to innovate before the Liberator's return. As a result, Páez began to suffer the desertion of some leaders and towns that previously backed him. Bolívar, then, finally reentered Venezuela, heading first to Maracaibo, which under the Bolivarian loyalist Rafael Urdaneta had stood aside from the rebellion; and there he proclaimed his intention to call a national convention for constitutional reform. Páez dispatched the practiced intriguer Miguel Peña to Bolívar's camp, to warn him to accept Venezuelan aspirations or run the risk of armed resistance, but Peña was arrested before he arrived at headquarters. Nevertheless, Páez's tactics had the desired effect. From Puerto Cabello on 1 January 1827 Bolívar made known his solution for the Venezuelan problem: a general amnesty for Páez and his followers and guarantee that no one would lose rank or property, in return simply for recognition of the Liberator's authority. Páez saw fit to accept the offer. He went to meet Bolívar in Valencia, taking a security escort in case the Liberator did not entirely mean what he said, whereas Bolívar approached Páez alone and warmly embraced him.

When the Liberator next made a triumphal entry to the city of his birth, he was enthusiastically welcomed by a population already growing tired of Páez. There were dances, reunions with friends and family, and not least an emotional reunion with the beloved Hipólita, the slave wet nurse to whom Bolívar had long since given freedom. Less agreeable were his encounters with aggrieved creditors. Although Bolívar was still a wealthy man, his habits of lavish spending and scattering of largesse—giving away properties, making generous gifts from his personal assets—created cash-flow problems at very least. (As Bolívar once wrote to a friend, "I have never seen an account, and I do not want to know what is spent in my house.") It would seem that only now did he become fully aware of the extent to which he had given people drafts payable out of funds (e.g., from the bonus voted by the Peruvian congress) that in practice never materialized.

Yet Bolívar was concerned with more than personal finances. His peaceful settlement with Páez was realistic when he made it, for he did not know exactly how far the rebel leader's position had deteriorated, and the chance to settle the dispute without firing a shot was not to be scorned. But Bolívar took appeasement of the former rebel to questionable extremes, calling him "savior of the republic" and showering favors on Páez's collaborators while offering little or nothing to those who had held out against the rebellion. Supposedly for the sake of public tranquility, he even prohibited criticism of Páez in the Venezuelan press. For the rest, he used his "extraordinary faculties" to issue decrees broadly similar to those he had recently issued at Bogotá but applicable solely to Venezuela. Among other things, he again raised customs duties, and he suspended the practice of accepting government debt certificates in payment. This last move put some merchants in an awkward situation, for they had bought up such certificates at heavy discounts precisely for use at the customs houses. No exceptions were made even for foreign citizens, so that one U.S. businessman was reduced to prison for not paying duties that he had thought to pay with already approved certificates.

Not surprisingly, Bolívar's actions in Venezuela raised a storm of protest in Bogotá. Somewhat veiled criticism of the Liberator began appearing in the official *Gaceta de Colombia,* but no holds were barred in the unofficial liberal press. The Caracas decrees of the Liberator were attacked as contrary to constitutional order and threatening to the nation's very existence; Bolívar's treatment of Páez and others guilty of sedition was seen as setting an extremely bad example for the future, quite apart from the implicit discrimination against those who had remained loyal. Santander himself wrote bitterly to Bolívar that, if Páez was savior of the fatherland, then he and all who had been upholding the laws must somehow be guilty. Santander did compliment Bolívar on his apparent decision to leave convocation of the promised national convention to congress instead of doing it himself by virtue of "extraordinary faculties," but the inability of the vice president to say anything favorable about Bolívar without slipping in a subtext of constitutionalist propaganda greatly annoyed the Liberator. In mid-March he wrote from Caracas to the secretary of war accusing Santander of "perfidious ingratitude" and broke off all correspondence with the vice president.

Even before he learned that Bolívar would write to him no longer, Santander had taken a step that immeasurably deepened the gulf between them. It resulted directly from the mutiny in late January of the Colombian Third Division, which Bolívar had left behind in Lima. Ostensibly this was a movement of constitutionalist officers, primarily New Granadan, against Venezuelan higher officers accused of intriguing to impose the Bolivian constitution. But the movement was abetted by Peruvian opponents of the regime Bolívar had created in their country, and either way it was frankly opposed to the Liberator. It is hardly surprising that Manuela Sáenz, also left behind in Lima, turned up at the mutineers' barracks brandishing a pistol in one hand and money in the other, in an unsuccessful effort to dissuade them. And when news of what happened reached Bogotá, the liberal friends of the constitution and of Santander celebrated it as a triumph of their cause: Santander himself ordered bells rung. But worse was to come. The revolt of the Third Division was quickly followed by a change of government in Peru and abrogation of the Peruvian version of the Bolivian constitution. With help from the new Peruvian authorities, the Third Division then left Lima for Guayaquil, where it deposed the pro-Bolivarian intendant, Colonel Mosquera, and replaced him with a man who was Colombian by birth but currently a marshal of Peru. To what extent the mutineers were actually working for Peru against Colombian interests is unclear, but their actions in Guayaquil were too much even for Santander. He ordered things put back more or less as they were before, although his response stopped short of unequivocally condemning the Third Division.

Bolívar, in any case, concluded that he must cut short his stay in Venezuela to return to Bogotá and conceivably from there to Quito and Guayaquil to confront the challenge of Peru. By the time Bolívar actually set sail from La Guaira for Cartagena, it was known that the immediate danger in the south had passed, because most members of the Third Division had deserted at the instigation of Juan José Flores, the officer to whom Bolívar had entrusted overall administration of the southern provinces. But Bolívar continued on toward Bogotá, with the force that he originally had said was needed to cope with the Third Division and Peru, and his approach naturally alarmed the New Granadan liberals who had been showering him with abuse in the Bogotá press. Santander tried to dissuade him from continuing his march, or at least from bringing all the troops he had gathered, with implausible arguments about the lack of means in Bogotá to support them. In reality, the vice president was afraid that his own political faction was now the target of the Liberator's advance, while Bolívar on his part was well aware that some members of that faction had been flirting with the idea of staging a preventive rebellion of their own to head off a possible Bolivarian dictatorship. They had been dissuaded by Santander's caution on one hand and the firm opposition of his entire cabinet on the other. Nevertheless, Bolívar was not sure the internal danger had passed entirely, and he further suspected that his political enemies would try to block the convocation by congress of the Great Convention (as it came to be known) for constitutional reform.

As things turned out, the fears of both sides proved unfounded. Congress did call elections for the convention, to meet the following year at Ocaña, in northeastern New Granada. It did so by a comfortable margin, with support not only from Bolívar's friends but from those dissatisfied for any reason with the nation's present organization—in particular federalists and partisans of local autonomy, not all of them Venezuelans by any means. And when Bolívar reached Bogotá, on 10 September 1827, he did not unleash the wave of military repression that some of his opponents expected. There were a few arbitrary acts committed here or there, but none truly noteworthy and all duly publicized in the opposition press. Some fervent liberals who had gone into hiding for safety's sake soon reemerged. Bolívar settled down to exercise the presidency with the help of the same executive cabinet that previously served Santander, and when elections were held for the Great Convention, they were as free and fair as any to date. Whether for reasons of political altruism or because of excess confidence in the outcome, Bolívar and his supporters made no concerted effort to impose the victory of official candidates.

What was from the standpoint of Bolívar's opponents his surprisingly good behavior reflected was among other things his hope that the coming convention would soon revamp Colombia's institutions more in line with his ideas. The hope was, however, rather unrealistic, because such ideas as life presidency and Andean Federation had gained little support, and though the more general idea of strong government that he always espoused enjoyed considerably wider support, there was no consensus as to the best way of achieving it. The elections thus produced no majority but rather three distinct minorities, and of these the unconditional Bolivarians were not even most numerous. Largest instead was the band of Santanderista liberals, headed by the vice president himself, who was elected deputy from Bogotá on the basis of a campaign dedicated to cultivating "the mere rabble of the country," in words of the British minister. Though a peripheral member of the landed upper class rather than true man of the people, Santander had gone around dressed like a peasant, picnicking with artisans in his successful quest for votes. Finally, there was a category of independent deputies, ideologically heterogeneous but sufficient in number to tip the balance. They included a group of New Granadan moderates, who distrusted both ardent liberal reformers and military men longing for dictatorship, and Venezuelans who were less interested in the fortunes of their native region's most illustrious son than in obtaining greater autonomy from Bogotá by any means available.

Even while waiting for the Great Convention to begin, Bolívar had to occupy himself with both high and routine affairs of government. One little-noticed action that he took was the decree, similar to one he had earlier issued in Bolivia, prohibiting the burial of cadavers in churches and ordering construction of hygienic burial grounds elsewhere in each town or city. In this matter he meant business: when a few days later a distinguished citizen of Bogotá was illegally buried inside one of the churches, Bolívar ordered the cadaver exhumed. Yet any offense to religious sensibilities was more than offset by another decree prohibiting the use in Colombian universities of the text on legislation by the English utilitarian Jeremy Bentham. This obviously had as its objective to protect the young from ideas contrary to strict Catholic doctrine and thereby win favor with the clergy and more devout lay Catholics. It is striking, even so, in that Bentham was a figure who had taken great interest in the building of new nations in Latin America and had numerous admirers and correspondents there—one of whom had been Bolívar. In fiscal matters, Bolívar again demonstrated a conservative bent. He further amended Colombian tariff legislation with a view to raising import duties, which pleased protectionists in Quito and elsewhere even though Bolívar normally presented his tariff policy as designed solely to generate income for the treasury. In effect, he espoused the somewhat simplistic notion that an increase in tariffs would automatically produce more revenue. Yet meanwhile, according to a senate committee report, the increases he had decreed for Venezuela during his stay in Caracas were causing numerous ships that reached Venezuelan ports after the changes took effect to simply take their cargoes somewhere else.

In the weeks just before the Great Convention, a number of concrete events served to exacerbate the fears of Bolívar's opponents. Some military troublemakers burned an issue of one Santanderista newspaper and then, when it reappeared under the new name of *El Incombustible,* sacked the press where it was printed. The guilty parties were ordered to give satisfaction to their victims, but the episode was disturbing nonetheless. And on 13 March 1828 Bolívar declared a state of emergency and assumed "extraordinary faculties" throughout the republic except for the canton of Ocaña, where the convention was to meet. This was officially justified on grounds of a possible Spanish attack from the Caribbean as well as outbreaks of banditry in Venezuela, some of whose perpetrators claimed to be acting in the name of the king. But domestic oppositionists suspected that the measure was intended for their intimidation—and for that of the deputies elected to Ocaña, who were being subjected to a flood of frequently abusive petitions and memorials from military units and others that called on them to save the republic from the snares set by Bolívar's enemies. Often as not the petitions were inscribed on printed forms distributed from a central location, clearly indicating orchestration by government officials or supporters.

Bolívar himself left Bogotá in mid-March, heading toward Venezuela ostensibly to confront the royalist menace. Before the convention opened, that danger had largely dissipated. However, he did not return to the capital, for another danger had arisen in the form of a political-racial disturbance at Cartagena, where Admiral José Padilla attempted to depose the military commandant of the region, General Mariano Montilla, who was a strong partisan of Bolívar. At bottom, this was a confrontation between the local creole elite that supported Montilla (a

Venezuelan *mantuano,* like Bolívar) and the coastal *pardos* who sympathized with Padilla, the highest-ranking New Granadan officer of that same social origin. Having lost out in his challenge to Montilla, Padilla proceeded to Ocaña to plead his case before the convention, but he then returned to Cartagena—and was arrested. His movements, in any event, gave Bolívar a pretext to settle down in Bucaramanga, a point in the eastern cordillera from which he could conveniently monitor events along the coast but which was not far distant from Ocaña.

When at last on 9 April the convention opened, Bolívar did not attend, but he sent a message in which he sketched a somber picture of the state of the nation:

> Colombia, which managed to spring to life, lies lifeless. . . .
> Colombia, which breathed an atmosphere of honor and virtue in
> the face of oppressive forces, now gasps for air as if it were
> unaware of its national dishonor. Colombia, which once thought
> only of painful sacrifices and distinguished service, now thinks
> only of its rights, not its duties. The nation would have perished
> if some remnant of public spirit had not driven it to cry out for
> remedy and drawn it up short of the edge of the grave.

Bolívar went on to offer his recommendations. He did not ask for dictatorship or call for either Bolivian constitution or Andean Federation, no doubt having come to realize that there was insufficient support for those solutions. But he did emphasize the undue power of the legislative and judicial branches vis-à-vis the executive under the existing constitution, and he even intimated that the judicial power should properly be considered a mere subtype of the executive. He mentioned a number of concrete ways in which the executive should be strengthened, and he called for giving the military more independence from civil officials. Conspicuous by its absence, however, was any reference to the threats to Colombian unity. He had at least been toying with the idea that greater Colombia could perhaps be saved, if at all, only as a looser union of Venezuela, New Granada, and Quito, each with a centralized government of its own; but he seems to have been genuinely uncertain what to do on this score.

Bolívar remained in Bucaramanga some seventy days, hoping that he would be summoned to Ocaña to further enlighten the deputies. However, no call came, despite the efforts of his supporters. Bolívar's liberal opponents adamantly opposed the motion, with Santander—who knew all too well the persuasive power of Bolivarian charisma—foremost among them. Hence the Liberator had to content himself with weeks of card playing, horseback riding, and regular attendance at church, although a French officer who became his confidant while the stay lasted once saw him taking a book to read during mass and noted further that he never crossed himself. Meanwhile the deputies at Ocaña debated constitutional reform in rather bad humor. The leader of the Bolivarian faction was Secretary of Finance José María Castillo y Rada, who when holding the same position previously under Santander had stood out as the most doctrinairely liberal cabinet member. But he had been a candidate for vice president in 1826 in opposition to Santander's reelection, and a factor of personal rivalry clearly influenced his present alignment. Castillo introduced a project for constitutional reform that strengthened the national executive in line with Bolívar's wishes and, though not specifying a life presidency, did not rule out the possibility of indefinite reelection. For the Santanderistas, Dr. Vicente Azuero presented another proposal that increased provincial autonomy but stopped short of outright federalism, despite the fact that Santander himself on the eve of the convention had declared his conversion—purely tactical and transitory—to federalism as a means of "restraining the colossal power that Bolívar exercises." Azuero's project attracted additional support from the band of Venezuelan autonomists at Ocaña, and when it became obvious that it was more likely to be approved than Castillo's, the Bolivarians did what had to be done to block it: they went home, making it impossible to assemble a quorum. The convention dissolved, and with it the last chance to reform Colombian institutions with some semblance of procedural legality. Dictatorship remained the only alternative.

The Last Dictatorship
(1828–1830)

As word of the dissolution of the Great Convention spread through the land, Bolívar's military and civilian supporters began issuing calls for him to assume unlimited powers and do whatever was now necessary to "save the republic." He was not unwilling to accept the challenge but let it be known that, before accepting the proffered dictatorship, he must be sure he had the consent of his fellow citizens. Bolívar's leading partisans in Bogotá therefore set out sheets of paper on which they invited the inhabitants to come forward and affix their names, indicating approval or disapproval of concentrating all political authority in the hands of this one man. Exactly four persons (two students, two petty officials) signed in opposition. A larger number did not sign at all, yet even in Bogotá, where the opposition had easily won the elections for delegates to Ocaña, there is little doubt that most people were by this point satisfied to give Bolívar whatever powers he felt were needed. The same could be said of the country as a whole, though Bolívar's adherents this time were leaving nothing to chance: General Montilla in Cartagena instructed a subordinate officer to extract a memorial calling for dictatorship from one locality "even if it costs blood." And well before Ocaña itself submitted such a memorial, Bolívar had in fact assumed dictatorial powers, which he would lay down only in 1830.

Admirers and detractors alike of Simón Bolívar agree that this final dictatorship brought him little glory even while embittering his days with personal disappointments and political frustrations. Otherwise their assessments vary greatly, in accordance with the authors' historiographical and ideological positions. Conservative traditionalists have been the most consistent and enthusiastic admirers of what Bolívar did in this last phase of his career, because of his action in suspending a series of earlier liberal innovations, especially in the area of ecclesiastical reform. Yet among the apologists of the dictatorship can also be found writers who consider Bolívar to have been a precursor of modern state interventionism of social revolutionary tendency and who find in certain of his dictatorial decrees an element of social reformism that has escaped most other observers. The same authors would classify such figures as Santander as constituting a small-minded oligarchy incapable of appreciating either Bolívar's continental dreams or his devotion to popular needs. The most widely read example of this last interpretation is the one implicit in *The General in His Labyrinth*, the novelized version of Bolívar's final days by Colombia's Nobel prize–winning author Gabriel García Márquez. It is quite explicit in the populist rhetoric of such contemporary political leaders as Venezuela's president, Hugo Chávez.

At the other extreme are historians of the conventional liberal school, who have viewed the last dictatorship as an aberration, a regime "absolutely regressive" in the words of Roberto Botero Saldarriaga. It was simply unworthy of the Liberator, who at this stage of life was supposedly misled by the nefarious influence of the people around him—military, clergy, backward-looking aristocrats. A similar view was expressed by members of Colombia's "old left," such as Ignacio Torres Giraldo, one of the founders of the country's Communist Party, who in his historical writing gives a version of Bolívar wholly different from that of the contemporary Colombian leftists who dubbed an umbrella revolutionary committee the Coordinadora Guerrillera Simón Bolívar, or "Simón Bolívar Guerrilla Coordinating Junta." Probably the most balanced assessment, in any case, is that given by the classic historian of Colombian independence José Manuel Restrepo, who served Bolívar as interior secretary and regarded the dictatorship as a necessary evil. It was an evil because of the arbitrary actions committed and because of the prominence in it of Venezuelan military, which annoyed Restrepo as a New Granadan civilian; but it was made necessary by the intransigence of Santander (whom Restrepo had also served) and his liberal supporters generally, who having stirred up opposition and unrest through premature innovations, refused to seek an amicable compromise with the party of Bolívar.

Once the dictatorship was established, its operation was governed by an "organic decree" that Bolívar issued at the end of August 1828. Virtually no limit was set on the executive power, but this did not mean that power was wholly concentrated in the hands of Bolívar and his immediate collaborators in the nation's capital, for a salient characteristic of the regime was the extent to which the dictator delegated power to regional chiefs, each of whom had control over one major part of the country. For Venezuela the chosen chieftain was inevitably Páez, who for the most part followed whatever guidelines were sent out from Bogotá, but not always—and yet the council of ministers (as the cabinet secretaries were renamed) took pains never to overtly disapprove anything Páez did. In the future Ecuador, a similar role was entrusted to General Juan José Flores. Only in the interior of New Granada did the central government exercise direct and immediate control, for along the coast General Montilla held a position analogous to that of Páez or Flores. Indeed his authority as *"jefe superior"* extended from Panama in the west through Maracaibo in the east, which was thus detached from Páez's bailiwick. The arrangement was hardly pleasing to Páez, but in a sense it harked back to the period before creation of the captaincy-general of Venezuela in the late colonial era, for only then had Maracaibo become a dependency of Caracas.

The peculiar status of Maracaibo underscores Bolívar's continuing ambivalence concerning the relationship among major sections of Colombia. For some time he had wavered between the possibility of frankly accepting the dissolution of greater Colombia; the maintenance of a centralized union; or creation of a loose confederation of Venezuela, Ecuador, and New Granada, or perhaps of interior and coastal New Granada as two separate states as suggested by the latest administrative divisions. At one point he came close to proposing the last of these alternatives to the Great Convention, but when his supporters at Ocaña presented a strictly centralist scheme, thinking it in line with his true preference, he desisted from the idea. The sweeping delegation of dictatorial authority under the "organic decree" suggested a reversion to the concept of Colombia as a three-part (or four-part?) confederation—but the fact remains that Bolívar never truly came to grips with the problem of just how to fit together the different sections of the country. The "organic decree" did, however, make clear that for Bolívar dictatorship was no permanent solution. Its very last article was a call for still another constituent assembly, to meet in January 1830, and for which the elections, it was hoped, would produce more satisfactory results than those held for Ocaña.

For the present, the principal victims of the dictatorship were the men responsible for thwarting the Liberator's wishes in the assembly just ended, who variously suffered intimidation or outright persecution. Their treatment was not wholly unjustified, because, after the convention ended with nothing accomplished, the hard core of oppositionists drew up a public statement to the effect that an odious tyranny was about to be established and therefore even armed resistance was just and necessary. The signers included Venezuelan federalists (in reality cryptoseparatists) as well as New Granadan liberals loyal to Santander. Several of the former were refused reentry to Venezuela by order of Páez, who in this matter did follow guidelines from Bogotá. The New Granadans suffered less outright harassment on returning home, but a few did lose jobs. Santander lost his when the vice presidency was simply abolished by the "organic decree," although in practice he had not exercised it since Bolívar's return to Bogotá in September 1827, and for consolation he was offered diplomatic exile as Colombian minister to the United States, which he did not hesitate to accept. In sum, no odious tyranny occurred, and in general, tranquility reigned, for the regime enjoyed at least the tacit consent of a majority of Colombians. The fact that official agents committed occasional arbitrary acts did not mean that Bolívar personally ordered them or that in this respect his dictatorship was wholly different from any previous government.

Bolívar himself settled down to live in Bogotá, spending as much time as possible in the suburban villa ("Quinta de Bolívar") that a grateful citizenry had presented to him after the Battle of Boyacá. It was hardly luxurious—luxury being then almost nonexistent in the Colombian capital, where the wealthiest families aspired at most to approach the degree of comfort enjoyed by the British or French middle class—but it had ample corridors and the requisite braziers and fireplaces for protection against the Andean chill. Behind it was a garden with an outdoor tub in one corner, where Bolívar, a fanatic of personal cleanliness, could take his daily bath. In the villa he also met socially with his friends, mostly military officers (including a number of British) and members of the local aristocracy. He passed many hours there, too, with Manuela Sáenz, though she kept a house of her own downtown.

Bolívar's continuing relationship with Manuela, not to mention her unconventional ways, provoked murmurs of disapproval in a good many quarters, but he paid little attention. Among those unconventional ways—for a woman—was her obvious willingness to dabble in politics, whether giving solicited or unsolicited advice to the Liberator or doing her best to make life difficult for his adversaries. Manuela felt a particular dislike for Santander, so that one of her more outrageous pranks was to enliven a party she was hosting by staging his mock execution. For this purpose an effigy of Santander was made out of old rags, and an ultraconservative cleric was enlisted to give the effigy extreme unction, while one of Bolívar's British officer friends organized the firing squad. Bolívar, who was not present, realized that this time Manuela had gone too far and resolved to finally break off his relationship with the *amable loca* ("loveable madwoman"), as he called her. But he could not bring himself to do it, nor did he punish the others involved despite promises to that effect.

There was more to the dictatorship, however, than the intimidation of opponents. Early on, Bolívar had sketched a larger agenda for it in a letter to Páez: "My plan is to rest my reforms on the solid base of religion, and as far as is compatible with our circumstances to act in conformity to the old laws, less complicated and more sure and efficacious." The most notorious examples of return to "the old laws" did in fact have to do with religious issues, in particular the orders of monks and friars, which were a target of early liberal reformers in Colombia as elsewhere in Latin America on grounds of their supposed general uselessness and immorality. There was both truth and exaggeration in the allegations, but the monks and friars in any case had friends among the population at large, so that measures inimical to their interests aroused significant opposition. For the latter reason, and not because of any sudden religious conversion, Bolívar decreed the restoration of the smaller male convents that had been suppressed by the Colombian constituent congress, which then earmarked their assets for the support of public education. He likewise suspended a later law that set a minimum age of twenty-five for religious vows in the hope that by that age any young man would know better than to want to become a monk. Yet there was a bit less to these dictatorial decrees than met the eye. Buildings and revenues formerly belonging to the restored convents were *not* to be given back if they were already being used for educational purposes; and the decree on religious professions specified that in the future any new friar had to spend five years in mission work among the Indians, something not necessarily to the liking of the religious themselves, to judge from the overwhelming concentration of existing friars in Bogotá, Quito, and other major cities. It should be noted that some of Bolívar's closest friends were displeased with the restoration of convents—to which he replied, according to his Irish confidant O'Leary, "It is necessary to oppose religious fanaticism to the fanaticism of the demagogues." Worth noting also is the fact that it never occurred to Bolívar simply to turn the church loose to manage its own affairs, even though he was on record as favoring religious toleration: in Spanish America the tradition of a state-controlled and at the same time state-supporting church was too deeply ingrained to be swiftly abandoned.

Neither would all Bolívar's friends have been in sympathy with his policy in the matter of slavery, which is invariably cited by those who attribute social revolutionary content even to the measures of his final dictatorship. Turning a deaf ear to the complaints of wealthy slaveowners that the modest antislavery legislation of the constituent congress did not sufficiently respect the rights of property, in one of his first decrees after accepting dictatorial faculties Bolívar introduced some changes to improve the working of the manumission juntas set up to administer the special inheritance taxes used for buying the freedom of slaves born too soon to benefit from the free-birth principle. The taxes in question were not very productive, and as long as the persons whose inheritances were being taxed still enjoyed substantial social prestige and political influence, it was illusory to expect much more. Even so, Bolívar's persistent abolitionism was fully in accord with comments he had made during his recent sojourn in Bucaramanga about "the state of slavery in which the Colombian people finds itself" and about the local magnates who profited from that servitude. In this he referred, of course, to more than just the legally enslaved. The magnates in question were for the most part his political allies, but the antislavery principle had to be upheld, and history, he knew, would see to its final implementation.

The reiteration of Bolívar's antislavery stance neither turned his slavocrat backers against him nor won over his liberal opponents. The latter were more concerned with his coddling of friars and with various official actions that lessened the independence of the judiciary or further removed the military from civilian control. They also deplored the dictatorship as such, and even if so far it had been a mild one, such episodes as the mock execution of Santander were scarcely calculated to inspire confidence. It is thus understandable that plotting to overthrow the regime was soon underway. In Bogotá, a so-called Philological Society appeared, ostensibly a literary discussion group but in reality a center of conspiracy. Its most representative figures were young liberal professional men from New Granada, but there was a sprinkling of others, civilian and military, including Commandant Pedro Carujo, the highest-ranking military officer to be implicated and a Venezuelan to boot. The detractors of Santander have always insisted that he too was involved, and it is undeniable that most of the conspirators were his friends or partisans and that he accepted the theoretical justification of their cause. He realized, however, that conditions were not ripe for a successful revolt, and having accepted the post in Washington, he would certainly have preferred to be summoned home at some future date to take charge of the country once others had rid it of dictatorship. It would even appear (though neither of the incidents has been fully clarified) that he personally frustrated two attempts on Bolívar's life prior to the definitive attempt, which was made on 25 September 1828 with Santander still in Bogotá.

The blow was not originally intended for that day but was moved up because indiscreet talk by one of the military conspirators gave warning to the authorities (and led to his arrest). Nor did the assassination of Bolívar necessarily form part of the original plan, but because of the sudden change in date, and the fact that not all preparations for a coup were yet in place, it seemed that only the terror sown by news of the dictator's death would provide some chance of success. Bolívar at the moment was staying not in his villa but at the presidential "palace," really just a large house some two blocks from the central plaza of Bogotá, and though duly advised that a plot had been discovered, he took no special precautions. Indeed he was not feeling well. He called for Manuela, who read to him while he took a warm bath. He went to bed and was asleep when a group of the conspirators broke into the "palace," overpowering the guards, then charged up the stairs shouting *"vivas"* to the constitution and wounding an aide. Manuela, still awake, rushed into Bolívar's room, and though he instinctively grabbed a pistol for self-defense, she convinced him to climb through a window to safety in the street below, which conveniently was empty because all the attackers were inside the building. The window is still marked by a plaque commemorating the salvation of the Padre de la Patria.

Manuela won Bolívar a little extra time by misinforming his would-be assassins concerning his exact whereabouts. They soon realized what he had done, but by then Bolívar, down in the street, had encountered one of his servants and with him took refuge under the bridge across a nearby stream. Early the next morning the servant went forth to reconnoiter, heard *"vivas"* being shouted not for the constitution but for the Liberator, and thus knew the coup had failed—and not just the attempt on Bolívar's life but a parallel attack planned against an urban barracks. After a needed change of clothes, Bolívar proceeded on horseback to the main plaza to receive congratula-

The Window through which Bolívar jumped to safety, with plaque reading (in Latin): "Spectator, stop for a moment and see the place where the Father and Savior of the Country saved himself on the ill-fated September night in 1828." (Author's collection)

tions from the assembled garrison. Even Santander came up to congratulate him, but he indignantly rebuffed the gesture, convinced that the former vice president and minister designate had been the brains behind the entire conspiracy.

Although he had survived one more attempt on his life, the experience sorely depressed Bolívar's spirit. He declared his intention to resign—apparently meaning it—and even to pardon the conspirators. But his immediate associates, the military especially, succeeded in changing his mind. Bolívar did not resign, and there was punishment not only for the guilty but for some who were not. It is quite true that all fourteen people who were condemned to death and executed over the next few weeks were at least guilty of something. However, the naval hero José Padilla, one of the victims, was in no way involved in the latest conspiracy; he was merely a strong Santanderista and conveniently at hand in a Bogotá prison, to which he had been sent by his archenemy General Montilla after his failed local uprising in Cartagena earlier in the year. The sentence of death handed down against Santander and then commuted to exile at the insistence of a majority of Bolívar's Council of State was in some ways comparable. There was no shred of evidence implicating him in the September 1828 conspiracy, but neither had he concealed his belief that resistance to dictatorship was morally justifiable, and undoubtedly he knew more about the plotting than he ever told the authorities. Bolívar remained convinced that Santander was chiefly responsible for what had happened; and though he agreed to commute the sentence, he was visibly annoyed to do so.

The wave of repression that followed the abortive assassination attempt was far from extraordinary by twentieth-century standards but did involve more than the fourteen executions. Other men were expelled from the country or ordered to go live in distant and unhealthy parts of Colombia on vague grounds of suspected complicity or because they were close friends of Santander or any of the known conspirators. Interior Minister Restrepo stated frankly that Bolívar was determined to root out "the party of General Santander," and several subsequent decrees aimed to prevent the occurrence of similar troubles in the future. Secret societies of Masonic type, which tended to be centers of liberal activism, were formally prohibited; various ardent liberals had their teaching licenses canceled; and the prefect (the Napoleonic-sounding new title for intendant) of Cundinamarca imposed the requirement to carry a passport even for traveling from one municipality to another. At least there was no need to take action against the opposition press: none existed, potential anti-government journalists being either in exile or sufficiently intimidated.

Alongside instances of political repression there was a continued rollback of supposedly premature institutional reforms. A significant example seldom mentioned by those who would interpret the dictatorship as a reaction against scheming lawyers and irresponsible oligarchs was the October 1828 degree reestablishing Indian tribute. This was done in large part for fiscal reasons in line with Bolívar's conviction that the old taxes were easier to collect and therefore more productive, and the occasional petitions from the Indians themselves for its restoration were naturally cited in justification. But as noted in a previous chapter, the tribute was at the same time a mechanism of social control, which is why large landowners of Quito and Popayán had lobbied to bring it back. Bolívar's outspoken supporter Tomás C. de Mosquera, now serving in his native Popayán as prefect-intendant of the Cauca department, insisted that it was necessary to impose the tax in order to force the natives to work, because without the need to earn money to pay it they had been returning to "an almost savage state. . . . [T]hey have done nothing except abandon themselves to their brutal pleasures." Bolívar was well aware that the creole elite in areas of significant Indian population wanted the tribute for just this reason, and though it was clearly not his prime objective, he can hardly have imagined that he was restoring the tribute for the Indians' sake. More clearly intended for their benefit were the restoration of the colonial office of "protector of Indians" (for reasons of political correctness now redesignated "protector of indigenes") and circulars for the founding of schools in indigenous parishes. Resurrection of the separate "protectors" for the native population at least showed that Bolívar rejected the doctrinaire liberal fiction that they should now be considered equal citizens with exactly the same rights and obligations as anyone else, but the record of such officials in the colonial period often left something to be desired, and as for the schools to be founded for native children, they were to be paid for by the natives themselves.

Another forward-looking if largely ineffective measure of the dictatorship was a decree Bolívar signed for conservation of the nation's forest resources. Then there were measures indefinitely suspending the elected municipal councils as a useless expense and further reducing civilian control over the military. And it need hardly be added that the military were, politically, a key pillar of the regime. All the more important officers—until the defection in mid-1829 of José María Córdova, and with the obvious exception of Santander, a general of quasi-civilian mentality—were strong partisans of Bolívar. Much the same could be said of the clergy, whose members backed the government with pastoral letters and even by sharing secrets of the confessional. Their attitude was based in part on gratitude for the reversal of anticlerical policies and in part on bureaucratic ambition, exactly as was the case with civil officials, most of whom were as eager to hold their jobs and, if possible, rise to the next higher level after as before the installation of dictatorship. In the matter of clerical appointments concretely, the system of ecclesiastical patronage inherited from the colonial regime and still in force gave the state the final power of decision. Thus Father Juan Fernández de Sotomayor, an ardent Santanderista up to the end of the Ocaña convention, just one year later was being effusive in praise of the Liberator. One of Bolívar's correspondents shrewdly attributed the turnaround to "the scent of the mitre," for Sotomayor was eager to be appointed bishop of Cartagena—and he was.

The British minister to Colombia, Patrick Campbell, summed up the social basis of the dictatorship by observing that Bolívar enjoyed the support of "all that is respectable in point of talent, birth, and wealth." Bolívar did indeed have the firm allegiance of the highest social sectors in Quito and New Granada; the backing of his own social element in Venezuela was, paradoxically, a little less firm. Members of the professional middle sectors were somewhat more critical of his government, and it is hard to say exactly what ordinary men and women thought, because they were not consulted save when herded en masse to take part in demonstrations of support for the Liberator. No doubt they continued to feel genuine respect for him, but there is little doubt that their respect was diminishing because of resentment over the cost of the regime's military apparatus, forced military recruitment, and any instances of misconduct by the dictatorship's officials. New Granadans felt a particular sense of grievance due to the identification of the military establishment with Venezuelans—while Venezuelans still resented their formal subordination to a seat of government in Bogotá.

It is perhaps significant that in the case of New Granada the few political leaders who had some undeniable popular appeal and grassroots following tended to be followers of Santander. The obvious examples are the unfortunate Padilla on the Caribbean coast and Colonel José María Obando in the southwest. Even after Padilla was executed, Bolívar continued to fear disturbances on the coast due to "the pretension of the *pardos* and friends of Padilla." But the friends of Obando proved a greater problem, when he and his sidekick, Colonel José Hilario López, launched a rebellion just a few days after the attempt on Bolívar's life. They had hoped to synchronize their uprising with a successful coup in Bogotá, which did not turn out as they hoped. However, thanks to Obando's personal influence with the region's masses, including former royalists who had been his comrades during the independence conflict until his own conversion to republicanism, and thanks to the overconfidence displayed by the government commander Tomás C. de Mosquera, they succeeded in taking both Popayán and Pasto. The two rebels proclaimed the constitution again in force; but their fortunes began a rapid decline once Bolívar dispatched a sufficient force from Bogotá to deal with them.

By that time, an even more serious problem had arisen between Colombia and Peru. It had a variety of causes, of which the most concrete though not necessarily most important was the boundary dispute that would still be causing bloodshed between Ecuador and Peru in the late twentieth century. Other sore points were the help Peru gave in 1827 to the mutinous Third Division and (particularly objectionable to Bolívar personally) Peruvian interference in Bolivia, which had hastened the departure of Sucre, Bolívar's favorite general, from the Bolivian presidency. The conduct of the Peruvian minister in Bogotá, who publicly aligned himself with Bolívar's domestic enemies, was a last straw that caused the Liberator to break relations with Peru. The Peruvian response was a naval blockade of Colombian Pacific ports and the seizure of Guayaquil by a substantial armed force. Because of the apparent gravity of the situation, Bolívar resolved to leave Bogotá and go south to confront the invaders, meanwhile delegating to Sucre, who was now back in Quito, discretionary power to deal with the problem. This time Bolívar's journey was painful in the extreme because of his deteriorating health—he could ride for barely two hours at a time. He was also greatly worried by the Obando-López revolt, for the rebels were in a position to cut communication between Bogotá and the south. Accordingly, Bolívar agreed to give them full pardon (as he earlier did with Páez) and even promoted Obando to general. However, this generosity turned out to have been not quite necessary after all: with fewer troops at his disposal but far better generalship, Sucre had already decisively defeated the invaders in the Battle of Tarqui in late February 1829, slightly before the arrangement made with Obando.

Bolívar continued on to Quito and remained in that part of the country for a few months, both because he was in no condition to face the journey back to Bogotá—one correspondent affirmed that at age forty-six he appeared already a man of sixty—and because the Peruvians, in violation of an agreement signed the very day after Tarqui, delayed the evacuation of Guayaquil. But it was also precisely during Bolívar's stay in the south that a political crisis erupted in the rest of Colombia that would hasten final collapse of the union. Its origin was a monarchist intrigue that from Bolívar's day to the present has generated far more controversy than its intrinsic importance warrants and that in truth was only the Colombian aspect of a broader continental phenomenon, because monarchist schemes were broached in virtually all the new Spanish American nations following independence.

As regards Bolívar specifically, did he by any chance see in the establishment of monarchy a last chance to preserve both social stability and something of his political achievement? If so, did he propose either to wear a crown himself or assume the presidency for life, meanwhile preparing to be succeeded by a European prince? He had, of course, never concealed his admiration for constitutional monarchy as a system or his skepticism as to its feasibility in his part of the world, so that his attitude was clearly ambivalent. And what he actually did, in April 1829, was to write from Quito to his ministers in Bogotá, urging them to explore the possibility of a British protectorate for Colombia, an idea that he had toyed with before and that they did not consider at all feasible unless, conceivably, Colombia itself adopted a monarchical form of government. The cabinet ministers accordingly proceeded to sound out Great Britain and France on the possibility of importing a European prince, and together with other highly placed Bolivarians they sounded out opinion makers within Colombia concerning the proposal. Bolívar could hardly have avoided hearing about this, however much his ministers carefully refrained from asking him for an overt endorsement. They merely assumed, from the lack of protest on his part, that they had his tacit consent for what they were doing. Thus when, after receiving clear indications that there was still deep opposition to monarchy in Colombia, Bolívar finally declared his opposition to the scheme, his ministers felt disillusionment, to say the least. Nevertheless, Restrepo took pains in his later history to emphasize that Bolívar never gave any explicit approval to the monarchist negotiations and much less showed the desire for a crown on his own head. Nor has any evidence been produced to contradict either Restrepo's assessment or the Liberator's basic ambivalence.

Quite apart from Bolívar's degree of personal responsibility in the matter, the mere specter of monarchy not only angered many of his fellow citizens—the negotiations being an ill-kept secret—but adversely affected his image abroad. In Europe some who had praised Bolívar as an example of true republicanism, as contrasted with the reactionary monarchies of their own continent, were taken aback by his assumed complicity. Even worse was the impact in the United States, whose people and government had the presumption to look on themselves as guardians of the republican cause throughout the hemisphere, and where the Bolivian constitution with its life presidency had already aroused suspicion as to Bolívar's intentions. Several U.S. representatives in Latin America fully shared that suspicion, including the minister to Colombia, who was the future president William Henry Harrison. Convinced that the Liberator had become the chief enemy of Hispanic American liberties, Harrison was indiscreet in his association with opponents of the dictatorship, and only the prospect of his removal by a new administration in Washington saved him from being declared persona non grata and invited to leave. Harrison's anti-Bolivarian activity, in the guise of exalted republicanism, along with that of other U.S. agents and publicists, was what chiefly moved Bolívar to make one of his best-known aspersions on the North American neighbor: "The United States appear destined by Providence to plague America with miseries in the name of liberty." The words in question—dear to the hearts of contemporary Latin American leftists and even inscribed on a postage stamp of revolutionary Cuba—were contained in a letter to British minister Campbell, who unlike Harrison was a good friend of Bolívar.

For the Colombian friends of Harrison, it was Bolívar who threatened to "plague America" with the "misery" of monarchy; and one of those who frequented the same social circles was José María Córdova, the preeminent New Granadan military hero of independence. Córdova had some personal reasons for disaffection, but the issue of monarchism was a factor when, in September 1829, he launched a constitutionalist rebellion similar to that of Obando and López (which as a matter of fact he had personally helped suppress), though in his own native province of Antioquia. Improvised and premature, the uprising was easily defeated; Córdova himself, wounded in battle, was afterward shot and killed by one of Bolívar's British auxiliaries. The rebellion was duly followed by another burst of repressive measures—even including the expulsion from Bogotá of Santander's longtime mistress Nicolasa Ibáñez. When the party of Santander returned to power in New Granada after the death of Bolívar, they would take their revenge by exiling Manuela Sáenz.

At the time of the Córdova affair Bolívar was still detained in the south: it was during a stop at Popayán, on his return journey to Bogotá, that he frankly condemned the monarchist initiative. Bolívar remained uncertain in his own mind, however, about what should be done instead. He wavered between the view at one extreme that some form of his Bolivian constitution was still the best solution and, at the other, a willingness to accept even the formal dissolution of the Colombian union. He rested his hopes, such as they were, on the constitutional convention that was due to meet in January 1830, and for which elections had already been held in mid-1829. They were held under a regulation that made it easier than before for the military to vote but raised the minimum voting age to twenty-five and altered the socioeconomic requirements in a manner whose practical effect is hard to determine. In any case, Bolívar and his collaborators proposed to leave nothing to chance and not to repeat what they considered to have been their grave error of overconfidence at the time of elections for the Great Convention at Ocaña. Bolívar himself wrote to Páez, Montilla, and other regional officials urging them to exert a wholesome influence on the electoral process, and the efforts were successful, as government supporters were everywhere victorious. Especially noteworthy was the outcome in Bogotá, where Santanderista candidates received a mere handful of votes. Because the party of Santander had swept the capital by a substantial margin in the previous voting, it is unlikely that the difference reflected solely a change of thinking on the part of qualified voters. Certainly the orchestration of the soldiers' vote played a part, as did the exile of the principal opposition leaders and absence of an opposition press.

The nationwide victory of pro-government candidates was reinforced by a series of instructions to the deputies drawn up by the local electoral assemblies, in accordance with an express requirement imposed at Bolívar's insistence. Distrustful as always of deliberative and legislative bodies, he explained that he had more faith in the patriotism of the average citizen than in the wisdom of those who might be elected. And his faith was vindicated, as far as the responses from New Granada and Ecuador were concerned: they were uniformly favorable to the regime in power. Some even asked explicitly for life presidency or the institution of monarchy. Venezuela, however, was a different matter. Although Venezuela's electors had chosen government supporters to represent them in the coming convention, they soon began adopting declarations in favor of Venezuelan independence from the Colombian union.

One reason for the upsurge of Venezuelan separatism was the reaction against monarchist intrigues. But this merely amplified a regional discontent that already existed. The greater part of Venezuela had not accompanied Páez in his 1826 rebellion in order to obtain a conservative dictatorship, still based in Bogotá, such as Bolívar now headed; it had been seeking greater autonomy and in practice had obtained this thanks to the sweeping delegation of powers made to Páez by the dictatorship itself. Yet that did not represent a permanent solution, and as it happened, Venezuela was not only the part of the republic least inclined to accept monarchy but the one least inclined to support the general orientation of Bolívar's dictatorship. For the important agroexport sector of its economy, tariff protectionism was more a burden than a help. As intellectually the most liberal part of the country, it had little sympathy for the measures favoring clerical interests, while its influential slaveowning minority was not necessarily happy with Bolívar's refusal to backtrack on the manumission law. (The latter would be watered down just as soon as Venezuela did in fact separate.) In sum, according to the U.S. consul at the port of La Guaira, no part of Colombia was now so hostile to the Liberator as was Caracas, the city of his birth.

One factor that weighed less in Venezuela because of its distance from the war theater was the unpopularity of the recent conflict with Peru. That this was a war of Spanish American brother against brother had been bothersome even to Bolívar, but there was also widespread unhappiness over recruitment and over the special taxes and contributions levied to pay for the war. All this, in addition to the looming separation of Venezuela, gave heart in late 1829 and the beginning of 1830 to the New Granadan liberals who had been followers of Santander, who now began to emerge from hiding or regain their repressed courage and make their voices heard. The more moderate Bolivarians, furthermore, were convinced that it would be necessary to reach some compromise with them. For Bolívar the political outlook was thus increasingly unfavorable. He nevertheless continued his return trip to Bogotá and entered the city for the last time on 15 January 1830, through streets decorated in his honor but with few signs of the old enthusiasm and excitement. Five days later the convention formally opened, and Bolívar duly submitted a message to it, which unlike his message to Ocaña two years before, contained chiefly generalities. Bolívar carefully avoided anything that might appear to suggest an imposition of his own will on the deputies, but he was relieved when Sucre was chosen to serve as president of the gathering. He even made a point of congratulating the deputies on their choice, describing Sucre as the most worthy of Colombian generals. The description was true enough—but not well received by the general who had been functioning in Bolívar's absence as strongman of the dictatorship, war minister Rafael Urdaneta.

The convention that met in 1830 is known in Colombian history as "Congreso Admirable," but it was "admirable" more for the distinguished caliber of its members than for what it accomplished. It did produce a new constitution, which bore a striking and somewhat surprising resemblance to the original Colombian constitution of 1821 that Bolívar disliked: there were changes in the relationship between branches of government and in other details, but at bottom the Constitution of 1830 was another conventionally republican text, with no semblance of life terms or other special features of the sort once favored by the Liberator. At the same time, there was a note of unreality in all the convention did, because it was writing a fine new constitution for a nation in process of dissolution. Even without a formal declaration of independence, Venezuela was already in practice a separate nation with Páez as its leader, and while a few voices were raised in favor of keeping Venezuela in the union by force, the notion was wholly impractical, both because of the military strength at Páez's disposal and because the population of New Granada would have overwhelmingly opposed any such attempt. If anything, New Granadans were more relieved than grieved at the departure of Venezuela.

The thought once or twice crossed Bolívar's mind that, if only he were granted sufficient powers, he could again put things in order; at other times, he appeared resigned to the collapse of his political creation. In any event, his opinion carried less and less weight, as his ministers and other subordinates increasingly managed affairs on their own. By the end of April, exhausted physically and spiritually, Bolívar formally resigned the power that had already largely slipped from his hands and prepared to go into voluntary exile. He gave his suburban villa to a close friend and liquidated many of his other possessions in Bogotá—silverware, horses, and so on—that he would no longer need or could not conveniently take with him. By now his patrimony was reduced to little more than the copper mines of Aroa in Venezuela that he had been trying, so far unsuccessfully, to sell to English investors. To be sure, Bolívar was not leaving office a pauper, for in addition to the proceeds of all he had sold, the congress had voted him a life pension of 30,000 pesos a year, a huge sum for the period even though its exact and punctual payment could not be taken for granted.

On 8 May, having said a sad farewell to Manuela, Bolívar left Bogotá for the coast. Some insulting shouts could be heard as he passed through the city, but he reached the Magdalena River without incident and after a few days' rest embarked downstream. People living along the banks of the Magdalena received him with respect and honor, which lifted his spirit somewhat. By the 25th he was already on the outskirts of Cartagena, where he planned to take ship for Europe or at least to the Antilles. However, for lack of ships going where he wanted to go or simply lack of suitable accommodations on board, he did not embark after all. For several months he remained waiting and suffered both from the heat and from the bad news that kept pouring in—the separation of the southern provinces, to become the Republic of Ecuador; the assassination of Sucre, as he was returning from Bogotá to Quito after the convention, in a crime whose authorship is still hotly debated and that eliminated the one man whom Bolívar had looked upon as his political heir; and the vote of the separatist Venezuelan congress forbidding him even to set foot on the soil of his homeland.

Bolívar eventually moved to Barranquilla, near the mouth of the Magdalena River, where he busied himself with correspondence to friends and supporters. To General Flores, now head of the new nation of Ecuador, he penned his final cry of despair:

> You know that I have been in command for twenty years; and from them I have derived only a few sure conclusions: first, America is ungovernable for us; second, he who serves a revolution ploughs the sea; third, the only thing that can be done in America is to emigrate; fourth, this country will fall without fail into the hands of an unbridled multitude, to pass later to petty, almost imperceptible tyrants of all colors and races; fifth, devoured as we are by all crimes and destroyed by ferocity, the

Europeans will not deign to conquer us; sixth, if it were possible for a part of the world to return to the primeval chaos, the latter would be the final stage of America.

At length the Liberator continued to Santa Marta, ostensibly to embark from there for some foreign port but in reality to die. He found lodging at the hacienda San Pedro Alejandrino, ironically the property of a Spaniard, and a French doctor who happened to be in Santa Marta at the time diagnosed his condition as an advanced stage of tuberculosis. It was apparently an old infection whose full effect had been retarded thanks to the physical vigor he enjoyed during most of his life. Bolívar proceeded to draft a will, in which he left most of the property he still possessed to his sisters and nephews, and he accepted the last rites of the Roman Catholic church, from the priest of a nearby rural parish. Some modern Catholic authors, seeking to co-opt Bolívar retroactively, have suggested that, in the end, he thus abandoned his freethinking ways. Other writers suggest that he decided to take the last rites, just in case. . . . Whatever the exact truth of the matter, he probably also realized that if he died outside the fold of the church, it would cause a bad public impression that would redound to the discredit of his political followers. Bolívar then died, on 17 December 1830.

Just before his death, Bolívar drafted a final proclamation "to the people of Colombia" in which he implored them "to work for the supreme good of a united nation." Whether the unity he referred to was that between Venezuela, New Granada, and Quito or peace among contending factions, it was a constant aim of Bolívar; and by now it was, of course, too late to attain it. Despite a rhetorical emphasis on strong government and national union, the administrative system he implanted during his final dictatorship was in fact a first step in the process of dismantling Colombia, or second step if the revolt of Páez in 1826 is considered the first. Moreover, Bolívar never found the ideal balance between order and freedom, and as he recognized in the letter to Flores, his life's work had numerous unintended, even regrettable, consequences.

Bolívar was in fact better at analyzing the ills of Latin America than at devising remedies. He was keenly aware of the region's poverty, the lack of popular education, and the stark

Everyone loves Bolívar: Honored (a) on a Cuban stamp, with his warning that the United States would "plague America with miseries in the name of freedom;" (b) the U.S. Cold War "Champion of Liberty" postage stamp series. (Author's collection)

social and racial divisions that vastly complicated the nation-building process. He further recognized the paradoxical situation of leaders like himself, members of a privileged minority who had fought for independence in the name of liberal and democratic principles that they did not honestly believe the mass of their compatriots were ready for. His solution in the short range was to equip himself with dictatorial powers that he used with moderation and never intended to last. Yet for the long term his proposals were as exotic in the Spanish American context as those of the doctrinaire liberals whose work he derided. Bolívar was quite unlike the Argentine Juan Manuel de Rosas, who ruled with a strong and often bloody hand for almost a quarter century, but he failed to approximate the system of the man who was perhaps most successful of all the postindependence national leaders, Chile's Diego Portales, who behind a conventional republican façade developed a strong government ultimately resting on the collaboration of the social "forces of order" and the subservience of their inferiors.

Among Bolívar's myriad talents and accomplishments, what is best remembered (as he himself would have wanted) is his role of Liberator. Had there never been a Simón Bolívar, it is still hard to conceive that the Spanish flag would wave today over Caracas, Bogotá, or even Lima; neither did he fight single-handed, and his success as a warrior is due as much to invincible determination as to brilliance as a commander. Where he unquestionably stood out (much as did San Martín in the south and unlike such men as Páez and Santander) was in his commitment to Spanish America in its entirety. His flexibility of movement between Venezuela and New Granada and indiscriminate use of the human and material resources of both former colonies certainly hastened the final victory in that part of the continent, and without his intervention the war in Peru could hardly have ended when it did. Bolívar's dream of a permanent association of Hispanic American nations quickly proved unworkable. However, his proposal retains validity today as an agenda for Latin American integration. Bolívar's ideas and actions have likewise been cited in modern Latin America as precedents for pretty much everything from the Sandinista revolution in Nicaragua to assorted military dictatorships. This involves often lifting things out of context or overlooking inconvenient details (such as his proposal to give Nicaragua to Great Britain), but the fact remains that Bolívar is and for some time will surely continue to be the highest authority to which anyone in Latin America can make appeal.

A Note on the Sources

The student of Simón Bolívar and his times fortunately has available a large quantity of published source materials, including the voluminous correspondence and official papers of Bolívar himself. There are two classic collections of his writings and other documents relating to him: the confusingly titled *Memorias del general O'Leary*, Simón B. O'Leary, ed., published in thirty-two volumes (Caracas, 1879–1914; reissued in thirty-four vols., Caracas, 1981); and *Documentos para la historia de la vida pública del Libertador*, José Félix Blanco and Ramón Azpurúa, eds., published in fourteen volumes (Caracas, 1875–1878; reissued in fifteen vols., Caracas, 1977–1979). Both are in the process of being superseded by the definitive Sociedad Bolivariana de Venezuela, *Escritos del Libertador* (Caracas, 1964–).

But there are many shorter compilations too, including several in English. Most extensive of the English-language compilations is *Select Writings of Bolívar*, compiled by Vicente Lecuna and edited by Harold A. Bierck, Jr., in two volumes (New York, 1951); most of the citations from Bolívar's writings in this work are either from the Lecuna-Bierck compilation or from *El Libertador: Writings of Simón Bolívar*, a new translation by Frederick Fornoff (New York, 2003).

Biographies of Bolívar are vast in number, but for reasons suggested in the preface there is no surfeit of good ones. In English, the most useful are Gerhard Masur, *Simon Bolivar* (2nd ed., Albuquerque, 1969), the work of a distinguished German scholar that is somewhat dated in its style and approach but is comprehensive and generally reliable; Salvador de Madariaga, *Bolívar* (London and New York, 1952), the well-written and well-researched if also tendentious study by a Spanish author who was not one of the Liberator's outspoken admirers; and Augusto Mijares, *The Liberator* (Caracas, 1983), in many ways the best of all, by a Venezuelan historian who avoids the worst excesses of his nation's Bolívar cult. Also worth consulting are the articles in a special edition of *Hispanic American Historical Review* (February 1983) prepared in commemoration of the bicentennial of Bolívar's birth. For a study of Bolívar's thought, especially political, the classic treatment by Víctor Andrés Belaunde, *Bolívar and the Political Thought of the Spanish American Revolution* (Baltimore, 1938), remains worth reading, but one can also consult with profit the essay by David A. Brading published in pamphlet form, *Classical Republicanism and Creole Patriotism: Simón Bolívar (1783–1830) and the Spanish American Revolution* (Cambridge, 1983). Bolívar's relationship with the poet, publicist, and jurist (and much else) Andrés Bello is the subject of Antonio Cussen, *Bolívar and Bello: Poetry and Politics in the Spanish American Revolution* (Cambridge, 1992).

For a general overview of the independence struggle in Colombia (taking the name primarily in the contemporary sense and not that of Bolívar's larger republic), a reader may consult the recent treatment by Rebecca Earle, *Spain and the Independence of Colombia 1810–1825* (Exeter, UK, 2000). On Peru there is Timothy Anna, *The Fall of the Royal Government in Peru* (Lincoln, NE, 1979), and the creation of Bolivia is covered by Charles Arnade, *The Emergence of the Republic of Bolivia* (Gainesville, FL, 1957). And for the general history of Venezuela, the standard English-language source is John V. Lombardi, *Venezuela: The Search for Order, the Dream of Progress* (New York, 1982). On the colonial background specifically of Venezuela and modern Colombia, we have Michael P. McKinley, *Pre-Revolutionary Caracas: Politics, Economy, and Society, 1777–1811* (Cambridge, 1985), and Anthony McFarlane, *Colombia before Independence* (Cambridge, 1993). Covering Peru as well and extending in some of its essays into the independence era itself, there is John R. Fisher, et al., *Reform and Insurrection in Bourbon New Granada and Peru* (Baton Rouge, 1990). And focusing on the role of foreign soldiers, see Alfred Hasbrouck, *Foreign Legionnaires in the Liberation of Spanish South America* (reprint ed., New York, 1969).

To place the story of Bolívar in the larger picture of Latin American independence, much the best source is John Lynch, *The Spanish American Revolutions, 1808–1826* (2nd ed., New York, 1986), although there are briefer, more recent overviews by Jaime E. Rodríguez O., *The Independence of Spanish America* (Cambridge, 1998), which gives strong coverage to Spanish background, and by Jay Kinsbruner, *Independence in Spanish America* (2nd ed., Albuquerque, 2000). Also helpful are a number of collaborative volumes with topical chapters devoted to different aspects of the period, often including late-colonial antecedents and the early postwar years. A good recent example is Víctor M. Uribe-Uran, ed., *State and Society in Spanish America during the Age of Revolution* (Wilmington, DE, 2001). But see also Kenneth J. Andrien and Lyman L. Johnson, eds., *The Political Economy of Spanish America in the Age of Revolution, 1750–1850* (Albuquerque, 1994). For the international relations of the period, there is a notable lack of recent studies, but a number of standard older treatments are readily accessible: for example, Arthur P. Whitaker, *The United States and the Independence of Latin America, 1800–1830* (Baltimore, 1941), and William W. Kaufmann, *British Policy and the Independence of Latin America, 1804–1828* (New Haven, 1951).

Some works dealing with other figures of the period naturally add light on the career of Bolívar. Among works in English concerning Francisco de Miranda and the beginnings of Venezuelan independence, William S. Robertson, *The Life of Miranda* (2 vols., Chapel Hill, 1929), is still essential but was lately joined by Karen Racine, *Francisco de Miranda: a Transatlantic Life in the Age of Revolution* (Wilmington, DE, 2003). My own *The Santander Regime in Gran Colombia* (Newark, DE, 1954; reprint ed., Westport, CT, 1970) is not a biography of Santander but primarily a study of the domestic history of the greater Colombian union of which Bolívar was principal founder. On

Bolívar's favorite lieutenant and chosen successor (who however did not outlive him), there is John P. Hoover, *Admirable Warrior: Marshal Sucre, Fighter for South American Independence* (Detroit, 1977), which is a short version of the original work that appeared in Spanish (Cumaná, 1975). Looking at the war of independence from the enemy's perspective, Stephen Stoan produced a study of Bolívar's ablest adversary in *Pablo Morillo and Venezuela, 1815–1820* (Columbus, OH, 1974). R. B. Cunninghame Graham published *José Antonio Páez* (London, 1929), which is heavily dependent on Páez's own *Autobiografía* (1st ed., 2 vols., New York, 1869). Another participant who left an account of the struggle is Bolívar's aide Daniel F. O'Leary; the English translation of his memoirs, *Bolívar and the War of Independence* (Austin, 1970), is a good abridgement of the original Spanish version. Not least, there is even a novelized biography of Manuela Sáenz by Victor W. Von Hagen, *The Four Seasons of Manuela, a Biography* (New York, 1952).

If it appears that most of the titles in this bibliography are not very recent, the reason is that the independence of Spanish South America—as distinct from that, say, of Mexico—has in recent years attracted little attention from foreign scholars. It has not even been a leading concern of professional historians, it would seem, in the Bolivarian countries themselves. However, for an annotated listing of the principal publications in the field, in all languages, the interested reader can consult the *Handbook of Latin American Studies,* published yearly by the Hispanic Division of the Library of Congress and conveniently available online as well as in print version.

Glossary

afrancesados: Spanish admirers of things Fench, including the monarchy of José Bonaparte, imposed on Spain by his brother Napoleon.

Alcabala: traditional Spanish sales tax

cabildo abierto: an open town meeting.

Campaña Admirable: "Admirable Campaign," the liberation of Venezuela in 1813.

Captaincy-General: a major territorial subdivision in the Spanish colonies, often corresponding to one of the presentday Spanish American republics (e.g., Venezuela); though included in a larger Viceroyalty, the subordination of its high officials to the viceroy was often only nominal.

corsair: private seaman licensed by a government to prey on enemy shipping; also "privateer."

creole: person born in America of Spanish descent.

fuero charter of privileges granted to a particular group of subjects (e.g., clergy or military).

grandes cacaos: "big cacaos," term sometimes applied to the leading cacao planters in Venezuela.

llanos: "plains," in this work referring to the plains of the Onoco Basin in Venezuela and New Granada.

llaneros: "plainsmen," that is, people of the llanos.

mantuanos: the cream of the cream of the Venezuelan aristocracy, so designated because of the *manto,* or cape, worn by the ladies.

pardo: "brown," referring to someone of partAfrican descent.

pastuso: native of Pasto.

peninsulares: Spaniards from the parent country, that is, from the Iberian Peninsula.

Presidency: another major subdivision of the Spanish empire, such as Quito (modern Euador), whose administrators enjoyed slightly less autonomy visàis the viceroy than those of a captaincygeneral.

quiteño: native of Quito.

real: monetary unit equal to oneeighth of a peso.

Upper Peru: a Presidency in the Viceroyalty of Río de la Plata that became modern Bolivia.

Viceroyalty: largest of the territorial subdivisions of the Spanish empire, including one or more captainciesgeneral or presidencies, over which the viceroy exrcised limited authority, as well as a central core that came directly under his jurisdiction.

Index

A

Adams, John Quincy, 159
Afrancesados, 19–20
Afro-Latin Americans, 3, 7, 30, 37, 56, 61–62, 75, 125, 135, 141. *See also Pardos,* Slavery
Agrarian reform
  attributed to Bolívar, 87
  Haiti, 75
Alcabala, 27, 122
Andes
  ascent in Boyacá campaign, 103–104
  coastal range, Venezuela, 6
  New Granadan interior isolated by, 44
  royalist stronghold in Peru, 131, 142–143, 146
Anderson, Benedict, 119, 130
Angostura (Ciudad Bolívar), 83, 85–86, 90, 94–95, 110, 113–114, 136. *See also* Congress Angostura
Angostura Address, 96–98, 158
Anticlericalism, 194
  Spain, 127

Venezuela, 164, 200
Anglo-American Revolution, 5, 14, 18, 23
Antioquia, province, 63, 121, 198
Antilles, 5, 61, 69, 76, 86, 202
  British, 14, 34, 59–60 (*see also* Jamaica, Trinidad)
  Spanish, 29, 44, 48, 118 (*see also* Cuba, Puerto Rico)
Apure River, 90
Aragua, valley, 4
Arauca, 89
Arauca River, 103
Araucanian Indians, 73
Argentina, 2, 92, 93, 118, 129, 139. *See also* Río de la Plata
  independence historiography, 133
  and Panama Congress, 150, 153
Arismendi, Juan Bautista, 77
Aroa, copper mines of, 202
Armistice, 115–116, 126, 144
Artigas, José Gervasio, 87
Assembly, Bolivian national, 155–156, 158–159